INCLUSIVE EQUALITY

A vision for social justice

Sally Witcher

First published in Great Britain in 2015 by

Policy Press
University of Bristol
1-9 Old Park Hill
Bristol
BS2 8BB
UK
t: +44 (0)117 954 5940
pp-info@bristol.ac.uk
www.policypress.co.uk

North America office:
Policy Press
c/o The University of Chicago Press
1427 East 60th Street
Chicago, IL 60637, USA
t: +1 773 702 7700
f: +1 773-702-9756
sales@press.uchicago.edu
www.press.uchicago.edu

British Library Cataloguing in Publication Data
A catalogue record for this book is available from the British Library.

Library of Congress Cataloging-in-Publication Data
A catalog record for this book has been requested.

ISBN 978 1 44730 004 5 Paperback

Cover design by Policy Press
Front cover: image kindly supplied by www.alamy.com
Printed and bound in Great Britain by CMP, Poole
Policy Press uses environmentally responsible print partners

Contents

Acknowledgements

My warmest thanks go to Alison Shaw at Policy Press for her support and patience with me, as I learnt the hard way just how long it takes to write a book while also trying to earn enough to pay the bills. The same qualities were exhibited by her colleagues at Policy Press, all of which made my first experience of publishing something like this considerably less traumatic than would otherwise have been the case. The two anonymous reviewers of the first draft each helped by drawing attention to areas of weakness while giving me the confidence to persevere.

This book started life around twelve years ago. The basic idea for it was thrashed out via a PhD thesis and, although much revised and up-dated, this book could not have been written without the luxury of time for extended study and reflection that this provided. I would like to thank my long-suffering PhD supervisors, Professor Ruth Jonathan and Dr Ian Dey at the University of Edinburgh, for many challenging and stimulating discussions that maintained my interest over the years, and helped me to focus and refine my thinking. I would particularly like to thank Ruth for introducing me to social and political theory when I studied for my Master's degree, and for inspiring a passionate interest in it. In terms of practical support, the ESRC awarded me a very welcome studentship to support my studies. I (and the work) also benefited greatly from a three month user-fellowship at the Centre for Analysis of Social Exclusion (London School of Economics and Political Science) for which I would like to thank Professor John Hills and his colleagues.

I could not have attempted this project, and certainly would not have finished it, without the support of my friends and family. I am very grateful to my mum who fed me, brought me cups of tea, helped check the references and put up with me for weeks on end, when I installed myself at her house in the country, away from the many distractions I would otherwise have found. I would like to thank friends and colleagues too numerous to mention, but in particular Danny McShane, Marnie Roadburg, Susan Elsley and Cameron Paton, for listening to me enthuse and grumble (mostly the latter) about the thesis over the six years it took to complete it, then for putting up with more of the same when I went back to it a few years later to set about updating it, rethinking it and turning it into something more book-like. I am sure that they are even more relieved than I am that the ordeal is now finally at an end.

Preface

Before launching into the book I hope it is helpful to provide an indication of what you are going to find – and what you will not. First, although it is an academic study, in some ways it is not typical of such works, any more than I am a typical academic. It is primarily an exploration of ideas, theories, discourses and concepts (although occasional use is made of empirical data, particularly when setting the context in the introduction). Whether the end result amounts to anything as sophisticated as social theory is another matter.

Second, the book is perhaps unusual in that its focus is upwards and outwards, in an attempt to create a vision of the 'bigger picture', rather than on burrowing down into microscopic exploration of any one of its features. While it draws heavily on a wide variety of academic work, it makes no claims to coming anywhere close to a comprehensive literature review. Given the range of ground covered, such an exercise would run to numerous volumes. In my hunt for raw material with which to build an overarching framework, I have roamed across topics and disciplines. While I hope the resulting edifice stands up to general scrutiny, some parts of it are more robust than others. For example, I know that there is a lot more that could be said (and has already been said by others) about socio-economic class, network theory, identity and the literature on participative democracy. The sociology greats, in fact sociology in general, do not get the attention they deserve.

I may have discovered rather too late in the day why microscopic burrowing is generally preferred! Not only has the enormity of the task sometimes felt overwhelming, it is fraught with dangers. I may have spent most of my working life exploring the fields of poverty, inequality and social exclusion, but I cannot – and certainly do not – claim to be expert in everything to do with them. The bigger the picture, the more likely it is that limitations will be exposed. I am acutely aware that I am boldly going, not just where others have gone before, but into well-trodden terrain on which eminent academics have built life-long careers, founded on in-depth study of any one of the many areas touched upon within these pages. There are, therefore, a lot of people who will be extremely well placed to point out all the book's weaknesses and all the important authors and angles I have undoubtedly missed. I realise that I may well have unwittingly ridden roughshod across sensitive intellectual territory, trampling carefully honed, nuanced argument in my wake. If so, I can only apologise and promise to learn from my mistakes.

Yet I hope that there is some merit in this foolhardy mission, even if it is just to show what other perspectives might have to offer. It may be that concepts can only really be grasped in terms of how they are positioned in conjunction with each other. Perhaps the resulting arrangement could tell us more than any one of them in isolation about the nature of disadvantage and how it operates. This reminds me of the fable (which a quick consultation of Wikipedia reveals to feature in a variety of religions) about people who cannot see, each holding a different part of an elephant, who separately understand 'elephant' very differently but who collectively can build up a picture of the whole beast.

Like most people's literary endeavours at some level, this one was prompted by experiences in my professional and personal life. This book has been informed by a number of perspectives that I have largely acquired through an (in all other senses) erratic career-path. I have explored its subject-matter from the angle of campaigner, academic, civil servant and disabled person. I mention the last with some trepidation, not because I am at all uncomfortable with that aspect of my identity, but because I know to my cost that it can distort the expectations of even fair-minded, honourable people. Indeed, the expectation may now be that this book is all about disability. It does make an appearance, along with much else, in the context of the more widely experienced phenomenon of misrecognition.

As the director of the Child Poverty Action Group, I found myself inextricably immersed in endless debates about the meaning of poverty and its measurement. Yet, while each form of measurement had its strengths and weaknesses, it was, of course, perfectly clear to everyone that the picture they collectively painted amounted to clear evidence of the existence of poverty, its extent and its devastating consequences. Much energy was expended in attempting to nail jelly-like meaning to the wall; to make the case for government action to tackle poverty – to a government that refused to acknowledge that poverty existed in Britain. Absurdly, to stand any hope of engaging them, the word 'poverty' had to be banished from all submissions, and replaced with 'financial hardship', which, for some reason, was deemed more palatable.

When I later went back to university, I discovered how meaning can also fall down the gaps between disciplines. Confusingly, concepts can be reinvented and renamed by people working in separate academic silos. A brief stint in the civil service revealed analogous phenomena. In spite of the mantra of 'joined-up government', the imperative is often unavoidably to focus down onto the particular policy issue and priorities of the Minister in question, regardless of their wider interface – contemporaneously, with what went before or with what might come next.

In whatever setting, regardless of the skills and the good intentions of those concerned, there are dynamics that militate against a holistic approach. The power of institutional culture and systems to drive behaviour is very considerable. Complexity, rapid change and just sheer overwhelming scale create a bewildering spectacle that is more than enough to prompt anyone to avert their gaze onto more immediate, familiar, comprehensible surroundings. Furthermore, no matter how hard we look there are some things that are difficult to see. Experience tells me how valuable it can be to generate dialogue between different stakeholder groups. What a problem looks like from one perspective can bear no resemblance to how it looks from another. Similarly, what appears to be an obvious solution to one party can, to another, be unworkable – or just completely misses the point.

This book makes the case for having regard to the bigger picture, whatever we are engaged in and wherever we are placed. It means understanding how individual identity is formed and conveyed by social and cultural context. Each policy initiative needs to be set in its wider context, to ensure that they do not unhelpfully cut across each other. Similarly, narrowly focused academic study (and I am not disputing the value of this) can usefully confer with its neighbouring disciplines, which may have fresh light to shed on the subject, or light that reveals much the same conclusions in another guise.

This also applies at the macro level, where the impact of global events on our daily lives is becoming hard to refute. The scale of inequalities and concentrations of economic power and wealth that are occurring in our world, and the apparent absence of any clear pathway out of the situation, is deeply worrying. It is becoming clearer, to those who choose to look, that power, including our ability to hold those with it to account, has shifted beyond our grasp.

It seems also to lie increasingly beyond the reach of national politicians, who find themselves demoted to a middle management role, obliged to enact their overlords' agenda and charged with keeping the masses on-side. Those who cannot, or will not, risk finding themselves replaced by unelected former employees of Goldman Sachs and their ilk. No longer is the litmus test for policy what the voters will think of it, but how the markets will respond. Evidence suggests that they respond well to privatisation, cuts to welfare benefits and services, the removal of protection for employees/consumers/citizens/the environment, and anything else that enables the rich to get richer.

Where does that leave the vast majority of us? Must we accept that we will not benefit proportionately from economic growth and that we must disproportionately pay the costs of economic recession? Whatever happened to democracy? Where is social justice to be found? This bleak scenario is not one which, naively or otherwise, I am willing to accept. In this book I try to set out an alternative; sketching out a vision for social justice, exploring how to widen the social mainstream, remove barriers to engagement and thereby promote inclusion for people with diverse characteristics on a more equal basis. I also discuss the sorts of policy and practice that could bring this about.

This book is not comprehensive and it is far from perfect. Yet, whatever its limitations, my hope is that it has something to offer and that, in the spirit of co-production, readers with different perspectives and knowledge will see ways to strengthen it and take it forward.

Sally Witcher
February 2013

ONE

Introduction

In search of social justice

Regardless of their affiliation, politicians down the ages have avowed their commitment to the pursuit of fairness or, more grandly, social justice. While at face value this might be cause for celebration, there are of course less happy interpretations of the apparent consensus. Either politicians all share the same goal, or terms such as 'fairness' and 'social justice' can mean whatever the utterer wants them to mean, thereby rendering them completely meaningless. They become reduced to 'feel-good' words that all can unite behind (Piachaud, 2008), even if what people understand by them is diametrically opposed (see Burchardt and Craig, 2008). Certainly no politician seems likely to declare a commitment to unfairness and social injustice (and any contemplating it might be well advised to rethink their choice of career). Whether the electorate is being offered a startling lack of choice, or different unarticulated choices, it bodes somewhat ill for democracy.

The elusive nature of much political discourse is nothing new and is in many ways unsurprising. There is the obvious risk that potential supporters may be deterred if meanings and intentions are more precisely spelt out. Moreover, where it pertains to disadvantage, the vaguer the concept the more difficult it becomes to demonstrate its extent, thereby dissipating pressure to act and evidence of failure to do so. However, not only can the same language mask significant differences, it is possible for difference to be proclaimed where in fact little exists. Familiar concepts may be renamed as politicians strive to demonstrate progress; to distinguish their efforts from those of their predecessors. Policies can be tweaked and re-branded to demonstrate supposed newness. At a time when the span of political terrain narrows, policy substance may be very similar and thus the scope to differentiate relies increasingly on the manner of its presentation:

> The degradation of politics to a state where it is a matter of the competing marketing policies of parties which at all levels of governance are essentially indistinguishable in their relation with corporate power and supine attitude to that

> power means that we have no say in the determination of future social trajectories. (Byrne, 2005, p 173)

In contrast, the imperatives in the academic arena are generally to strive for exact specification, to analyse and promote in-depth understanding. To achieve this in a highly complex environment points to the need to select narrow, tightly-defined subject matter to put under the intellectual microscope. A wide-angled charting of the landscape is abandoned in favour of archaeological investigation of a discrete area. Yet this approach too can result in lack of clarity and inconsistency. The same terminology can be used to describe entirely different phenomena. For example, social exclusion has variously meant detached from the labour market, not covered by state national insurance schemes, or without access to citizenship rights. Each has very different implications for social policy. On other occasions, different versions of much the same concept coexist without being acknowledged, as is the case across the literatures on discrimination emanating from the separate fields of disability, gender and race. Sometimes approaches are contested and furious disagreements ensue (the exchanges between Peter Townsend and Amartya Sen on the subject of poverty being a case in point – see Chapter Three).

Not only are there multiple discourses to be found in academic study of social justice, poverty, discrimination and social exclusion respectively, there are few clues regarding how they might inter-relate, or even the extent to which they are distinct from each other. At a mundane level it seems plausible to suggest, for example, that discrimination results in poverty and social exclusion and that all three are inimical to social justice. However, this apparently straightforward statement rapidly descends into complexity on a moment's reflection. Must discrimination cause poverty? Can it have disadvantageous consequences irrespective of levels of income and wealth? What anyway is the difference between poverty and social exclusion? Are there circumstances in which discrimination, poverty and social exclusion are compatible with social justice? And what role does inequality play with regard to any of them?

It seems self-evident that clarity and consistency matter a great deal in both political and academic arenas. For democracy to function, people need to know what they are voting for, to have options and to be able to understand them. They need to know what commitments mean if they are to hold politicians to account (see Burchardt and Craig, 2008). For social policy to come up with effective solutions, it is necessary not just to describe a social problem but to understand its causes. This indicates a need to delve beneath political sound-bites and empirical descriptions of disadvantage, to clarify meanings and formulate theory respectively.

However, before condemning lack of clarity and inconsistency out of hand, we might pause to consider if anything can be said in their favour. Perhaps it makes sense for politicians not to be overly specific about future action at a time of rapid change, when flexibility to respond to unpredictable events is likely to be necessary. It is not, however, a matter of prescriptive detail versus total vagueness. Somewhere in between it must be possible to articulate distinct goals, priorities and strategic direction. Clarity and consistency here could be seen as particularly important at such a turbulent time, if there is to be any hope of proactive intervention, not to mention democratic accountability. Moreover, there are occasions when politicians have demonstrated that they can achieve this. New Labour's Child Poverty Act 2010 set out an unambiguous goal of eradicating child poverty by 2020 and identified four forms of measurement with which to gauge progress (though, of course, it could be suggested that as any party is most unlikely to be in power for such a length of time, this was a target against which they were most unlikely to be held ultimately accountable).

A better reason for lack of clarity and inconsistency might reside in the nature of what is being described. If disadvantage has many causes and effects, different terminology will logically be required to distinguish between them. Furthermore, new concepts and coinages may be needed to make sense of new evolving manifestations of it. However, in practice, even where a concept is held constant, its meaning can shift subject to time and place. Poverty in the nineteenth century seems unlikely to be the same experience as it is today, any more than contemporary experience of it in Britain is likely to be the same as in Ethiopia. Whether this signals a change in the concept of poverty or just in its manifestation is debatable. Perhaps both are relative to time, place and culture. Alternatively, it may be possible to distinguish a consistent basis for comparison that respects difference and enables it to be gauged.

Concepts and discourses originate in different countries at particular times. Each reflects the historical context and prevailing cultural values, explaining economic, political and social issues of the day (see Veit-Wilson, 1998). For example, the concept of social exclusion originates from France as a product of an intellectual tradition founded on notions of the 'social contract' and solidarity, with seminal thinkers such as Rousseau and Durkheim (Silver, 1994). Meanwhile, from the heavily market-orientated US comes the discourse of 'the underclass', of ghettoisation and marginalisation (Burchardt et al, 2002a; Murray, 1996). The language differs, reflecting those contextual differences, but to what extent do they describe the same phenomenon? Is the 'underclass' a consequence of a breakdown in solidarity? Is understanding obscured or enhanced by separate discourses?

Different language might be used to denote the same phenomenon; the same language to denote different phenomena. While either scenario is evidently a recipe for confusion, it does not neatly follow that using the same language to describe the same phenomenon must always aid understanding. At one extreme, the experience of every individual is unique. For each person to articulate their experience via unique, albeit consistent, terminology would make it difficult to draw comparisons, to recognise common ground and to empathise. At the other extreme, to remark that people across the world experience the phenomenon of social injustice may well be true, but it tells us nothing regarding the similarity or diversity of those experiences, their underlying causes or potential courses of redress.

This suggests a number of challenges to establishing the right level of clarity and consistency of meaning that is necessary to promote understanding, steer action and permit accountability. First, there is the question of the appropriate degree of generality or specificity regarding the relationship between the concept and its expression. This might be envisaged as a spectrum, with 'general' at one end, 'specific' at the other, with a point somewhere between indicating the balance required to maximise understanding. A further factor might be the breadth of subject-matter, whether macro or micro, global or more local. Depending on the lens employed, the location on the general/specific spectrum might shift. It seems reasonable to suggest that the greater the proximity, the more can be seen, and the more precise it is possible to be while sustaining accuracy; and yet, to get too close can also compromise understanding. It might eclipse all context and make it hard to draw comparisons; both of which are important for establishing meaning.

A key consideration is whether a given concept serves as a universal benchmark against which empirical evidence, political intent or policy success can be evaluated and understood. It may instead be intrinsically relative, to the norms of a given society or a particular vision for society (whether or not articulated). We might all want social justice but our vision for how society should be is not the same. If the former is relative to the latter, then what we mean by social justice will similarly differ. Alternatively, a universal benchmark of social justice could be used to demonstrate that some visions for society are more socially just than others. If it were feasible to conceptualise such an entity, then what would a vision for the ideal, most socially just, society look like? Given the difficulties in capturing meaning, how could its features be unambiguously described? In a world of diverse people and cultures, does not any attempt to place one vision above others carry risks of imperialism and oppression? Even if such obstacles could be satisfactorily overcome, what could be done about it in practical terms? These are challenges with which this book will need to engage, though whether it proves possible (or indeed necessary) to resolve them all, remains to be seen.

Inequality versus social justice

Perhaps a good place to start is by attempting to identify the sorts of features of any society that might be deemed universally positive. Conversely, it is then worth pausing to consider whether there might be some interests that the features posited might not serve; some purposes that they could thwart rather than progress. The aim is to explore what might get in the way of consensus, not to state what does or must take place.

It would seem uncontroversial to suggest that social cohesion is likely to be a universally desirable characteristic. An absence of civil unrest and good relations between different communities must surely be to everyone's advantage. It is, however, possible for social friction to be deliberately generated. 'Divide and rule' might be an old cliché, but that does not mean it is without foundation. The demonising of certain groups (such as benefit claimants or immigrants), setting one against another, might be a way of manipulating public opinion and distracting public attention. While the spotlight is directed onto the alleged morals and behaviours of the least powerful, those of the powerful fade from view. Fragile group identity might become more distinct, and loyalty strengthened, by the exaggeration of difference and the creation of social distance. In such a situation, social cohesion might still be achieved, albeit by the oppression (whether by overt enforcement or by whipping up social disapprobrium) of people, behaviours and agendas that do not advance, or threaten the privileged position of those who hold power.

Similarly, and relatedly, it might seem self evident that it would be desirable for social arrangements to maximise the wellbeing, and minimise the suffering, of the populace. Yet if all are content with their lot, if they do not need, covet or fear anything, how are they to be incentivised to do what the powerful require of them? How are they to be controlled when both sticks and carrots (even the inconspicuous ones) are rendered redundant? Without competition; without winners and losers; without need or on-going dissatisfaction with one's lot, how is economic growth to be generated? Perhaps inequality is, as Walker contends Thatcher governments viewed it: 'an engine of enterprise, providing incentives for those at the bottom as well as those at the top' (1997, p 5); a driver as well as a consequence. Needs and wants promote (or compel) engagement with the means of satiating them. Yet there may be many or few such means available, and inequality might be expressed in the form of unequal opportunities to engage.

Such arguments do not necessarily show that cohesive societies comprised of contented, fulfilled, diverse people are undesirable. Instead, they are intended to suggest that where inequality of power prevails, such a scenario may not further the aims of the disproportionately powerful should they wish to retain and enhance their status. Neither does this necessarily mean that these are not universally desirable qualities of any society. Rather, it suggests that they may not be compatible with inequality. If so, then where inequality prevails, (honest) consensus on what an ideal society looks like seems unlikely to be achievable. More problematically still, if inequality can be shown to be compatible with social justice, would it mean that the proposed universally desirable features of a society are not?

Surely the democratic process is designed precisely in order to guarantee the justice of an inequitable distribution of power. It bestows equal power on each member of the electorate, legitimises the unequal power distribution that arises from the expression of their preferences and sets the strategic direction for its deployment. This may be more persuasive if a) it were incontrovertible that power resides with elected politicians, b) there were real choices about strategic direction on offer, c) these choices and their implications were unambiguously communicated, d) it were possible to bring the powerful to account should they wander off the agreed path, e) it could be shown that voting made a difference, f) large swathes of the electorate did not consequently abstain. Perhaps disengagement too is deliberately cultivated; another ploy to protect and promote unequal privilege.

As Byrne asserts:

> throughout the modern history of politics, market-orientated political ideologues and practitioners have sought to limit the political engagement of the mass of people and to restrict the capacity of political systems in relation to economic life. In mass democracies, achieving popular

> political disengagement is an important means to this end. (2005, pp 31, 32)

While inequality might provide incentives to engage (to satiate needs and wants), it seems it can have the opposite effect, perhaps because engagement is impossible, pointless, or perceived to be so. Whether proactively engineered or a natural consequence of inequality, a connection between degrees of inequality and disengagement has been established (Wilkinson and Pickett, 2010). With disengagement comes exclusion and inequality and exclusion would thus appear to be interconnected. Byrne's allegation also points to a relationship between political systems and market economies, and the mechanism through which power might shift (or be proactively shifted) from the former to the latter, or become conflated with it. Again, which is cause and which consequence is hard to discern.

Another possibility is that even a very inequitable distribution of power and resources could nonetheless be fair. In contrast to the view that our equal humanity imparts equal worth, perhaps human beings are intrinsically very unequal in their deservingness. If so, then inequality might be a socially just reflection of that fact. Yet the case for the justice of inequality is undermined by the pre-existence of inequality. Unequal starting points, access to opportunities, and so on can reasonably be expected to result in unequal outcomes. Unless all inequalities can be shown to mirror the degree of unequal deservingness, then surely they cannot be proclaimed to be just. It presupposes a system where disadvantage and advantage do not disproportionately lead to an accumulation of more of the same (unless deservingness is similarly accumulative). A further consideration is the definition of deservingness, who has the power to define it and how fair and impartial their definition is likely to be. An obvious consequence of inequality is that it is open to those who wield the power to set in place systems and benchmarks that will both perpetuate and justify their own advantage.

It is all very well to build a case that equality and social justice are closely intertwined (although there remains a great deal more to say on the subject), but surely it will serve little practical purpose if it can be shown that unjustifiable inequalities are unavoidable. If today's unjust inequalities (un-related to the deservingness of the individuals experiencing them) have their roots in past unjust inequalities and will in turn spawn future unjust inequalities, how is that trajectory to be altered? If inequality is not just continued but exacerbated over time, as inequalities accumulate and entrench ever deeper, how is that dynamic to be reversed? Perhaps the escalation of inequalities is a natural and inevitable phenomenon (Nozick, 1974) rather than one deliberately created by the self-interested privileged.

When it comes to inequalities in wealth, the stock answer is to redistribute in order to equalise – not that this will necessarily change the underlying dynamic – as Nozick has argued, to maintain equality would require repeated intervention (1974). Immediately this raises another issue that could weaken the foundations of the case for social justice. Is it always possible to distinguish between just and unjust in/equalities? If not, there is a risk that people who deserve their privilege are wrongly penalised, while those who deserve their disadvantage are wrongly rewarded. To make accurate judgements about deservingness must surely require intimate knowledge of people's lives, the reality of the opportunities available to them and the barriers which they face. Once again, inequalities intervene to make this proposition intrinsically problematic: 'When income differences are bigger, social distances are bigger and social stratification more important' (Wilkinson and Pickett, 2010, p 27). The more socially remote we are from each other, the harder it becomes to see clearly the situation of people with very different lives, experiences and perspectives: 'Empathy is only felt for those we view as equals' (Wilkinson and Pickett, 2010, p 52).

Underpinning these lines of argument are hints of a profound difference of view concerning the scope for everybody to forge their own destinies. Where inequalities prevail, those who disproportionately benefit may be expected to have a vested interest in asserting that the scope for agency is equal and hence arising inequalities are a just reflection of its deployment, for better or worse. More charitably, as previously suggested, social distance may simply render them oblivious to the possibility that not all share their freedoms and opportunities. Conversely, those who are disproportionately disadvantaged might draw attention to the obstacles that restrict their scope to improve their situation and compare this to the freedoms enjoyed by those more privileged. Thus the privileged might be inclined to attribute their good fortune to their own personal qualities, while the disadvantaged attribute their misfortune to the intervention of external factors that curtail their capacity to act as they would otherwise choose. Whether the aforesaid dynamics towards increasing inequalities are a natural or a created phenomenon, they might indeed constitute just such an obstacle.

Building up the capacity of disadvantaged individuals (for example to increase their employability) might make them better equipped to tackle the obstacles in their path. Without wishing to discount this potentially beneficial strategy, it does not necessarily do anything to change the environment that generated those obstacles in the first place. Instead of focusing on individuals and attributing their predicament to their own inadequacies, an alternative approach might be to take them out of the equation altogether and instead explore the social barriers which people might encounter and whether anything could be done to remove them. Instead of attributing all detrimental outcomes to the inadequacies of people (self-inflicted or otherwise), what would be the implications of attributing them to the nature of their environment? This is not necessarily to make a case that one or the other is solely responsible; it may be a matter of addressing both.

If social justice is contingent on an accurate fit between deservingness and outcomes, then it is imperative to flush out any hidden factors that might skew that relationship, otherwise people could be unfairly held accountable for disadvantage that is not of their making and from which they are powerless to escape. The equal availability of opportunities becomes meaningless if social barriers prevent some from taking them up. Whether or not unavoidable, if there are aspects of the way society operates – its systems, structures, cultural norms – that could intervene to promote qualitatively different outcomes for equally deserving individuals then these need to be disinterred. Without that awareness, judgements regarding deservingness cannot be confidently made. Yet it is one thing to recognise social injustice and another to tackle it. Unless such barriers are not just identified, but also removed, or reduced to the maximum extent possible, inequality cannot be socially just.

From this discussion it is possible to detect quite different approaches to equality. Baker et al (2004) identify three. Their first concerns minimum standards for basic equality: 'the idea that every human being deserves some kind of basic minimum of concern and respect' (2004, p 23), even if inequalities exist beyond this. Yet, instead of defining minimum standards, would it not be instructive to explore what maximum standards might look like? Their second, liberal egalitarianism, adds a concern for equal opportunities to the mix and focuses on individuals rather than groups or external factors. Inequalities are accepted as inevitable – the task is to make them fair. Yet, as argued, how can they be fair if external barriers prevent some from taking up so-called equal opportunities? Those who advocate 'equality of condition', their third approach, go further; aiming to eliminate major inequalities or at least reduce them significantly. They see inequality as also affecting groups and as rooted in social structures, particularly those of dominance and oppression. If so, then we need to know more about what these structural factors are, where they come from and how they operate. We need to explore how the space for diversity can be maximised through minimising dominance and oppression.

There is more to explore concerning types of inequality and its impact. There has already been considerable discussion of inequality of power and resources. For Baker et al (2004) they are two of five 'dimensions' of equality: respect and recognition; resources; love, care and solidarity; power; and working and learning. These are 'key factors that affect nearly everyone's well-being or quality of life' (2004, p 24). They are conditions that enable people to pursue their own – potentially diverse – aims and conceptions of well-being.

Before proceeding to conclude that inequality is the key issue to be explored, we need to distinguish its impact from that of disadvantage (in its various forms), irrespective of the extent of inequality in the society within which it occurs. For example, is it the unequal distribution of resources or the lack of resources that is the issue? The seminal work of Wilkinson and Pickett (2010) demonstrated that it is inequality within countries (and also US states), not the overall wealth of each that is the key determinant of outcomes: 'differences in average income or living standards between whole populations or countries don't matter at all, but income differences within those same populations matter very much indeed' (2010, p 13).

Although material conditions like bad housing, poor diets or lack of educational opportunities are generally associated with poor outcomes, it is the extent of inequality of income and wealth within a country that explains why 'some of the richest countries do worst' (Wilkinson and Pickett, 2010, p 25). They found that this inequality has an adverse impact on a range of outcomes, including level of trust, mental illness, life expectancy and infant mortality, obesity, homicides and imprisonment rates.[1] If, as previously discussed, it also erodes engagement and the capacity to empathise (Wilkinson and Pickett 2010), inequalities in income and wealth would also appear to have an adverse impact on other 'dimensions' of inequality (Baker et al, 2004) like respect and recognition, and love, care and solidarity. Meanwhile, inequalities in working and learning may well contribute to generating resource inequalities. The extent to which all dimensions appear to be bound up with resource inequalities underlines the latter's central importance. Whether or not this conflation is inevitable remains to be explored.

The relationship between 'lack' and inequality of resources requires further consideration. This includes the question of how 'lack' is to be defined and what benchmark of adequacy is to be used. Is it best established as a point within the span between extremes, comparison with the norm or average, the requirements for bodily survival or the pre-conditions (perhaps 'dimensions') for autonomous action? Questions remain concerning how inequality and/ or 'lack' of resources might be redressed. Failing that, perhaps their disadvantageous impact might be mitigated or even neutralised, thereby lowering the adequacy benchmark. Issues like distribution and mitigation might arise with regard to other forms of disadvantage, whether associated with resource levels or in their own right. To get to the bottom of this we need to obtain a firm purchase on the nature and impact of different forms and ranges of disadvantage and advantage. Consideration will be necessary of the entire span of inequality, as well as averages and norms..

An alternative vision

Earlier a question was posed concerning the feasibility of conceptualising a vision for the ideal, most socially just, society. The previous section then began with an attempt to sketch out some features that might be considered obviously and universally desirable. Rapidly, it became clear how inequality could intervene to undermine them. This would seem to imply that the aim should be to diffuse the dynamics of inequality and to equalise as much as possible. Yet, if the aim is to promote engagement, and thence inclusion and social cohesion, there have to be reasons to engage. If equality were fully achieved (casting aside for now the practical feasibility of the proposition), where would be the incentive? If all have the same resources, how is effort to be justly rewarded and destructive behaviours admonished or prevented? If all have the same amount of power, does anyone actually have any power? The vision is not for a stagnant pool of sameness. Equality does not have to mean 'the same'. It can also mean equivalent: different but of equal worth.

The starting point for this book is a vision for mainstream society where diversity – of people, cultures, forms of contribution, and so on – is recognised, valued, and accommodated to the maximum extent possible. It follows that inclusion must be on a basis of empowerment to express difference, rather than conditional on its oppression. However, there will be limits to what can be included without jeopardising social cohesion and causing society to fragment. Exclusion on other grounds would contravene social justice.

If this proposition sounds straightforward, it is deceptive. It raises many questions, including how such a society is to be depicted, the nature of the space available for individual agency to operate within, and what binds people together or cuts them adrift. The pivotal relationships between difference and equality (in its many guises) and between equality and inclusion require in-depth exploration, as do the roles of different forms of disadvantage. Having developed a theoretical model, the practical implications for policy need to be extracted.

The form disadvantage takes may be consequent on the way in which a given society operates and the barriers this creates. It might therefore be possible to minimise its prevalence and/or its impact by 'adjusting' social structures, institutions, systems and cultural norms. To achieve social justice in accordance with the vision described could, therefore, entail taking action to widen access to the social mainstream – or the concept of the social mainstream itself – by identifying social barriers and exploring whether and how they might be removed. Conversely, where the terms of inclusion are narrowly drawn, to be included might require the oppression or repression of difference rather than enable its expression. Inclusion on any terms, at any cost, is not the aim.

Of course, some alternatives will be mutually exclusive. Removing social barriers for one group might in turn create new barriers for another. Disadvantageous outcomes might not be attributable to external factors but to the personal characteristics or behaviours of the people experiencing them. Rather than removing social barriers, social justice might instead (or as well) be a matter of equipping individuals to improve their outcomes, for example by increasing their skills or facilitating new behaviours. Theoretical and practical limitations may arise, to the extent that the environment and the people within it can – or should be – be 'adjusted' to achieve a better fit. It may transpire that some barriers must be retained and some people need to be excluded, if social cohesion is to be preserved and social justice respected.

The extent to which people do, or should, integrate into wider society are matters for debate. Integration often has connotations of imposition or enforcement (see Ratcliffe, 2000), which is clearly at odds with the notion of expression of difference. The central issue for this book, though, is the extent to which the inclusion of diversity into the mainstream is possible, if differences are enabled rather than oppressed. It explores how inclusion on a basis of equality (of various types and guises) can be maximised, and what this implies for the ways in which society operates: a vision for social justice as inclusive equality.

Contemporary reality

Discussion so far has been at a somewhat theoretical level. It is all very well to hypothesise about the impact of inequality and to posit an ideal, but if these exercises bear no relation to the 'economic, political and social issues of the day' (see Veit-Wilson, 1998) they serve little purpose. If the forms that disadvantage takes are consequent on the nature of society and the way it operates, how are we to describe the nature and operation of society today? In particular, what evidence is there that this creates inequalities, disengagement and exclusion?

This section starts by briefly considering the impact of globalisation and developments in IT that have enabled it. Drawing on recent data it then drills down to explore how emerging themes have played out in Britain, albeit situated within its global context. In effect, this exercise reveals some of the weaknesses of over-proximity and attempts at precision. To focus on one detail risks failure to see neighbouring landmarks that it would be relevant to include. A full survey of the landscape at this level of detail would require a book in itself. Similarly, even if accurate today, it may not be so tomorrow. The best that can be done here is to provide a blurry snapshot of a rapidly unfolding narrative. Hopefully it is sufficient to convey something about the starting point for the journey towards a vision of inclusive equality.

The big picture

How is 'society' to be delineated in today's world? No longer can it neatly be equated (if it ever really could) with a homogenous nation state, encircled by co-terminus economic, political, cultural and geographic boundaries. The forces of globalisation operate to detach financial and political power from their former moorings at that level, leaving in their wake all manner of social repercussions. Greater migration means that nation states become increasingly heterogeneous, their populations comprised of a rich mix of diverse peoples and cultures. The ongoing revolution in the field of information technology is both eroding the significance of national boundaries and fundamentally changing how we interact with each other: the way we work, buy and sell, learn, entertain ourselves, form communities, socialise and mobilise politically. It is also changing how we convey our identity, enabling anonymity or total reinvention.[2]

All of these might be considered features of globalisation, 'the shrinking of time and space' (Deacon, 2007, p 8), as geographically defined boundaries and physical distance cease to impose limits on interaction. Held highlights the highly interconnected nature of the world we are in, as can be measured by 'mapping the ways in which trade, finance, communication, pollutants, violence, among many other factors, flow across borders' (2010, p 298). The impact of globalisation has been described in terms of the triumph of capitalism, 'American style' (Stiglitz, 2002, p 5; also Giddens, 2002), where the rules of the game protect the rich at the expense of poorer nations. The 'Washington consensus' promotes the view that the role of government is to be 'fundamentally distrusted in core areas of socio-economic life – from market regulation to disaster planning' (Held, 2010, p 296). The thrust of that consensus is 'to adapt the public domain – local national, global – to market leading institutions and processes' (Held, 2010, p 296).

Contrary to the contention that globalisation shrinks time and space, it seems very much to extend the distance between the powers that have an impact on individual citizens and those citizens themselves. The institutional infrastructure does not exist for democratic governance of global institutions (see Held, 2010 and Archibugi, 2010). There is no mechanism through which they can hold to account multi-national corporations, global markets and structures such as the International Monetary Fund, World Bank, United Nations or European Union. Whatever the advances in communication technology, institutions like the International Monetary Fund and the World Bank are neither transparent in the way they operate nor democratically accountable (see Stiglitz, 2002). Individuals are not necessarily aware of the actions of global institutions and how they affect their daily lives. Direct causal connections may anyway be far from clear-cut.

In turn, it is argued, globalisation curtails the capacity of national politicians to act, and hence the scope for the ordinary citizen to exert democratic influence and accountability at that level too. According to Habermas:

> The political autonomy of citizens acquires concrete content only to the extent that a society is capable of influencing itself by political means...the expansion of the domains of political responsibility and the new forms of corporatism have placed the channels of legitimation of the nation-state under intolerable strain...with a switch-over to a neoliberal economic regime these channels have definitively reached breaking point. (2010, p 276)

He comments on the impact of the extensive privatisation of formerly state-provided services and how this removes them from political supervision and control – and hence democratic accountability. Risks increase where privatisation extends to 'core areas of sovereignty' such as public security, the military, the penal system or the energy supply – processes vital for 'maintaining the rule of law, freedom, distributive justice, and equal rights'; leading to ever more pronounced asymmetry between the responsibilities accorded to the democratic state and its scope for action (Habermas, 2010, p 276).

As power appears to be drawn upwards to global level, where does that leave regional or local-level political structures? Giddens (1998) has suggested that globalisation moves power downwards, to devolved structures and the formation of local community identities, as well as upwards to supranational institutions. This proposition might open up the possibility of a more equitable distribution of power at lower societal levels, in the form of greater scope for influence and accountability. Of course, in accordance with Habermas's account of the impact of globalisation and its dominant economic agenda on nation-states, localisation might just mean devolvement of responsibility and accountability, but not necessarily the power and resources to act.

Globalisation seems to have profound implications, not just for equality of political power and economic resources, but in terms of how we respond to increasing contact between people who live and think differently (Giddens, 2002). Whatever our differences, 'cosmopolitanism' concerns the acknowledgement of 'moral obligations owed to all human beings based solely on our humanity alone, without reference to race, gender, nationality, ethnicity, culture, religion, political affiliation, state citizenship, or other communal particularities' in the context of our 'increased human interconnection' (Brown and Held, 2010, p 1). Their focus is on the universal equality we share beneath our differences.

Yet, whether exposure to difference does in fact result in increased connection or in rejection depends on whether it is seen as enriching or threatening, regarded with respect or contempt, or dismissed as irrelevant. Increasing interconnection in terms of exposure does not necessarily result in positive connection: in some cases 'the sight of difference is the portent of danger, horrifying for being unfamiliar and unspeakable' (Bauman, 2000, p 82). It might result in homogeneity, as cultural norms and practices interweave, or in a hardening of cultural boundaries, to polarisation rather than integration, as per the rise in religious fundamentalism, both Islamic and Christian. Giddens (2002) goes so far as to describe the battle between cosmopolitan tolerance and fundamentalism of various sorts as the 'battleground of the 21st century'. As will be explored, both entail risks of social disintegration.

Globalisation may thus have economic, political and social consequences. It seems to change the distribution and location of political power and economic resources, and compels us to confront and respond to social and cultural diversity. For ordinary citizens, the complexity, pace of change and sheer scale of what occurs at global level could understandably make the prospect of engaging with it overwhelming. Their inability to exert influence would seem to make it pointless to try and the lack of infrastructure through which to engage anyway makes it impossible. Greater interconnection in some respects appears to be accompanied by disconnection in others.

However, we should be careful not to leap too readily to the conclusion that globalisation is the whole story or that national governments are powerless to do much about it (Hirst et al, 2009). True, its role in the near-collapse of the international banking system seems difficult to dispute. According to Hutton, the interdependence of the New York and London offices of the five largest US investment banks has been so close that they were 'operating a financial axis that, for all practical purposes, was one market' (Hutton, 2011, p 152). Yet, as will be explored, there remains much that national and local government can do to promote equality in its various forms, widen scope for engagement and hence help foster inclusion.

What this tells us is not that society as nation state no longer exists, but that it needs to be understood within its global context. National social policy 'can no longer be *understood* or *made* without reference to the global context within which the country finds itself' (Deacon, 2007, p 3, emphasis in original). However, nation states remain clearly delineated geographical territories. The nature of local neighbourhood communities continues to have an immediate bearing on quality of life, and face-to-face interaction remains both necessary (such as in the delivery of social care) and, surely for most of us, highly desirable.

National politicians and national policy remain the primary focus for managing external and internal pressures and the economic, political and social issues these generate within their domain. Whether they retain the power proactively to forge an altogether different direction to the one demanded by global markets and their political allies seems less certain – even where conforming to it brings devastating social costs to great swathes of their electorates (the fate of Greece being a case in point). Yet, to make 'reference to the global context' (Deacon, 2007) does not have to mean that all is determined by it. While their room for manoeuvre may have diminished – and it might suit politicians of a certain ideological persuasion to exaggerate its reduction (Hirst et al, 2009) – it should be helpful to our purpose to investigate what autonomous action can be taken in the space that remains. That is the primary focus for this book – though it is not to deny the critical importance of the cosmopolitan project to define social justice in terms of global justice (for more on this see, for example, Brock, 2009; Brooks, 2008; Mandle, 2006).

Under the spotlight

Economic crisis

It seems a fairly safe assertion to make that much of the situation in which we find ourselves today stems from the widespread financial crisis that erupted in 2008. Yet, according to Hutton that crisis was 'a generation in the making' (2011, p 155). Driven by sheer greed and fuelled by globalisation, at its heart lay 'delusional self-deception among bankers about the risks they were running' made possible by 'laissez-faire ideology' and 'the collapse of social and political forces committed to fairness' (Hutton, 2011, p 155).

Wilkinson and Pickett assert that: 'there is now evidence that inequality played a central causal role in the financial crashes of 1929 and 2008' (2010, p 296). Income inequality in the UK, as in the US, is among the highest when compared to other developed countries (Wilkinson and Pickett, 2010). Today, widely reported figures proclaim that the richest 400 Americans own more wealth than the bottom half of the American income distribution – 150 million people. This phenomenon too did not spring from nowhere. For example, a report from the US Congressional Budget Office published in October 2011 revealed that between 1979 and 2007, the income of the top 1 per cent of households grew by 275 per cent, whereas the bottom 20 per cent saw an increase of just 18 per cent.[3] This suggests that what occurred in 2008 was both symptomatic of wider, longstanding problems as well as the cause of many more.

While economic growth in the UK continues to prove elusive, and the threat to it posed by the Eurozone debt crisis still looms large, not all have been equally adversely affected. The High Pay Commission's independent inquiry into top pay showed that 'In the last year alone, as economic growth has slowed, executive pay in the FTSE 100 rose on average by 49 per cent compared to just 2.7 per cent for the average employee' (2011, p 9). Justification for such a divergence – just what those at the top have done (or indeed could do) to merit it – is not always apparent.

According to the High Pay Commission, excessively high pay and pay inequity promotes employee disengagement and this damages companies. Yet the negative impact of excessive high pay extends further; it is also 'bad for our economy and has negative impacts on society as a whole' (High Pay Commission, 2011, p 8). Unsurprisingly, 'the growing pay gap, with rewards meted out to those at the top, often for failure, has increased public disillusionment and distrust of business'

(High Pay Commission, 2011, p 10). Public trust in the way our banks are run has plummeted, from 90 per cent in 1983 to just 19 per cent (Park et al, 2010).

If times are hard for many people in work, it is certainly no better for the increasing numbers who find themselves unemployed. The quarterly fall in the number of employees is the largest since records began in 1992, with figures for September 2011 showing an unemployment rate for the preceding three months of 8.3 per cent – the highest since the three months to January 1996. The number of unemployed people (2.62 million) has not been higher since September 1994. Meanwhile, unpaid work (much carried out by women) receives little acknowledgement, despite the fact that it is valued at around a third of Gross Domestic Product in OECD countries (OECD, 2011).

Figures show that certain groups have been disproportionately affected by the downturn (Office for National Statistics, 16 November 2011). Female unemployment is at its highest for 23 years and the total number of 16–24 year olds out of work (an unemployment rate of 21.9 per cent) has risen to 1.02 million; both unemployment rate and number being the highest since comparable records began in 1992. Meanwhile, unequal pay remains an issue for women in paid employment. Despite the Equal Pay Act, according to the Fawcett Society, they are still paid 14.9 per cent less on average than men.[4] There is also considerable evidence of the disproportionate economic inequalities experienced by people from black and minority ethnic communities.[5] It seems that economic inequality can have more than one axis, creating distance between people segmented not just by socio-economic status and income distribution, but also by groups founded on characteristics such as gender, age and ethnicity.

Democratic failures

If the conditions leading up to the financial crisis arose over a period of several decades, it seems reasonable to ask why our politicians failed to intervene to prevent it. Another good question might concern their apparent inability to deal with the consequences. In the US, the Joint Select Committee on Deficit Reduction, charged with finding a way to reduce the US deficit by $1.2 trillion (out of a total $15 trillion),[6] failed to meet its deadline for reaching agreement on a way forward.[7] In the UK, the massive deficit in the public accounts gave the Coalition government a green light to roll back the frontiers of the State, [8] and with it democratic accountability, on a scale and at a speed that Conservatives of past eras could have scarcely dared imagine. They have seized the opportunity: withdrawing state subsidy from higher education and opening up the National Health Service to private providers. Yet alarm bells should be ringing. The self-inflicted collapse of private care home provider Southern Cross in 2011 left the fate of its 31,000 residents hanging in the balance. If, as with the banks, private companies delivering essential services cannot be allowed to fail, might the tax-payer repeatedly be called upon to foot the bill for their mismanagement? How might the knowledge of an ever-present bail-out skew market behaviours and dynamics?

Meanwhile, in Europe, despite the politicians' apparent best efforts, the euro continues to teeter on the brink of catastrophe. Their response has been to push for greater centralisation of fiscal power. In Greece and Italy, the two countries in most serious trouble, democratically elected governments were replaced with technocratic administrations. Italy's Silvio Berlusconi was replaced by Mario Monti, a former senior adviser at Goldman Sachs – a company with far-reaching influence, both economically and politically.[9] As political power becomes ever more closely enmeshed with (or usurped by?) economic power, a concentrated, centralised nexus takes form, increasingly remote from the vast majority of people.

In the UK, public disillusion with the banks appears to be accompanied by loss of trust in our politicians, which was never particularly high. It fell to an all-time low in the wake of the MPs' expenses scandal – it is not just the bankers who have been perceived as taking whatever they can get away with. According to the British social attitudes survey (Park et al, 2010), four in ten people say that they 'almost never' trust governments to put the national interest first. This was six points above the 34 per cent recorded in 2006 – a previous all-time high.

Perhaps as a consequence of lack of choice provided by the mainstream parties, and/or loss of confidence in them, nationalism is emerging as a focus for political divergence. In keeping with the proposition that power is shifting downwards, pressures towards devolution may well increase, with the Scottish National Party gaining a majority in the Scottish Parliamentary Election in 2011 (despite an election process designed to prevent majorities from occurring) and swingeing cuts in the pipeline, imposed by a very different brand of politician in Westminster.

Evidence is mixed regarding trends in engagement with the political process. Party allegiance has been in long-term decline and there has been a weakening of a sense of civic duty to vote (Park et al, 2010). Nonetheless, while still low by historical standards, turnout at the 2010

General Election at 65 per cent was a little higher than previously. Representation of different groups in Parliament remains unequal, but there are some signs of improvement. Less than a quarter of the MPs in the House of Commons are women, although the percentage of female MSPs in the Scottish Parliament is higher at over a third. While they remain under-represented, in the 2010 UK Parliamentary election the number of minority ethnic MPs almost doubled, reaching a total of 27 (EHRC, 2011 – triennial review).

What is perhaps more striking is the extent of political activity taking place outwith formal political structures. Strikes, demonstrations and 'occupations' can be seen as another way in which people attempt to make their voices heard by their political rulers. Austerity measures have prompted major protests in many European countries, including Greece, Spain, the UK, France and Romania. The 'Occupy' movement emerged in a matter of months, with a global day of action on 15 October 2011 reportedly marked by protests in 951 cities in 82 countries.[10]

It could be considered ironic that just a few years ago the US and its Western allies campaigned to bring democracy to the Middle East. Now it is claimed that the 'Arab Spring' uprisings in Egypt and Tunisia inspired the Occupy movement to fight back against 'the corrosive power of major banks and multinational corporations over the democratic process, and the role of Wall Street in creating an economic collapse that has caused the greatest recession in generations'.[11]

Social disengagement

It is evident that economic and political events will have social repercussions. The backdrop to current social developments in the UK are the so-called austerity measures, in the form of massive cuts to essential public services and welfare benefits. It is not just the poor who are bearing the brunt of the recession. The middle classes too are 'squeezed' by, among other things, the above-inflation rise in costs imposed by the privatised utilities and rail companies. Claims that we are 'all in this together' ring hollow, however, as the wealthiest somehow contrive to increase their wealth.

In keeping with the paradox of increased global interconnection and disconnection (enforced or otherwise) from economic and political systems, evidence is mounting that we are also disengaging from each other. Despite a widespread view that the income gap between rich and poor is too large, the latest British social attitudes survey (Park et al, 2011) indicates a hardening of attitudes towards people in poverty.

The percentage attributing their predicament to laziness or lack of willpower rose from 15 per cent in 1994 to 26 per cent in 2009 while the percentage giving the cause as injustice in society fell from 29 to 19 per cent. This is consistent with Wilkinson and Pickett's findings that 'With greater inequality, people are less caring of one another, there is less mutuality in relationships, people have to fend for themselves and get what they can' (2010, p 56). However, it seems that such attitudes can be fuelled by factors other than poverty or income inequality. Once again, there is evidence that particular groups are disproportionately likely to be disadvantaged.

There is talk of a lost generation of young people unable to find jobs, saddled with large debts acquired in order to pay newly introduced tuition fees, unable to save for the higher deposits now required for a mortgage, and with the scope to put aside something towards a pension but a distant dream. Fifty-five percent of 18–29 year olds reported being treated with prejudice due to their age compared to just 20 per cent of those aged 60–9 (Park et al, 2010).

A study into what led young people to become involved in the sudden outbreak of rioting in English cities in August 2011 revealed a mixture of motivations (Morrell et al, 2011), ranging from 'something exciting to do', 'the opportunity to get free stuff' and 'a chance to get back at the police'. Some cited anger and resentment at authority figures, particularly politicians, lack of job prospects and the constant struggle to make ends meet in the context of a materialistic culture. Deciding factors included the nature of their local communities, whether low-level criminality was the prevailing norm; whether they had a stake in the local area via voluntary and community work, and family and peer attitudes. While it may be too simplistic to attribute destructive behaviours to inequality and disengagement, they clearly had significant roles to play.

At the other end of the age spectrum, a report from the Equality and Human Rights Commission (EHRC) revealed that care services for older people in England were often so poor that they breached human rights. While half those surveyed were happy with the service received, others experienced treatment that was dehumanising and left them stripped of self worth and which promoted rather than redressed social isolation. The report highlights examples of failure to provide basic support to enable people to eat, drink or go to the toilet, money being stolen, physical abuse, and patronising behaviour. It stressed the importance of how services are delivered, the attitude of the carer and the quality of the relationship between care and service user. Problems arise when the focus is overwhelmingly on the completion of tasks for which insufficient time is allowed, both likely to be symptomatic of financial cutbacks. Such findings, and the reasons for them, are echoed in the Care Quality Commission's report 'Dignity and nutrition for older people' (published 13 October 2011), concerning the experiences of older people in NHS hospital settings.

Meanwhile, hate crime towards disabled people is increasingly evident (see Quarmby, 2011), arguably fuelled by political and media portrayals of disabled people as benefit scroungers. Another EHRC report claims that disability-related harassment – covering bullying, physical violence, sexual assault, financial exploitation and institutional abuse – is a part of everyday life for many disabled people. The inquiry exposed systemic failure on the part of local authorities when it came to recognising its extent and impact and taking action to prevent it. Surveys commissioned by disability organisation Scope showed that nearly half the disabled people questioned felt that attitudes towards them had worsened over the previous year, while 66 per cent said that they had experienced aggression, hostility or name-calling.[12] Hate crime is even to be found in care settings. Broadcast on 31 May 2011, secret filming in a residential hospital for people with learning disabilities exposed horrific levels of bullying, systematic brutality and even torture.[13]

Racism was given fresh impetus by the so-called 'War on Terror'. Fears about opening the flood-gates to asylum-seekers and economic migrants are easily ignited at a time when jobs and services are on the line. Race and religiously-motivated attacks remain a persistent phenomenon. Yet there are some more positive signs, as reported in the EHRC's first triennial review (2010). This shows that people are increasingly comfortable with the idea of working with and for people from ethnic backgrounds other than their own. Black Caribbean and Bangladeshi pupils are starting to narrow the achievement gap at GCSE level. The gender stereotype of a women's place being in the home has softened. Civil partnership legislation enabled lesbian and gay couples to acquire legal recognition and status, an important step towards equality. Overall, they say that Britain has become a fairer place. However, as discussed, there remain significant and increasing inequalities, notably of income, wealth and power.

Review

Whatever its acknowledged limitations, the data presented here begins to indicate a way of conceptualising 'society' as a multi-layered structure, from global, to national, to regional and local, right down to individuals. Power and resources can be seen to concentrate at certain levels and shift between levels. There seems to be a close interplay of power, causes and effects between economic and political dimensions, and how they play out in social dimensions.

Throughout society, from wealthy bankers and MPs to young people rioting in the streets, there is evidence of an 'everyone for themselves' attitude. Fairness for some seems to mean whatever you can get away with. Similarly, there is a loss of respect and empathy all round, both for authority figures and for those deemed weaker or needier. This could be taken as both causative and symptomatic of disengagement from the wider collective, or rather the dissolution of the latter resulting from inequality.

Undoubtedly, our world has become more complex, more subject to rapid change and more culturally pluralistic, notwithstanding the crude polarisation of so-called Western Christian and Islamic cultural values arising in the aftermath of 9/11. There is evidence of inequality across all five of Baker et al's dimensions (2004) and of the consequences of inequality, like loss of empathy and trust, identified by Wilkinson and Pickett (2010). While there are indications that attitudes towards some groups are becoming more tolerant and respectful, they have become very much less so towards others. To reverse the on-going increase in concentrations of wealth and power (and their counterparts) becomes ever more challenging. It means those who have them continue to strengthen their ability to protect and expand their assets and those without become increasingly less able to stop them. Yet, if we do not want to see a future scarred by social fragmentation, disregard – even contempt – for others, increased poverty, exclusion and disempowerment, the inequalities arising from the way our society currently operates have to be addressed. We urgently need to find shared commonalities amid diversity, around which to forge social cohesion.

Approach

In the quest to establish meaning, and identify action that would take us towards the vision for inclusive equality described, one (entirely valid) approach would be to gather further empirical data to flesh out this sketch of contemporary society, look at how it operates and the disadvantageous social consequences that ensue. Another approach, and the one that this book will take, is to delve more deeply into theory. As Lister remarks, 'Facts don't speak for themselves: they have to be interpreted' (2010, p 2). For example, we may all accept that data show an escalation in wage inequality. However, perhaps particularly in a very unequal society, socially distant people may attribute this to different causes – to the prevalence of skills and their market valuation, differing degrees of effort, or the curtailment of opportunity by social barriers. To get a purchase on what lies beneath superficial manifestations, we need to excavate the theoretical strata that lie beneath: 'Only by abstracting from the complexities of the real world can we devise a conceptual schema that can illuminate it' (Fraser, 1997, pp 12–13; Mandle, 2006).

Although the aim of this book is to develop a vision for social justice that is relevant to today's world, it does so by abstracting back to create a heuristic model – a generic theoretical framework against which to focus debate and steer the collection, arrangement and assessment of empirical data, through which to identify implications for policy and policy-making processes. Models are usually simplifications or abstractions, screening out superficial detail to reveal the underlying skeleton. They can fulfil many purposes: to propose a way of looking at something, to illustrate how something works or to test out how it might work. The purpose of this model is primarily the first of these. While acknowledging that theory and discourse may emerge from social context rather than precede it and direct it, that goals are not necessarily explicit any more than actions are strategically and rationally oriented towards their achievement, the model constructed here explores how to classify and codify types of goals, systems, processes and relationships.

The book is concerned with the relationship between theory and what it implies for policy, in particular for social policy. As previously discussed, economic and political factors generate social repercussions. Adjustments to economic policy and political systems should therefore be capable of bringing social benefits. However, those policy levers seem to have been somewhat decommissioned with regards to that goal, by an absence of political will – or capacity – to regulate the markets, the diminishment of democracy that accompanies large-scale privatisation, and the increasingly remote centralisation of political and economic powers. Of course, the counter-argument is that unregulated markets and privatisation bring economic growth, which in turn brings social gains, as does the promotion of economic participation through the removal of state-funded social protection. To the extent that economic issues dominate the social arena, it seems likely they will also drive social policy, in terms of its goals and delivery. Moreover, social policy can be understood to have a remit well beyond such matters as the design of public services (health, education, social security and so on), but instead to be intimately bound up with wider sociological concerns about how societies manage changes in structure (Townsend, 1975). This blurring of disciplines is controversial, but this is the approach that will, nonetheless, be pursued. In fact others too will be brought into the mix where this helps to illuminate discussion.

Social welfare policy plays a pivotal role in promoting or impeding inclusion, operating at the boundary (or boundaries?) between exclusion and inclusion, supporting people who are ill-equipped to operate, or prevented from operating, in the market. The design and delivery of welfare goods and services, notably social security, employment services, education, health and community care services, are of critical importance. They can facilitate participation, not just in the market but in wider society, or they can be dead-ends, reinforcing social exclusion with unnecessary stigma, segregation and failure to promote wider social connections. Even if they ultimately hold the key to inclusion, prospective recipients are likely to avoid engaging with services that confirm incapacity, invade privacy, and further disempower.

Of course, whether theory is what steers policy is open to challenge. Policy is often claimed to be 'evidence-based'; rooted in empirical evidence of the problem it seeks to address and of the impact of potential solutions. As previously discussed, theory can play a key role in steering the collection of evidence and in its interpretation. Yet, political economists responsible for theory and people involved in developing social policy do not always speak the same language (Wolff, 2008). The line of sight from abstraction to implementation can be very blurred.

It may persuasively be argued that social policy development is not driven by theory – or empirical evidence for that matter – but by political imperatives to reduce public expenditure, enable tax cuts, promote economic growth and, of course, win elections. Policy may be made reactively in response to unforeseen events, or used opportunistically to lend credence to pre-existing ideologically derived intentions or assumptions. In such cases, it may appear that theory has no role to play. Nevertheless, whether or not those responsible are conscious of it, whether or not *post hoc*, some form of theoretical underpinning is always discernible, even if just at a level of broad assumption. The more considered and substantial that underpinning is, the greater the chance should be that policy will achieve its goal.

Key themes

The first task will be to grapple with the meaning of 'social justice' and concepts of 'disadvantage' – poverty, discrimination and social exclusion – to try to extract the distinguishing features of each. Even if their expression is relative to the society in question, what exactly are those concepts that are expressed in relative terms and how do they differ from, and relate to, each other? It is possible that respective meanings and interactions will become clearer when each concept is viewed in the context of the others.

Discussion of inequality weaves throughout those literatures, as do other themes that need to be unpacked – and perhaps reframed and realigned – in order to draw conclusions. By abstracting back from their expression in the contemporary context to explore such themes in generic 'ideal' terms as they apply to the vision for social justice described, it should be possible to develop a framework through which to examine it in greater depth, to gauge distance from the intended destination and to identify action to take us forward.

This book casts a wide net, drawing not just on theory commonly discussed in relation to social policy, but sociological, political and psychological theory as well as 'group-based' theory emanating from Women's Studies, Disability Studies, and so on. This is not intended as an in-depth literature review; the aim is to pull out key themes and consider how they might come together. The quantity of material that could be included is vast and what follows is necessarily highly selective and incomplete.

The following section briefly outlines key cross-cutting themes.

The nature and operation of society

As may be expected, the thinking of Durkheim, Marx and Weber informs the literature in various ways and aspects of it will be discussed at various points. However, particular themes that emerge include the conceptualisation of society in terms of economic, political and other spheres or dimensions (Walzer, 1983; Rodgers, 1995a; Berghman, 1995), social and systems integration (Lockwood, 1992) and how social operations promote the interests of dominant groups. There is also a strong emphasis on social processes and relationships, particularly in the social exclusion literature. One way of conceptualising social inclusion is in terms of participation in social processes.

This seems to be consistent with a loose definition of social structure as 'the pattern of social arrangements within a society or social group' (Deacon, 2002, p 138). It can be conceived, not just in terms of spheres or dimensions, but as systems, institutions, class relations and other forms of social categorisation and inter-relationship. However, whether social categories form social structure or are formed by the dominant 'pattern of social arrangements' is challenged by the discrimination literature in particular. Whether social structure is what frames social processes or is formed by them is a further consideration. Giddens' structuration theory positions structures as both the means through which social practices are enabled and the outcome of social practices: '"structure" is regarded as rules and resources recursively implicated in social reproduction; institutionalised features of social systems have structural properties in the sense that relationships are stabilized across time and space' (1984, p xxxi).

The relationship between structure and agency (the autonomous action of individuals) is a major preoccupation of social theory in general. It is a central theme in the literature on social justice and poverty, in terms of explaining whether disadvantage is the outcome of the constraints imposed by social structures, or the freely-chosen actions of individuals. Bound up with this is a raft of moral and status issues, and questions around motivation and policy direction. This debate surfaces in the discrimination literature which, in various guises, explores the impact of structural forms and their rules on the characteristics, capacity and behaviours of individuals, and of the processes connecting each to the other.

Engagement and connection

If participation in social processes is an aspect of social inclusion, questions arise regarding motivations and objectives for it, and what would encourage or dissuade people from engaging (Doyal and Gough, 1991; Dean, 2010; Goffman, 1967; Turner, 2002). The quality of one-to-one interaction and its implications for each party concerned – what they expect to gain, how they consequently feel about themselves – is likely to be key. How the motivation and capacity of each party are regarded by the other may determine the style of interaction and the stance of those concerned. Le Grand (2003) memorably characterises human motivations and behaviours in metaphorical terms: whether the other party is assumed to be honourable, altruistic and benevolent (a knight), dishonourable and self-interested (a knave), passive and helpless (a pawn) or autonomous and proactive (a queen).

There are other factors that affect the quality of interaction, such as the balance of power between the parties, perhaps a consequence of the degree to which the interaction is a necessity for each. It has also been shown to be contingent on inequality. Harking back to the structure versus agency debate, inequality means that people may be too far apart to see the realities of each other's situation (or even their humanity) to recognise the barriers and opportunities which they face, the degree of autonomy which they can exercise and thence to gauge desert. They rely on rough outlines, broad stereotypes, of each other. Attitudes to difference, and the ability to recognise shared commonalities, assumes critical importance.

Identity

To assess and judge each other requires a means of conveying identity. There is much to be found in the postmodernist literature on how identity is formed and communicated, some of which has directly contributed to thinking about the subject within the discrimination arena, particularly with regard to 'queer theory'.

Postmodernists have much to say on the significance of discourse. It is through discourse that needs, perspectives, priorities and identities are recognised or rendered invisible (echoing early discussion about the difficulty in pinpointing meaning).

> Sexists, racists, and imperialists all use similar techniques – they make *their* 'normalizing' discourse prevail, and, in doing so, they can actually create or bring into being the deviant or what many postmodernists call *the other*. Their discourse actually helps to *create* the subordinate identities of those who are excluded from participation in it. (Butler, 2002, p 46, emphasis in original)

Discourse is the means through which social positions are enacted, understood and connected: 'no self is an island; each exists in a fabric of relations that is now more complex and mobile than ever before' (Lyotard, 1984, p 15).

The notion of 'the self' is intrinsically fluid (Foucault, 1986) and identity is multi-faceted: 'What postmodern theory helps us to see is that we are all constituted in a broad range of subject positions, through which we move with more or less ease, so that all of us are combinations of class, race, ethnic, regional, generational, sexual, and gender positions' (Butler, 2002, p 56).

Postmodernists' insights into the complexity and fluidity of identity, enhance understanding of the challenge when it comes to maximising the inclusion of people with diverse characteristics. As will be explored, this can be seen as presenting opportunities as well as challenges.

Book structure

Chapter Two opens with an exploration of key themes from the literature on social justice, covering distributive justice, the case for cultural recognition and how these two approaches might fit together as aspects of distributive (or more general social) processes. Arising insights and themes are then developed in Chapter Three, which discusses the nature and origins of needs, definitions of poverty and their implications for social structure and inclusion. The emerging framework is then used as a basis for proposals concerning the operation of discrimination and oppression in Chapter Four. Consistent themes across the literatures are extracted and what they say about the structuring of society, the conveyance and interpretation of identity and the role of social barriers is explored. Chapter Five explores the contributions of the literature on social exclusion to the accumulation of conclusions from preceding chapters, in particular on social structure.

Throughout all these chapters, a theoretical framework gradually takes shape, built around social processes as the vehicles through which people interact with each other and with other levels and spheres of society though its institutions. Chapter Six then pulls together and further explores how those institutional processes might be structured if they are to maximise the inclusion of diversity on a basis of equality. Chapter Seven then considers issues arising from their enactment, the nature of relationships and face-to-face interaction. No matter how well structured a process, the way in which it is delivered is of critical importance to engagement.

Finally, Chapter Eight attempts to encapsulate and distil what has emerged in the course of exploration, and what it means for social justice. The implications for social welfare policy and practice are signposted throughout.

Notes

[1] The full list is given as: level of trust; mental illness (including drug and alcohol addiction); life expectancy and infant mortality; obesity; children's educational performance; teenage births; homicides; imprisonment rates; social mobility (not available for US states). See Wilkinson and Pickett, 2010, p 19.

[2] Susan Greenfield (2008) has gone so far as to suggest that it affects the neurological formation of human identity itself, blurring distinctions between reality and the cyber-world, and programming us to opt for short-term, immediate gratification in preference to more demanding intellectual activities, potentially leading to changes in human nature.

[3] *Trends in the distribution of household income between 1979 and 2007*, Congressional Budget Office report, published October 2011, www.cbo.gov/publication/42729.

[4] Fawcett Society: www.fawcettsociety.org.uk/.

[5] See for example: www.bteg.co.uk/index.php/Publications-Downloads/BTEG-Reports.html.

[6] As reported on the BBC news web-site, 22 November 2011: www.bbc.co.uk/news/world-us-canada-15830176.

[7] See, for example The New York Times: http://topics.nytimes.com/top/reference/timestopics/organizations/c/congress/joint_congressional_committee_on_deficit_reduction/index.html.

[8] Margaret Thatcher's declared aim was to roll back the frontiers of the State, see for example her speech to the Conservative Party conference, October 1986, 'This Government has rolled back the frontiers of the State and will roll them back still further': www.margaretthatcher.org/document/106498.

[9] The Independent, 20 November 2011, 'What price the new democracy? Goldman Sachs conquers Europe' www.independent.co.uk/news/business/analysis-and-features/what-price-the-new-democracy-goldman-sachs-conquers-europe-6264091.html.

[10] As of 21 November 2011 the Guardian had managed to plot 750 protests www.guardian.co.uk/world/occupy-movement.

[11] See Occupy Wall Street's web-site: http://occupywallst.org/about/.

[12] Com Res surveys commissioned by Scope published on 8 September 2011: www.scope.org.uk/news/paralympics-attitudes-survey.

[13] BBC Panorama: 'Undercover care: the abuse exposed'.

TWO

Social justice

Introduction

What is a just society? Presumably it is one where outcomes reflect norms of fairness. Bound up with this will be cultural views on human nature and appropriate behaviours, expectations about roles, and what characteristics and/or skills are valued. Views on the capacity of individuals to forge their own destiny, and hence their responsibility for outcomes both good and bad, will also be relevant. Goals need to be defined. Are we aiming for equality? If so, why? Equality of what and with what (or whom)? Can inequality be just if it mirrors unequal effort or skills? Perhaps inequality should not be the central concern and instead social justice should simply be a matter of addressing outright destitution. Maybe the protection of liberty is the key issue rather than anything to do with equality. This in turn prompts questions about rights, of ownership to the fruits of one's labours, or to what is needed to enact full citizenship. Linked to this will be beliefs about the appropriate balance between market and state intervention.

At one end of the spectrum, the unfettered market is seen as the instrument of social justice; a view which casts unequal outcomes as a natural (and hence just) consequence of skill and effort. In this scenario, individuals have the moral right to use their skills how they please and to own what ensues from their labour. State-enforced redistribution is coercive and tantamount to theft (Nozick, 1974; Hayek, 1976). Conversely, at the other end, is the view that individuals cannot be held neatly accountable for outcomes because they do not have equal (or sometimes any) power over their situation, and hence cannot be held responsible for it. They may be constrained by factors beyond their control, by structural barriers arising from the way society and its institutions operate, pre-existing disadvantage, bad luck or unequal access to opportunity. Meanwhile, others are similarly, fortuitously advantaged. State enforced redistribution is necessary to level the playing field. Without it, advantage and disadvantage will be unjustly perpetuated and exacerbated.

Differences in conclusions are underpinned by competing visions of society and views on human nature, whether or not explicit, perhaps reflecting the perspectives of people occupying very different positions within the one they inhabit. Rich and poor cannot easily empathise with each other across a widening gulf of inequality (see Sandel, 2009; Wilkinson and Pickett, 2010). People from minority ethnic backgrounds lead 'parallel lives' (Cantle, 2001), their communities culturally, and often economically, cordoned off from the mainstream. Barriers to participation and to success are often (understandably) invisible to people who have never experienced them. Yet we may, as some have argued, have an innate ability to detect unfairness (Hutton, 2011). Alternatively it may be that sound reasoning is a means of identifying justice (Sen, 2010). In either case, to draw accurate conclusions we need information and understanding about the circumstances and perspectives of others, their capacity to exert agency and the context in which it is exerted.

There are some obvious challenges. First, in unequal, multicultural societies, it seems implausible that there will be one unifying norm of fairness. Second, as discussed in Chapter One, the definition of society becomes less distinct in a globalised world. The capacity of international institutions to redistribute is open to question, as would be the legitimacy of their actions in the absence (perhaps impossibility) of democratic accountability. Third, it is unclear whether universal principles of social justice can be found or whether social justice must be assessed against whatever the dominant view of fairness is in a given society (however that society is defined). It may or may not be possible (and helpful) to construct a generic blueprint for social justice, even if the nature of disadvantage is relative to the society in question. Fourth, there is nothing to say that the dominant view must be the majority view, that all have equal voice – or, even if they do, that the majority must necessarily find intolerable the outright destitution of a blameless minority.

Whatever the difference in conclusions, it is clear that central to social justice lie questions of the relationship between equality and liberty (Lister, 2010), of judgements regarding the responsibility for outcomes of structure or agency, of the morality of re/distribution, of value and access. It is not just the outcome of distribution but also the process; not just the moral case for redistribution but also its practical feasibility. Questions of value concern goods, cultures, and personal characteristics including behaviour. Power, voice and accountability have roles to play in legitimising redistribution, granting access and influencing what emerges.

The vision for a just society proposed in this book is one where the maximum has been done to widen its mainstream, to open up access to people with diverse characteristics, cultures and contributions to make, and where diversity is recognised and valued, as well as accommodated. Equality of various types and degrees will be required. However, while including diversity can strengthen cohesion, or have a neutral effect on it, there will be limits to what can be included without jeopardising social cohesion, causing society to fragment. We need to know what these limits are, to understand what barriers intervene and how to remove them, and where they prevent choice, inclusion and equality within those parameters.

One obvious barrier might be lack of resources: of whatever particular type and quantity of goods is the route to access. Another revolves around the question of attitudes to difference and the significance imputed to it: whether valued, respected, tolerated or rejected. Of course, this assumes that it is noticed at all. How identity is constructed, conveyed and assessed would seem to be important.

Before proceeding to explore the treatment of these themes in the social justice literature, the introduction to this chapter has raised some fundamental questions which need to be addressed to establish a view on what constitutes a just society and thence what social justice is. These need to be considered first, to ascertain their implications for the vision, or vice versa.

Defining a just society

According to Sen (2010), to ask the question 'What is a just society?' is the wrong place to start. He argues persuasively that the aim of achieving consensus on what the all-time perfect socially just society would look like – what he terms the 'transcendental' approach to social justice – is doomed to failure, in a setting characterised by inequality and plurality. To paraphrase rather crudely, this approach is typically (although not necessarily) concerned to design socially just institutions, which would distribute according to socially just principles, on the presumption that this would elicit socially just behaviours. Sen draws a distinction between social justice concerned with institutional rules and arrangements, and social justice in terms of the lives people actually manage to live – 'social realisation' – recognising that the former has an impact on the latter, but that it is not the whole story (2010). Given our aim, it would seem that the latter should be our primary concern. However, there is no obvious reason why appropriately designed institutions should not support and enable social realisation.

Furthermore, he contends that a definition of a perfectly just society is neither necessary nor sufficient as a device for identifying injustice and action to address it, for making comparisons and ranking them. Again, to précis his arguments rather crudely, it is perfectly possible to decide which of two alternatives would be more just without introducing a third 'supreme' alternative into the equation. You can work out which of two mountains is the higher without needing to know the height of the highest mountain in the world. If the Mona Lisa were pronounced the most perfect picture, this is of no help in choosing between a Picasso and a Dali. To try to rank them against an ideal cannot be done because objects have many dimensions of difference. Furthermore, the degree of proximity in appearance is not necessarily matched by a proximity in value (a mixture of red and white wine would look closer to red wine than white, but white wine might be preferable, even to someone who preferred red). Sen also cites the abolition of slavery as an example of where injustice was identified without recourse to a transcendental ideal notion of a just society. In summary, he draws a distinction between a transcendental approach to social justice and a comparative approach, arguing that to progress social justice the latter does not require the former and that anyway the former 'ideal' would be impossible to agree upon (2010)

His arguments on the feasibility of such a project echo earlier points made regarding the impact of inequality on understanding and empathising with others who are differently placed, and the task seems unlikely to be made easier by an explicit goal of maximising diversity. The risks of drawing conclusions on value (or other qualities for that matter) on the basis of superficial appearance, similarly appears consistent with previous observations on the gap between words and meaning, or between empirical data and the scope for multiple interpretations. His challenge regarding the limitations of a narrow focus on perfecting institutions is helpful. However, some of Sen's remarks on the redundancy of such a quest require further examination.

First, if objects (or concepts) have many features, to pick out one of them for the purpose of comparison between two alternatives may well be straightforward. Should you wish to know, you could establish easily enough which of two paintings was the longer (assuming you could work out which way up they went), or the more colourful or had thicker paint. You could compare the number of people in one country who have incomes below £15,000 a year with the number in another and conclude which of the two had more. However, this approach tells you nothing about the significance of your findings. One mountain may be higher than another, but are they both high mountains, both low mountains, or is one high and one low, as mountains go? Are the people in either country poor?

Some qualities cannot be measured so straightforwardly, either because they are a composite of a number of variables or because they are intrinsically intangible – and possibly changeable. For example, which of the two mountains is the most rewarding to climb? Which dress is the most fashionable? Which painting is the most artistic? Judgement is required if two alternatives are to be ranked, and there is vast scope for disagreement. That judgement is likely to be subjective, even though it may be influenced by wider cultural norms (implicitly if not explicitly). The challenge might be how to find a way of coming to objective conclusions. The question then arises as to whether judgement, subjective or objective, would be assisted by universal conceptions of the most perfectly rewarding mountain to climb, fashionable dress or artistic painting. Stepping back further, would it be assisted by conceptualisations of what rewarding means, what fashion is and what art is, or perhaps of the perfect mountain, dress or painting?

The possibly unhelpful answer might be that it depends on the question; what the purpose of the questioner is, what the object or good is intended for, and the outcome they are seeking to achieve with it. Comparisons between two alternatives, in the absence of any additional form of reference point, might answer your question, but devoid of any context, conclusions may not be reliable or tell you very much. The difficulty of gauging the proximity between appearance and value seems in some situations more likely to be unreliable if comparisons are limited to two alternatives, using only one means of comparison (the academic research practice of triangulation would seem to support this[1]). If you want to assess the value of a mixture of red and white wine against an ideal of red wine, comparing appearance might tell you something, but why not compare the taste too, or review the way each was made? None of this is to suggest that reference points are always explicit and consciously acknowledged. Neither does it imply that the reference point must always be a conception of the perfect ideal. It might be more immediately contextual.

For example, a universal conceptualisation of the meaning of art and what a perfect painting is might not be terribly useful if your purpose (as the questioner) is to choose which of two paintings (which good) goes better with the sitting-room wallpaper (the immediate context), to create maximum impact (the outcome). The conclusion would be a matter of subjective judgement (informed by cultural norms). If instead, the task concerned selection, by the staff, of a painting to go in the waiting room of a medical centre, more objective judgement might be helpful to selecting the painting that patients might prefer to look at. The conclusion would at least be the outcome of multiple, subjective points of view, though the question of whether it is art or not is unlikely to be paramount. Alternatively, if the questioner was the curator of the National Gallery and her purpose was to pick which of two painting to purchase on behalf of the nation, then a universal conceptualisation of what art is and of a perfect painting might be more helpful to making the objective, non-parochial decision required.

To draw analogies with discussion of social justice, this might seem to call into question the proposition that even extreme examples of injustice can be identified without recourse to some form of reference or references. For example, at one time, for it to have happened at all, slavery must have been seen as compatible with social justice. The realisation that it was profoundly unjust marked a shift in reference points concerning the meaning of justice. Indeed, Mary Wollstonecraft's opposition to slavery appears to have been founded on 'her central point that justice, by its very nature, has to have a universal reach, rather than being applicable to the problems and predicaments of some people but not others' (Sen, 2010, p 117). This would seem to make the case for a universal – dare one suggest transcendental – principle of justice that should apply in all contexts, in a perfectly just society.

The need for an ideal against which to compare objectively seems to increase in proportion to the numbers who will be affected and the degree of impact a decision would have on them. Though you might wish to consult any other members of your household who will have to live with it, what picture you choose to hang in your own sitting room is hardly a matter of survival and is really only going to have an impact on you (and, if your taste is poor, your unfortunate guests). However, it is not automatically obvious why the objective judgement of the medical centre staff should be the basis for a decision when it would seem entirely possible to get the views of patients. You might still want objective confirmation that the process was fair – that each had been given full information about the alternatives and an equal chance to express a view, and that the conclusion represented the weight of opinion. The logistics of gathering, synthesising and distilling the views of the nation on picture choice might be a greater challenge. Certainly, some kind of framework around which to organise them seems likely to be necessary – perhaps a questionnaire – to ensure information received is pertinent to the issue to be decided, to enable comparisons to be drawn and a conclusion to be reached. However, would members of the public have the expertise necessary to make such a selection? Perhaps expertise is not the issue and it is sufficient that they all know what they like (and what they do not). Perhaps they consider the impact on them too inconsequential to bother expressing an opinion.

There seem to be two, possibly contradictory, approaches here. This might broadly be characterised as decision-making with reference to a 'top-down' 'objective' definition by powerful experts of an ideal conceptualisation versus a 'bottom-up' democratic expression and distillation of the subjective views of the people who will be affected. Problems arise when the two are widely divergent and a decision will have a significant impact on those people. Questions arise as to whether the two can be enabled to converge. It could be argued that in fact, they do and always must converge, even if the outcome is a discontinuous division.

Another way of visualising this would be as a pyramid, with (to continue with the art example) an ideal conceptualisation of what art is at the pinnacle, which then extends down the scale from macro-, to meso-, to micro-level concerns, allowing increasing scope for more immediate and diverse contextual reference points to intervene as it descends. The fundamental question of 'what is art' does not necessarily cease to be relevant at what we might term 'sitting room level', though it would if a discontinuance disjuncture had occurred en route. Art might, though, be expressed in an increasing number of ways, and other considerations might well supersede it. The degree of the match between top and bottom would seem to say something about cohesion between the levels. It is possible that turning the pyramid on its head might strengthen that cohesion. Either way, by analogy, this might start to shed light on Wolff's observation (2008) concerning the different language spoken by political economists responsible for theory and people involved in developing social policy, and why the line of sight from abstraction to implementation can be so hard to trace.

Transcendental plurality

Casting aside the preceding discussion for the moment, if it is indeed the case that the quest for consensus on a perfectly just society is both impossible and pointless, this would seem to be devastating news, not just for the project in hand, but for some very eminent political philosophers (Nozick, 1974, and Dworkin, 2000, being among their number). Arguably, the foremost among them, John Rawls, asserts that 'the nature and aims of a perfectly just society is the fundamental part of the theory of justice' (1973, p 9). He aims to develop a set of principles for just distribution: a standard against which 'the distributive aspects of the basic structure of society are to be assessed' (1973, p 9).

To that end he conducts a thought experiment, conjuring up an idealised, self-contained society where moral judgments on principles for distribution are made by people behind a 'veil of ignorance' concerning their own class or social status, or their own natural personal characteristics like strength and intelligence. Under such conditions (the 'original position'), he contends, self-interested rational people would reach the same conclusions on the principles for just distribution. Those principles would be first that 'Each person is to have an equal right to the most extensive total system of liberties, with a similar system of liberty for all'. Second, 'Social and economic inequalities should be arranged so that they are both a) to the greatest benefit of the least advantaged, consistent with the just savings principle, and b) attached to positions and offices open to all under conditions of fair equality of opportunity' (see Rawls, 1973, p 302). In effect, the 'difference principle' – clause a) of the second – stipulates that it is acceptable for some to be better off, so long as this benefits the least well off most. Such a proposition could be taken to imply that society should be judged according to how it treats the worst off, or perhaps to support (dubious) claims that the rich must be incentivised to generate more wealth for themselves as this will trickle down to the poorest to their disproportionate benefit.

There are many criticisms of Rawls' approach which can and have been made; for example, that it takes insufficient account of inequalities for which individuals can be held responsible or their unreasonable behaviour (Dworkin, 2000; Sen, 2010), or how it would allow for extra costs incurred by some due to a medical condition or disability (Dworkin, 2000). Perhaps rather than focus on amounts and types of resource as determining what a person can do, it would be better to start with what a person should be able to do and then identify the resources they need in order to do it (Sen, 1983, 1985, 1999; Piachaud, 2008 – discussed further in Chapter Three). It is also far from clear how Rawls would deal with the postmodernist proposition that characteristics are not fixed, or the notion that disability is not a personal characteristic but the result of how society operates (see Chapter Four).

Among Sen's many criticisms is his contention that Rawls' approach is insufficient to guarantee consensus on distributive principles. Contrary to the approach of rational-choice theorists, 'defining rationality simply as intelligent promotion of personal self-interest sells human reasoning extremely short' (2010, p 194). He argues that it is perfectly possible for a plurality of impartial, equally well-reasoned claims and choices to exist (2010).

Sen provides a neat illustration in the form of a (much summarised here) scenario in which three children are arguing about who should have a flute that one of them has made and only one can play. Meanwhile a third is so poor that, unlike the other two who are better off, he has no toys. The flute would give him something to play with, which he desperately needs. Each illustrates a claim appealing to a different distributive principle, leading theorists of associated persuasions to draw different (equally rational) conclusions. The economic egalitarian would equalise resources by giving the flute to the child with no toys, while the libertarian would give it to the flute-maker on the grounds that she made it so it is up to her what she does with it. The utilitarian, whose interest is in whose pleasure would be stronger, would have more of a dilemma, but might reasonably conclude that it should go to the only one of the three who knows how to play it.

However, what is striking about this scenario is not just that the three claims and their underlying distributive principles could quite reasonably lead to different and mutually exclusive conclusions, but that they also suggest routes to compromise. For example, perhaps they could share the flute, each having it for an equal amount of time. Perhaps all three children could be taught how to make a flute, or the supply of flutes could be increased by some other means. In the context of this example, chopping the flute into three equal parts is unlikely to prove a terribly satisfactory solution. A flute is not a very interesting toy, in fact it is not really a toy at all. Maybe the child without toys would get more pleasure from something more toy-like. Maybe the other two children could give him some of theirs and he would relinquish his claim to the flute. Perhaps the child who can already play the flute would prefer to extend her skills by learning how to play another instrument. Furthermore, we do not know what the motivations are of the child who made the toy, or what she now wants the flute for. Perhaps she made it because the child who can play the flute has something she would like to have in exchange, or because she would like that child to teach her how to play it herself.

Further information and negotiation might reveal a number of different but equally just outcomes. What this seems to show is that injustice is likely to be generated by rigid adherence to any one of the distributive principles in isolation. Whichever one is unquestioningly pursued, one child will win and the other two lose, risking the fracturing of any pre-existing friendship (and by analogy, social disintegration). To take it further, it might suggest that justice requires a balancing between the three principles, as well as negotiation. To take it further still, it could be argued that the current global situation, as briefly discussed in

Chapter One, exemplifies what happens when libertarianism subsumes the other two, taking the form of rampant economic inequality and the alignment of pleasure with material wealth. This starts to point to the possibility that equilibrium is one form of equality required for 'inclusive equality'. If so, this requires further elaboration.

It might be the case that any one principle carried to extreme ceases to be sustainable – or that the cohesion of the society in which it is enacted, and the lives of a large proportion of the people within it, cease to be so. The question then needs to be asked whether the same would arise if the concept of inclusive equality is carried to extreme. If there are limits beyond which society starts to disintegrate, what are they? We could speculate that there will be logical limits, for example, where including one is contingent on the exclusion of another and no means of compromise exists. There may be practical limits, for example regarding the complexity of information that needs to be understood if informed choices are to be made. There may be trade-offs to make, for example, between the complexity created by a plethora of options or of parties within processes and the feasibility of choice and accountability, respectively. There may be moral limits too, or forms of universal benchmarks of needs or rights, that serve either to constrain the space for action or to define what it should permit. Again, these are not necessarily arbitrary conclusions. It might be quite possible to demonstrate that the vision cannot be realised without them.

Some limits are inevitable – they flow naturally and unavoidably from the proposition itself – namely the vision for social justice that this book aims to progress. Others will permit or require debate, interpretation and negotiation. Others again are artificial constructs that could be removed and to do so would be beneficial, to individuals and society. We need to identify what these limits are, and how the space between them within which diversity can be expressed is to be maximised.

The impact of agency

Moral limits are not just defined by conclusions on the resources and liberties that people should have. In the dispute about the flute, not only are the claims treated as equal, irrespective of the difference in the underlying distributive principle, but the children are treated as equally deserving. However, further information might indicate that one of them should have the flute, or at least that one of them definitely should not. For example, perhaps the other two are perfectly capable of making their own flutes, but have spent their time on something else. Maybe the flute-player broke her previous flute when she hit one of the other children with it. In both these examples, their behaviour – their failure to help themselves and make a social contribution, or socially destructive misuse of resources – undermines their claims.

To stretch the analogy a little further (possibly too far!) – perhaps the flute-maker knows how to make flutes because she comes from a family of flute-makers and inherited a large number of flutes, which she does not need and could never use. Meanwhile, in this somewhat unusual society in which the children happen to live, owning a flute and being able to make flutes are key indicators of social status and the route to acquiring other goods. This means that the impact of not having a flute escalates to the point where it compromises survival rather than merely provokes boredom.

Responses to these scenarios might reasonably be that the children who could make flutes for themselves should get on and do so, rather than rely on someone else's efforts. However, we do not know what is stopping them from doing this. It might be that they just cannot be bothered, or that they do not have access to flute-making equipment, or that they are engaged in some other more socially worthwhile activity. To have reasonable cause to think that an individual would use the flute for socially destructive purposes would suggest that awarding it to her would be a bad decision. Yet, again, we do not know the context to what occurred. Maybe it was an act of self-defence as the child she hit with it was attacking her. In the final scenario, there would seem to be a moral imperative to relieve suffering (where the sufferer cannot do it themselves) by a redistribution of flutes (though not everyone would agree with this 'theft').

In passing, we might also wonder at a society where only flutes are valued, given the wide range of musical instruments that exist, not to mention many other goods and skills that can contribute to personal and collective pleasure. We might also reasonably think that to be given privileged access to healthcare (for example) because you can make a flute would be nothing short of completely bonkers.

A framework for reasoning

The examples of negotiation, the need for objective judgement to avoid parochialism (Sen, 2010) and judgements about fairness all point to the importance of thinking beyond the confines of the immediate question to be resolved, to dig deeper and wider to gather more information which can serve as reference points. They showed that more information is needed about potential recipients, if effective and just conclusions or compromises are to be reached regarding conflicting claims.

As the scale of the question expands, from how to resolve a disagreement between three children to how to make the right decision for society, so the information demands can increase, along with the importance of objectivity. The challenge of collecting, sifting and focusing ever more information about ever more complex issues leads to the need to develop some form of framework or model around which to organise it. Sen makes the case for the 'crucial role of public reasoning', proceeding to argue that 'If the demands of justice can be assessed only with the help of public reasoning, and if public reasoning is constitutively related to the idea of democracy, then there is an intimate connection between justice and democracy' (2010, p 326).

Unfortunately, discussion in Chapter One seemed to indicate that democracy as currently operated does not always enable public reasoning to occur, voices to be heard, outcomes to be respected, or accountability to be enforced when they are not. Perhaps instead the aim should be to maximise participation in 'government by discussion' (Sen, 2010, p xiii): 'Democracy has to be judged not just by the institutions that formally exist but by the extent to which different voices from diverse sections of the people can actually be heard' (Sen, 2010, p xiii).

We do not have enough information to know which child would end up with the flute. It is the children themselves who have the necessary information and it is quite possible that they will come to a satisfactory agreement by themselves. However, to come to an objective judgement, it remains vital to get information that only the children have, and for each child to have an equal voice in the proceedings. Equal voice might be a key principle for justice, as might the proposition that for distribution to be just, those affected by decisions must be involved – although the mechanisms for this might require development. When transposed onto society-level concerns, such as the selection of a painting for the National Gallery, similar negotiation may ensue, and a variety of equally just alternative resolutions might emerge. By analogy, we cannot say exactly what a just society would look like (or which picture would be chosen), because, within certain parameters, it could take a number of different, if equally just forms that might change over time. Problems arise if the all-time perfect model for social justice does not permit such flexibility.

There is still more to consider: who should prevail (and why) in cases of irresolvable disagreement between objective and subjective perspectives; the location (and communication) of relevant knowledge and expertise, and whether the imperative to involve someone/people in a decision should be proportionate to the likely degree of impact or risk that decision could impose on her/them/others.

Processes and relationships

Reasons for engaging

According to Walzer, 'Human society is a distributive community. That's not all it is but it is importantly that: we come together to share, divide and exchange' (1983, p 3). Libertarianism, economic egalitarianism and utilitarianism have all been described in terms of principles of distribution: but distribution of what? There is much to be found in the social justice literature about the nature of goods and dis/advantages that could be the subject of distribution, though the capacity of institutions of any type to distribute some of them is questionable.

Walzer suggests that distributions might be of 'membership, power, honor, ritual and eminence, divine grace, kinship and love, knowledge, wealth, physical security and leisure, rewards and punishments' and, more mundanely, 'food, shelter, clothing, transportation, medical care, commodities of every sort' (1983, p 3). Miller proposes that a preliminary list of advantages must include 'money and commodities, property, jobs and offices, education, medical care, child benefits, honors and prizes, personal security, housing, transportation and leisure opportunities' (Miller, 2001, p 7). Disadvantages, or burdens which are not punishments, include 'military service, hard dangerous or degrading work, and care for the elderly' (Miller, 2001, p 7) – though the inclusion of the latter as a burden is instructive. To support older people to get the most from their lives could surely be a source of pleasure in a culture with more positive attitudes towards them.

It is striking how wide-ranging the concept of goods can be. The authors go far beyond thinking of distribution as necessarily requiring tangible, material commodities. They also include aspects or types of status, access to services, emotions, recognition for achievements, and personal security. While some goods take the form of objects that people might have; others are more action-oriented – or perhaps more about social realisation – concerning what people are enabled to do (get an education, acquire office, and so on).

Tangible and intangible goods

It is relatively easy to see how 'tangible' goods like food, clothing, property, jobs and offices might be subject to distribution. However, it is surely beyond the capacity of any institution to distribute love, personal security, or power. They might carry out rituals such as marriage ceremonies that publicly recognise the love between a couple. They might be responsible for police services which safeguard personal security. They may distribute roles to which powers are attached. However, whether the recipient can exercise them may hinge on their personal charisma or political skill, or external factors like the size of parliamentary majority or the availability of opportunities to demonstrate leadership. Opportunities for influence may be equally distributed, everyone may have an equal opportunity to speak, but not all will be equally persuasive. Distribution cannot easily bestow such 'intangible' goods, any more than education can guarantee knowledge, or healthcare, good health.

The intangible qualities or meanings conveyed by tangible goods can be similarly beyond institutional control, though they may well try to create associations through product-branding, for example. As Walzer suggests, clothes can convey status in a hierarchy (1983), and presumably also other aspects of identity. A house may convey wealth, poor taste, and so on. Possession of certain goods may in turn provoke intangibles, for example, self-respect or its opposite. Both possessions and action-oriented goods have the potential to convey symbolic information about status and identity. That is not to say that what they convey will necessarily be accurate (see earlier discussion of the possibility of gaps between superficial appearance and underlying meaning), that associations will be consciously made, or consistently understood. Much may depend on the prevailing (possibly multiple) cultural norms and the immediate context. Such factors clearly contribute to the difficulty of pinning down meaning.

Further complexity arises from the different ways of conceptualising intangible goods. For example, for Rawls (1973) self-respect is a good, while Sen (1983) portrays it (in terms of being able to live without shame) as a capability, or 'absolute need' (see Chapter Three). Williams (1969) describes power as a 'positional good'; one that not all can have; in fact its existence is contingent on others not having it. For some, power is not best conceived as an entity that people either have or do not have, but a property of interactions between individuals (Foucault, 1980, 1981): a potentially fluctuating feature of social relationships (Young, 1990). It can also be understood as constituting individual identity: 'the conflicting languages of power which circulate through and within individuals actually constitute the self' (Butler, 2002, p 51). Sibeon perceives it as 'emergent' in the sense of being an *outcome* of social interactions 'Actors may become more powerful, or less powerful: this is because their capacity to shape events or to obtain their objectives is not a structurally bestowed, predetermined or "fixed" capacity' (1992, p 35, cited in Thompson, 1998, p 76). Yet power may also be a precursor to social interactions, with the powerful defining how they are to proceed.

Thus, while acknowledging that they may be communicated by, and be outcomes of, the possession of tangible goods, it may also be productive to think of intangible goods such as self-respect, love, and power (or their opposites) as qualities of relationships. This might suggest that both the tangible good to be distributed and the nature of the relationship through which distribution occurs are factors in social justice. It also signals that motivations for engagement (or disengagement) can be emotionally-based as much as driven by pragmatic necessities. They could be compromised at any point throughout the process or by the outcome. For example, self-respect may be compromised by the admission of need that participation in a given process would demonstrate. Power and self-respect could be lost within the process by having to submit to the scrutiny of highly private matters. The perception of a process as adversarial or as supportive (the nearest to love that an institutional process might appropriately get!), could also have an impact on the decision to engage.

Walzer suggests that: 'The idea of distributive justice has as much to do with being and doing as with having' (1983, p 3). It follows that criteria for access to processes and relationships, and consequent distributions, may not just be concerned with what a person has, but with what they do and are – or are understood to be. Access may not depend on tangible, material resources, but on how relevant aspects of identity are selected, identified and understood. This begins to indicate that accurate recognition plays an important role in socially just distribution, and that the symbolic meaning of goods is one form of indicator of identity.

Priority goods

Not all goods will be equally important, whether in terms of the numbers and types of other goods and activities to which they grant access, their necessity for survival or to acquire social status and acceptance. Rawls identifies 'primary goods' as 'rights and liberties, opportunities and power, income and wealth' (1973, p 92). These have priority because they are necessary to pursue a variety of ends: whatever their personal goals, people can be assumed to want more of them. Rawls notes that goods, or the lack of them, tend to go together. Greater power and wealth often co-exist, as do lack of authority and lack of income, consistent with the discussion in Chapter One concerning the accumulative nature of inequality and its dimensions. This suggests that inequality in the distribution of primary goods would have a disproportionately significant impact on liberty (itself listed as a primary good): restricting inclusion for some and limiting the space available to them for diverse forms of social realisation.

The priority accorded to primary good might be due to their generic, multipurpose nature: the access they open up to a wide range of others. However, it could be this very feature that is responsible for multiplying and compounding inequalities. Alternatively there may be no logical or justifiable reason why a given good should grant access to others. For example, 'Money is inappropriate in the sphere of ecclesiastical office; it is an intrusion from another sphere' (Walzer, 1983, p 10). Superior education should not be the key to accessing superior healthcare. In these two examples, money and education are the dominant goods, respectively. Perhaps the 'flute society' discussed earlier was not so unusual after all.

Supply and demand

Equality of an egalitarian and purist sort might insist on an equal distribution of all dominant goods, or the scope to balance supply with demand. However there are both conceptual and practical reasons why this might be problematic, which have nothing to do with political acceptability. Not least, as various authors point out (including Walzer, 1983; Nozick, 1974), even if an equal distribution were established, inequality would rapidly ensue, as different people spent, saved, invested, traded and so on. Repeated intervention (theft, in Nozick's terms) would be required to re-establish that equal starting point.

It seems that some types of goods are 'unavoidably scarce' (Williams, 1969). The intrinsic social meaning of 'positional goods' like power or prestige resides in the fact that not everyone has them. If everyone did, he argues, they would cease to exist. In other cases, the social meaning of a good, like university education as a marker of advanced knowledge and skill or the capacity to acquire them, necessarily requires access criteria which not everyone will be able to meet – unless its meaning is to change fundamentally to become something less intellectually demanding. Finally, there are goods like national healthcare provision where, although potentially everyone meets criteria for access, there is not (and the implication is that there never can be) enough to go round.

It seems that dynamics ensue from the balance between supply and demand, the extent to which it is feasible to balance them, and the use of rationing in order to manipulate their inter-relationship. It is not always possible to increase the supply of a good, neither is it necessarily possible to increase the supply of suitably qualified prospective users without changing the meaning of the good or undermining its purpose. Furthermore, the more available the good, the less it will have 'positional' value, and the less desirable it will become. There are some goods which by their very nature cannot be equally distributed without compromising that good's essential nature and changing its meaning – with obvious implications for equality.

Yet, although the basic premise of this argument seems sound, it still allows for differing degrees of inequality when it comes to positional goods like power. Notwithstanding previous arguments concerning the impossibility of distributing power itself, there could be an equitable distribution of opportunities to express a view or to vote on a decision. The gap between those with most power and those with least could be of small or large dimensions. The power of some to act on behalf of others can be counterbalanced by making them accountable to those on whose behalf they act. Damaging social divisions occur when communication and connection between the powerful and the (consequently) powerless is lost.

The practicality of manipulating supply and demand to achieve something closer to equilibrium is challenged by globalisation, as discussed in Chapter One. Yet, social justice theory, and much social policy (Kymlicka, 2008), is framed to a considerable extent around a concept of society as the nation state – a bounded, closed system – with a determinate, homogeneous membership (Rawls, 1973; Walzer, 1983; Miller, 2001). There must be institutions that can deliver distribution, which must be capable of distributing in accordance with whatever principle prevails, and the impact on individuals must be clearly discernible. While it is highly debateable whether such 'perfect' conditions ever existed, in an increasingly globalised world of highly mobile finance, the power of individual nation states to tax, spend and redistribute is compromised. With remote, democratically unaccountable global institutions (Bertram, 2008), diverse and mobile populations, this premise looks even less secure, posing challenges both for theory and practice (see Burchardt and Craig, 2008), and for social justice at all levels.

Yet, while urgent action is certainly needed to connect global institutions democratically to the populations their actions affect, it is not necessarily the case that all hope for social justice at lower levels is lost. First, there is still much to do to formulate 'bottom-up' connection and engagement . Second, it signals that any account of social justice must be flexible enough to respond to diverse pressures, priorities and change. Indeed, there are obvious challenges to long-distance understanding of context and perspectives (Bertram, 2008, suggests that global justice can only confidently deal with damage limitation; the avoidance of conspicuous, unambiguous injustices). More may be visible at the level of nation state or region, and with greater awareness comes increased scope for social justice.

Complex equality

We might reasonably, if reluctantly, conclude that inequality is inevitable. Worse still, it seems so too is its perpetuation and exacerbation. Certain goods act as passports to the acquisition of others. Some are unavoidably scarce, which means that not everyone can have them. An equal starting point would inevitably become unequal, and require repeated intervention to re-establish.

Walzer's response is to argue for 'complex equality' which 'establishes a set of relationships such that domination is impossible', so that 'no citizen's standing in one sphere or with regard to some social good can be undercut by his standing in some other sphere, with regard to some other good' (1983, p 19). Broadly his argument is that 'Each social good or set of goods constitutes, as it were, a distributive sphere within which only certain criteria [for access] and arrangements are appropriate' (1983, p 10). These include security and welfare, money and commodities, education, divine grace and political power.

In each distributive sphere, so the argument continues, the shared social meaning of the good determines the principle for distribution, which Walzer describes as free exchange, desert or need (1983). Miller (2001) takes a different slant, proposing an association between distributive principle and mode of human relationship, rather than a good's social meaning. He proposes a number of distributive principles, focusing primarily on the social practice of those involved in distributive processes – on agents rather than structures. Need is the guiding distributive principle for the relationship mode of solidarity, where a community has a shared identity. Instrumental association – where interaction and collaboration occurs because they are deemed pragmatically necessary to reach personal goals – typifies market relations. Desert is claimed as the associated distributive principle – justice being determined by whether (for example) a person's reward matches their contribution. Finally, citizenship is the third way in which people can relate to each other, where the distributive principle is of equality, of (among other things) liberties and rights and personal protection.

A detailed exploration of the merits of their formulations of distributive principles (and whether or not they take us any further forward regarding the resolution of Sen's flute distribution dilemma) need not detain us here. However, what is helpful is the proposition of an association between distributive principle, social meaning of a good and the mode of human, or distributive, relationship. Distributions are 'patterned in accordance with shared conceptions of what the goods are and what they are for' (Walzer, 1983, p 7). The criteria for accessing a good, the manner of the good's distribution (perhaps mode of human relationship), and its purpose (which seems to be conflated with social meaning) all need to be consistent: 'different goods to different companies of men and women for different reasons and in accordance with different procedures' (Walzer, 1983, p 26).

For distributive spheres to be separate and autonomous, as required for complex equality, the underlying suppositions appear, first, to be that a shared understanding of a good's social meaning is achievable and, second, that the social meanings of different goods are distinct and inherently different from each other. Both are open to challenge.

Although Walzer acknowledges scope for variation in social meaning over time and in different societies this does not sufficiently account for the potentially vast variation, not just between but within multicultural societies. Even within the same culture, the purpose of a good (and hence its social meaning) will differ, depending on setting: in Christian culture, bread in a church means something very different to bread on a restaurant table.[2] Social context, whether broadly understood or as immediate setting, is critically important to establishing social meaning – as it might also be in generating group differentiation and resource needs.

Assuming that agreement can be reached on the social meaning of a good, complex equality might seem to suggest that the more precise that agreed meaning is, and the tighter its fit with distributive principle and access criteria, the more socially just the outcome. It might imply social justice is stronger, the narrower and more distinct from each other these are, and the closer the match between them. However, it might also suggest segregation: that people should only have access to spheres where they possess (or are attributed) narrowly defined, distinct characteristics or resources. It might also imply challenges to social mobility and incentives if, for example, only one way in which criteria can be met is recognised, and there is no place for transferable skills, development potential or risk-taking. Thus, although dynamics towards cumulative inequality might be successfully curtailed, complex equality is not necessarily inclusive.

However, instead of narrowly matching quality or resource of recipient to the social meaning of the good in question, subject to its availability it might be possible to expand social meanings up until the point at which they become meaningless or start to mean something else. Similarly, it may be possible to expand the ways in which a good might (justifiably) be accessed. For example, it may be the case that the purpose of a job could be fulfilled in many ways. Perhaps competency can be assessed through mechanisms other than formal qualifications. It may be possible to alter the job's location and contracted hours without in any way compromising the end result. If so, it would be socially unjust to exclude people by defining the terms of access unnecessarily narrowly, that is, more so than the purpose of the good actually requires.

Complex equality implies that the qualities or resources of recipients will be specific to each sphere of distribution. However, without compromising the social meaning or purpose of goods, are there some qualities, like intelligence, reliability or loyalty, which are transferable – for example, valued in a commercial as much as in an ecclesiastical setting? Might it not be reasonable to assume that, having been proven in one context, they would likewise prevail in another? While it remains the case that some qualities are specific to a good, and should not act as a passport to receipt of others that are un-related (wealth to ecclesiastical status, educational status to superior healthcare), others appear more generic and might therefore (in Walzer's terms) justifiably grant access to many spheres. It may not just be that goods become dominant; so, too, may particular personal characteristics (or the perception of them). Likewise, as with goods, both desirable and undesirable characteristics may cluster together, with obvious implications both for equality and inclusion.

Yet, there may be a way forward here too, albeit not necessarily comprehensive or complete. For example, taking the primary (and potentially dominant) good of power, it might be possible to have power (or a powerful position) in one sphere (for example, a university professor), but this should not act as a passport to power in another un-related sphere (for example, a hospital consultant). This might be conceptualised in terms of spreading power horizontally, across different spheres (equally powerful in different contexts), as well as vertically within each (more equally powerful within one context), for example, where a university or hospital boss establishes institutional policy in co-production with a students' or patients' council, respectively.

Cultural recognition

Over the last couple of decades, a new way of thinking about social justice has emerged. This places an emphasis on cultural recognition, with 'the cultural displacing the material' (Phillips, 1997, p 143), where 'group identity supplants class interest as the chief medium of political mobilization' (Fraser, 1997, p 11). Previously, traditional demographic divisions in the political economy had primacy – of socio-economic class including position in the labour market and decision-making structures (Young, 2008). Cultural recognition concerns positive affirmation of group identity and the valuing of difference. Whether cultural recognition is unconnected to issues of distribution, or how they might be intertwined, needs to be established. The meaning of cultural recognition also requires clarification, as do the implications of this paradigm for equality and social inclusion.

Group identities

The construction and deconstruction of group identities has been widely debated in feminist literature and in postmodernist theory more generally. According to Young, they are an 'expression of social relations', through which group identification arises 'in the encounter and interaction between social collectivities that experience some differences in their way of life and forms of association, even if they regard themselves as belonging to the same society' (1990, p 43). Presumably such 'cultural' connections built on shared experiences could apply to groups formed by socio-economic class too, as much as to those formed around gender, ethnicity and so on, but the emphasis of those writing on cultural recognition is on the latter.

While there may be associations between socio-economic class and other demographically-defined groups, in that people sharing particular group identities are typically to be found in certain parts of the labour market and income distribution (see Chapter One), this is not inevitable. Fraser describes gender and race as 'bivalent modes of collectivity', in that each contains both cultural and socio-economic components. Not all groups are 'bivalent', for example, groups defined by sexual orientation may have 'cultural' but not socio-economic class commonalities.

The shared experience of 'cultural' groups extends beyond the labour market: 'Gender affinities, if they exist, could have additional bases beyond their basis in the division of labour, for example in socialization, in culture, even in bodily experiences, such as menstruation' (Fraser, 1997, p 201). A further factor concerns the structural and cultural barriers that such groups may experience, created by the way that society and its institutions operate; the product of the dominant group in Western societies, namely white, non-disabled men (see Young, 2008). Indeed, such barriers could play a major role in group formation. There may be socio-cultural barriers that all members of a group share. It might be possible to increase access and equality for all group members by removing one such barrier, thereby moderating the axis for group differentiation and definition.

That is not to say that each member of a given group only has that one group identification: 'In complex, highly differentiated societies like our own, each person has multiple group identifications' (Young, 1990, p 48). It is inevitable that any two persons will have aspects of their identity that they have in common and others that differ. There are various ways of conceptualising this. Instead of membership of multiple groups, reflecting many possible points of commonality, sub-groups are created within groups founded on a dominant attribute. For example, the group 'women' includes black women, disabled women, lesbian women, and so on. Alternatively, each attribute can be framed separately: the women's movement exists alongside separate movements of black people, disabled people and lesbian and gay people.

Both conceptualisations may have something to contribute to strategies to promote social inclusion and cohesion. However, 'The culture, perspective, and relations of privilege and oppression of these various groups...may not cohere' (Young, 1990, p 48). If so, this would pose challenges both for the social integration of different groups around points of commonality, and for the coherence of individual identity. It is not inevitable that membership of different groups brings any inherent tension or contradiction. It may instead be a means of promoting social cohesion of a possibly complex kind, around multiple points of commonality – a proposition that will be developed in later chapters.

Approaches to difference

A group-based approach naturally raises the question of the fate of people who do not share (or appear to share) whatever commonality the group is founded upon. Group identification is objectively as well as subjectively determined. Criteria for group membership as much as criteria for distribution may be rigidly drawn and narrowly assessed, with potentially unjust exclusionary results. Attitude to difference – whether it is welcomed, accommodated or rejected – is critical in driving outcomes.

Difference might mean superiority, inferiority or different but equivalent (see Fraser, 1997; Young, 1990). Difference may simply be poorly understood, or elicit a variety of emotional responses such as fear, hostility or (a little more positively) curiosity. A further possibility is that difference is simply denied: what Taylor refers to as 'difference blindness'. This can be damaging: 'Non-recognition or misrecognition can inflict harm, can be a form of oppression, imprisoning someone in a false, distorted mode of being' (Taylor, 1992, p 25).

Alternatively, the focus might be on what is shared – on points of commonality rather than points of difference. A person may have, or be attributed, characteristics both relevant and irrelevant to a given setting, group membership criterion or distributional purpose. Williams stresses that reasons for differential treatment must be relevant: 'the fact that a man is black is, by itself, quite irrelevant to the issue of how he should be treated in respect of welfare, etc' (1969, p 156). In determining relevance, it is important to consider not just the qualities of the potential recipient but also the purpose of 'the good' in its setting. How to discern relevant from irrelevant characteristics is surely what recognition is about. To use disabilist terminology, it is possible not just to be 'difference-blind' (Taylor, 1992) but also 'sameness-blind' (Witcher, 2003): blinded by one overriding but irrelevant indicator of difference. It is also possible to be blind to the scope to reframe the good and the method of its distribution while remaining true to its social meaning. By reframing it might be possible to transform into irrelevance what was an ostensibly relevant difference that would have barred access.

Differentiation is not necessarily fixed: 'Class inequality lent itself to a strategy of elimination' (Phillips, 1997, p 143). At its simplest, this is to argue that inequalities experienced by socio-economic classes can be eliminated by redistributing income and wealth. Other forms of difference and ensuing group definitions are less amenable to erasure (Phillips, 1997; Fraser, 1997). This is an important point. In contrast to the proposition that identity is nothing but a product of socio-cultural context, it signals that there is something inherent to group members – perhaps their 'bodily experience' – that connects them and persists irrespective of it. However, that is not to deny the critical role of socio-cultural context in group differentiation and in determining the nature of much of their shared experience.

Group differentiation can be affected by strategies for addressing inequality. Some serve to affirm difference, accentuating it through targeting resources or special treatment. Others diminish its relevance by transforming the context that defines or even creates it. For example, difference is reinforced where flexible working hours are only available to a couple of people whose impairment results in fluctuating levels of stamina. However, to introduce flexible working hours for all workers would widen the mainstream, standard arrangement to accommodate difference. What was an axis of difference ceases to be so. The resulting destabilisation of group differentiation enables new groupings subsequently to emerge (Fraser, 1997). Groups are reframed around new points of commonality which cross-sect previous group differentiation. This seems worthy of further exploration, given the concern to promote inclusion and strengthen social cohesion.

Cultural confusion

There are different ways in which the characteristics around which groups are formed can be conceptualised as arising and this has the potential to be confusing. Characteristics like gender, race or disability can be construed as personal, as biological facts about an individual, and for many this is the obvious approach. However, as discussed, the formation of group identity can also be seen in terms of shared experiences, whether arising from socio-cultural – and in some cases economic – barriers or from bodily functions. Cultural recognition is concerned with the shared experiences that distinguish group members, rather than innate biological distinctions. In addition, characteristics may be ascribed to individuals by others – and this may be necessary in the context of distributions on behalf of the wider collective – or by individuals to themselves.

However, there are other understandings of 'culture'. Kymlicka (1995) equates it with 'a nation' or 'a people', indicating a geographical or ethnic characteristic. A wider definition of culture might also refer to music, art, theatre, discourse, as well as values, norms and expectations, shared experiences and lifestyles. As Barry remarks, 'Even if we want to say that there is a women's culture, a black culture or a gay culture, the extent to which members of the group identify with such a distinctive group culture varies greatly from one member to another' (2001, p 307). This is not to deny that groups cannot or do not develop their own culture in this wider sense.

The question arises of what exactly is the source of damaging misrecognition and subsequent unjustifiable treatment. As Barry puts it: 'we can identify people as women, blacks or gays without having to know anything much about their culture…discrimination may well be based on sheer identity as a woman, a black or a gay rather than on any associated cultural attributes' (Barry, 2001, pp 306, 307). He takes issue with Young's approach; what he terms the 'culturalisation' of group identities, pointing out that: 'groups can suffer from material deprivation, lack of equal opportunity and direct discrimination, and there is no reason for supposing these disadvantages to flow from their possession of a distinctive culture, even where they have one' (2001, p 315).

The phenomenon of mis/recognition seems logically to require someone to do the recognising or misrecognising and someone else to be recognised or misrecognised. The person doing the recognising is unlikely to have access to biological or genetic information about the individual s/he is trying to recognise, and so (except in very limited circumstances) this is unlikely to be what drives conclusions on identity. Cultural misrecognition might imply that it is the shared experience of group members that is being overlooked or devalued by the 'misrecogniser'. This might indeed be the case, whether attributable to lack of awareness or lack of concern. For example, misrecognition of disabled people's shared experience might be expressed in the failure to make adjustments to buildings, work patterns and so on to enable them to participate on an equal basis. A further possibility is that failure to act might arise from a misguided assumption about a shared group experience that an individual group member, indeed, the entire group, does not in fact share.

Yet this does not capture the full potential for misrecognition, neither does it explain how an individual becomes objectively deemed to be a member of a specific group. Where, for example, a person's appearance suggests a physical impairment, it may trigger all manner of inaccurate assumptions about their personal inability, inferiority or inadequacy. Even the disabled person's very humanity may be misrecognised, as hate crimes seem to suggest. The shared experience of the group in question is devalued because the members of that group are themselves devalued.

What is it, therefore, that someone keen to recognise another accurately and objectively has to rely upon? They seem to have little choice but to go on appearance and the symbolic information conveyed by what the person has, does, or is (or appears to be), as interpreted by cultural norms (explicit or implicit). Those cultural norms do not arise from the 'culture' of disabled people or the group in question, but from the culture of whoever is doing the recognising.

Multiculturalism

The acknowledgement of cultural alternatives, in terms of norms, values and so on, brings us to the question of multiculturalism: the claims of particular groups to 'special' treatment, such as exemption from the rules pertaining to the wider collective in which they are located. Irrespective of recognition, it may be that accommodation of cultural difference is logically limited (because one option precludes the other), perhaps because a culture explicitly insists on inequality. Certain cultures regard women as innately inferior, depriving them of access to political decision-making, education and employment. Homosexuality is viewed by some with great hostility, and disability is regarded as shameful. Some cultures practice the mutilation of children or the stoning of adulterers. Direct discrimination and violent treatment does not just arise where one culture confronts another. It can be meted out to particular groups within a culture.

Such behaviours come into direct conflict with laws prevailing in liberal societies, posing dilemmas for 'cosmopolitan tolerance'. Multiculturalism as special treatment could mean that 'liberal protections for individuals should be withdrawn wherever they interfere with a minority's ability to live according to its culture', with women, children and dissidents among the likely victims (Barry, 2001, p 327). The earlier proposition that apparently incompatible alternatives may be resolved by thinking beyond the immediate dilemma and through negotiation (as per the example of the children's claims to the flute) may have met its limit. So too may have the scope for inclusive equality.

Of course, not all differences are mutually incompatible and non-negotiable. It may be that the conflict concerns the wearing of a turban for cultural reasons versus wearing a helmet or hard-hat for safety reasons or wearing religious apparel that is not part of a school uniform. Such instances require negotiation, but compromise may be possible without great loss to either party. For example, could all individuals be empowered to make their own decisions about the risks they are willing to take? Why could school uniform not include the option of religious apparel, so long as it was in school colours? Or it may be that people have time constraints, because religious activities fall on a particular day, or they have caring responsibilities, or limited stamina due to impairment. These are factors which most service-providers or employers should reasonably be able to accommodate without too much inconvenience. They may even experience gains by opening up access to new customers or by increasing the pool of skilled staff. Moreover, as previously discussed, they could offer flexible working arrangements for all; widening the mainstream and reducing the need for special treatment.

Multiculturalism, or certain understandings of it, 'destroy the conditions for putting together a coalition in favour of across-the-board equalization of opportunities and resources' (Barry, 2001, p 325). If multiculturalism is understood in separatist terms – and claims for special treatment outwith the mainstream are intrinsically so – cultural recognition could work against distributive justice. It may also work against social inclusion and cohesion.

Instead, cultural recognition in its full sense might entail recognising that there can be different meanings and values to goods, relevant criteria and indicators. It points to the importance of dialogue, to raise awareness, find shared understandings and negotiate solutions in order to widen the mainstream, wherever possible.

Two paradigms into one

While both distribution and cultural recognition can be regarded as aspects of social justice, the general view seems to be that they constitute separate paradigms. They are different in terms of outcomes: distributive injustice results in exploitation, economic marginalisation into low paid, undesirable work (or unemployment) and deprivation, while cultural misrecognition can mean cultural domination, lack of representation and voice, and disrespect. Cultural recognition draws attention to the value of difference, while equality in the labour market (distributive justice) demands 'de-differentiation'; for example, the abolition of segmentation on grounds of gender. To make claims simultaneously on grounds of difference and sameness would seem contradictory – what Fraser calls 'the redistribution–recognition dilemma' (1997). Yet it is not necessarily so. A person could be the 'same' in that s/he is equally well able to do the job but 'different' in terms of the way s/he does it and the enriching perspective s/he brings to bear.

Along with debates about which should take precedence (Young, 1990; Honneth, 2003) there have been attempts to integrate the two paradigms of distribution and cultural recognition (discussed in Lister, 2008). Inequality could be a feature of either: as discussed in Chapter

One, Baker et al (2004) frame recognition, respect and voice 'in distributional terms as dimensions of equality'. As previously discussed, these intangible goods cannot literally be distributed, though the question remains as to whether qualities of relationship can be helpfully viewed in distributional terms.

Honneth (2003) argues that distributional injustice is an expression of social disrespect (of course, it can also be a cause of it) and that it is the latter that fuels claims for redistribution. It is certainly true that the possession of goods and social status are interconnected, but goods also serve important non-symbolic purposes, such as enabling people to keep warm and fed. Fraser (2003) proposes an over-arching framework to promote 'parity of participation'. The distribution of resources ensures independence and voice, people are treated with equal respect and recognition, and have equal opportunity to achieve social esteem, enabling them to interact as peers. Whether resources are (or have to be) what secures independence and voice; whether everyone is due equal respect regardless of their choices and actions, and the implications in practice, might benefit from further elaboration.

These proposals are all helpful. However, there is another alternative suggested by an approach that takes as its stating point misrecognition arising from difference and/or sameness 'blindness'; the inaccurate or unquestioning ascription of characteristics to individuals and all the assumptions about needs, capacity, status and so on that flow from it. By considering what exactly is required to create and enact a just distributive process, its components and stages, it becomes possible to identify where misrecognition of this sort might intervene to distort outcomes, and militate against engagement, inclusion and equality. It might even be the case that just distribution cannot happen *without* accurate recognition. This proposition, how it might be advanced and the limits to it, will be developed in subsequent chapters.

Conclusion

This lengthy chapter has begun the exploration of what a vision for social justice as inclusive equality might entail. Much builds on and chimes with Sen's thinking, but there are some notable departures.

The proposition that characteristics are formed by, and understood according to, a given socio-cultural context implies that an even greater feat of imagination is required of the folk behind Rawls' veil of ignorance. Such a contraption might be deemed necessary, not because motivations of self-interest are to be assumed, but in the acknowledgement that to arrive at a conception of justice requires the removal of the limitations to awareness inadvertently and inevitably created by one's own experience and cultural setting. Not only do they have to be ignorant of 'their own' characteristics, they have to be ignorant of the context that formed them, ascribed them and imbued them with respective values.

Perhaps, instead, they need to acquire awareness of how their own past experience and the cultural norms they have absorbed have implicitly formed their thinking and limited their understanding. This is less a matter of deliberation from behind a veil of ignorance and more a case of removing veils of ignorance that shroud awareness and distort understanding. A perfect conception of justice does not require ignorance; it requires omniscience! Having acquired it, the deliberators presumably would need to define the perfect socio-cultural context, identify its implications for characteristic formation and resource needs. Alternatively, in their supreme awareness they might explore whether 'transcendental' principles of justice could cater equally for any socio-cultural eventuality.

In practical terms (though also not without its challenges), breaking down barriers to awareness and understanding might be achieved by promoting dialogue and connection between differently placed people. For such dialogue to be just would require certain principles to be in place in advance, such as that participants should have an equal voice. Yet here, too, there will be limits, for example in terms of intrusion into privacy and resulting loss of self-respect, compromising equal voice and risking disengagement. Questions remain regarding the interface and impact of different perspectives; objective expertise informed by 'ideal' benchmarks versus (or in negotiation with?) subjective aspiration, opinion and day-to-day lived experience. All this has major implications for the role and operations of public institutions aiming to support social realisation.

Complex equality seems to offer a useful basis for developing theory on the role of inclusion in social justice. If the emphasis is on the inclusion of diversity, it may be a matter of relaxing or reframing the social meaning of goods or the way in which criteria can be met, depending on supply and demand and scope to balance them. This might be more achievable if awareness of alternatives was raised by ensuring that the design of goods, the definition of their social meanings and selection of access criteria were collective endeavours rather than imposed, top-down (as discussed). To reframe, to maximise inclusion in and between different settings, the principle of 'different yet equally valued' is likely to be key.

Permeating throughout is the notion that just distribution is contingent on accurate recognition – of the implicit influence of socio-cultural context, of scope for expanding and reframing social meaning, and with regard to understanding each other. Yet there will be unavoidable limits to accurate recognition. What appears is not necessarily what is (what might be termed the 'red wine phenomenon', as per Sen's example), yet understanding what is might have to depend on indicators of appearance. Meaning – as recognition and significance – can only be established through recourse to wider contextual information, perhaps with reference to setting, history, similar-appearing instances, ideal versions, or other types of benchmark. Moreover, it is not always possible to compare like with like, let alone identify the equal worth of different alternatives.

It may or may not be possible to establish a for-all-time perfect 'transcendental' understanding of a just society as one which accommodates and enables plurality, allows scope for balancing different principles of distribution within certain limitations (a principle of equality as equilibrium), permitting different but broadly equally just outcomes. This could be construed as an attempt to establish the case for curtailing the liberty of some in order to promote greater equality, or of finding ways to extend liberty – and pleasure – to larger numbers of people through promoting equality. It brings together the three principles discussed earlier; greater equality (egalitarianism) can lead to greater liberty for more people (libertarianism) and thereby promote the greatest happiness of the greatest number (utilitarianism).

This understanding of a just society would be founded on a variety of principles for different types of equality and on negotiation, with the aim of maximising the scope for diverse forms of social realisation. To structure the latter might require a 'transcendental' (or at least broadly consistent) framework for public reasoning. To help ensure that debate is well-informed, it might also serve as a framework to steer the collection of empirical data.

It may be a contradiction in terms to propose a transcendental model that allows for different outcomes and some degree of comparison between them, and that has a variety of intrinsic limitations (along with other types). It would be incomplete; while justice and degrees of it can be established in broad terms, only in certain circumstances will it be possible to confirm elements of it with anything like objective certainty (that is, in situations analogous to comparing the height of one mountain with the height of another to answer the question of which is the higher). A model with such features might anyway be a waste of time. Yet, if it draws attention to the need to bridge social divides by raising awareness, promotes a means of achieving negotiated solutions, identifies scope to increase the space for including diversity, and shows how equality of various kinds need not be the antithesis of liberty but the route to it, perhaps it might serve some useful purpose. Furthermore, if it can be shown how to put such a model into practice, so that it makes a real and positive difference to the lives of disadvantaged people (or enables them to make that difference for themselves) – and ultimately to the lives of everyone by strengthening social cohesion – this may be sufficient to justify its existence.

So far it is unclear that it could achieve anything of the sort. The rest of this book will develop the themes set out in this chapter, seek to identify limits to the model of 'inclusive equality' as social justice and develop a framework to support it through public reasoning and research.

Notes

[1] Triangulation is (in brief) a means of strengthening confidence in research findings by using three different methodologies to explore the same subject.

[2] Walzer, 1983, does discuss the multiple meanings of bread and the contingency of meaning on setting, but does so as an argument against the notion of primary or basic goods rather than an illustration of the potential for the elusiveness of social meaning.

THREE

Poverty

Introduction

We now turn to explore themes from the literature on poverty to get a firmer grasp of the goods people need to have and what they need to be able to do if they are to be included in mainstream society. The relationship between 'having' and 'doing' needs to be unpacked, as do their implications for identity, status and social acceptance (drawing on Walzer's observation that 'being' and 'doing' have as much to do with distributive justice as 'having'). As discussed in the previous chapter, tangible goods can convey intangible, symbolic information about personal qualities and it seems plausible that actions can do likewise. It may be the case that it is necessary to have a particular good in order to be able to act, or that particular actions are required in order to acquire goods.

A key issue that pervades much of the literature is whether certain types of good or level of resources and/or capacity for action will always be necessary, irrespective of the social context or whether requirements will always be relative to the society in question. If the latter is so, as with ideal models of social justice, it might be similarly debatable whether the quest for generic, universal approaches serves any useful purpose. Perhaps it is possible to distinguish between poor and poorer without recourse to any form of universal conceptualisation of poverty.

Of course, even if human beings are biologically much the same the world over – a fact that might seem to commend a universal approach – mainstream society can take many forms and evolve over time. It seems logical that so, too, will the requirements for inclusion into it. Yet, to attempt to pin these down; to itemise requirements for participation in mainstream living standards and life-styles surely risks missing – or inadvertently oppressing – alternative forms of social realisation. It might be possible to discern average or majority norms but this does not necessarily tell us about the extent of diversity (of life-styles, cultures, and so on) that these can encompass on a basis of equivalent worth. Moreover, while specification of what pertains today may be accurate, meaning and usefulness are left behind as time rolls on. Once again, the perils of 'over-proximity' come to the fore, particularly in an era of rapid social change.

If it is indeed the case that mainstream society can take many forms, and that what it takes for inclusion can similarly vary, then the challenge of maximising scope for inclusion implies that many different types of goods and activities can equally grant access, are accepted as equally valid and convey equal status. By taking a step back, it may be possible to set out in generic, universal terms the types of goods that people need to have and the capacities for actions that they should have, even if the forms they take and the purposes to which they are directed can vary considerably. Rawls' primary goods (1973) and Baker et al's dimensions of equality (2004) might provide helpful starting points. The poverty literature might also point to ways in which needs and/or wants are created by social structures and cultural norms and how they also determine the way needs and/or wants are to be met. This in turn might suggest how alternative structures and norms might eliminate or reduce needs and/or wants, and open up different, equally socially approved, routes to satiating them.

The previous chapter ended with the nascent proposition that scope for misrecognition might feature at different stages of a distributive process. There may be more to add from the literature on poverty and need. As we proceed, the relationship between poverty and inequality, and implications for inclusion, will also be tracked, building on the findings of Wilkinson and Pickett (2010) regarding the impact of income inequality (discussed in Chapter One).

The literature on poverty is vast. The work of Peter Townsend, one of its most eminent figures, alone runs to many volumes. It is therefore necessary to stand back to try to distinguish key themes, accepting that potentially important angles will have to be omitted. Such an overview reveals a confused terrain, with concepts, definitions, descriptions and measures not always consistently distinguished (Lister, 2004).

The difficulty in disinterring meaning may be partially attributable to the fact that people have different agendas when it comes to poverty; whether to describe it, to explain it or prescribe action to tackle it (Flaherty et al, 2004). Social scientists will generally be concerned to find objective, rigorous ways of defining adequacy, to provide a consistent basis for comparisons. Campaigners can be expected to apply pressure for action by drawing attention to the extent of poverty and its detrimental effects. Politicians, in turn, might have incentives to downplay what could amount to an indictment of their policies, and to resist the politically problematic call for redistribution.[1]

The battle does not just concern what the definition of poverty is, but whose definition prevails, and pursuit of the latter can be expressed via attacks on the former. Yet, it does not follow that social justice is necessarily on the side of the victor. If it is contingent on the outcomes of public reasoning (see Sen, 2010), opportunities for a definition of poverty to emerge from that source need to be found. It implies the provision of unbiased information, equal voice and negotiation. Alternatively, social justice may necessitate the ruling out of unreliable, competing perceptions and agendas through developing scientifically rigorous methods of drawing objective conclusions.

A further complication arises from the moral clout that a definition of poverty can deliver: that it signifies a level of deprivation that ought not to be tolerated. Justice concerns the location of moral responsibility to act, the discrediting via the media of poor people as idle scroungers being a classic means of deflection. If such accusations go unanswered, it may be because they are true. Alternatively, it may indicate that inequalities in voice go hand in hand with inequalities in resources; a scenario that the discrediting of poor people only serves to legitimise.

This chapter starts from the premise that poverty arises from unmet need. Before proceeding to explore definitions of poverty it should be helpful to get a purchase on the nature of needs and where they come from.

Defining needs

Need must surely arise in the context of an imperative, whether or not explicitly and consciously formulated. It might entail satisfying hunger, feeling useful, avoiding embarrassment, or buying the latest model of car. Needs might take the form of 'internal' physiological or psychological drivers, or be created by external factors, or by a combination of the two. They might be shared by all or associated with particular groups; they may be unchanging or vary according to place and time, unavoidable or artificially induced. They may be generated by whatever it takes for physical survival and/or to be socially included.

Human needs

What is it that human beings need in order to flourish? It seems safe to assume that their actions will be driven by imperatives to meet whatever those needs are. This suggests that one way of conceptualising need is in terms of human motivations; an approach adopted by Maslow (1943), who identified and ranked a series of motivations into a hierarchical order. The most powerful, he claims, are physiological needs (bodily requirements, like oxygen, water, nutrients, sleep and so on), followed by safety needs (including physical security and security related to livelihood, resources, family or world order), love and belonging (friendship, intimacy, family), esteem needs (self-esteem and self-respect and the confidence and respect of others) and finally the need for self-actualisation (self-fulfilment through achievement).[2] He proposed that only once the first (the strongest) had been met, would the second come into play, and so on down the ranking (discussed in Dean, 2010; Doyal and Gough, 1991).

This approach refines and weights biological and social needs; a distinction that might better be characterised in terms of physical 'bodily' requirements and those like self-esteem and self fulfilment which might be associated with mental health needs. The perspective taken seems entirely selfish. Rather depressingly, motivations appear uniquely concerned to achieve personal flourishing rather than with selfless contribution towards the flourishing of others, or of society more generally. If the latter two prosper it is but a fortuitous side effect of individual gratification.

Maslow's proposal concerning the order in which needs will be addressed has been roundly contradicted by empirical evidence that people do not adhere to his regimen. They do risk their personal safety in the interests of self-actualisation. They do prioritise keeping up appearances over satiating hunger (Dean, 2010; Doyal and Gough, 1991; Townsend, 1985). Moreover, it is plausible that opportunities for self-actualisation are required for esteem needs to be met, rather than the reverse. It is unclear why drivers for physical survival should always supersede mental health needs for emotional well-being, self-esteem and respect – and there is evidence that they do not. For example, older people living in dire poverty do not always exercise rights to means-tested benefits because of the stigma attached (see for example, Pudney et al, 2005). Neither is it apparent why safety needs should be met by the familiar and unchanging in as much as engaging with difference and fluidity could be the norm: where difference is familiar and change is continuous, and hence unchanging.

Others too have attempted to pinpoint 'essential characteristics of the human species and of its 'species being' (Dean, 2010, p 21). According to Dean (2010), four such characteristics (of a less individualistic nature than Maslow's) have been distilled by anthropologists from Marx's early writings on human need. These can be summarised as: work (as 'human beings' purposive interaction with the world around them', satisfying instrumental needs and building creative skills); consciousness (distinguishing us from other animals, making human action possible in that it is action that has meaning); sociality (meaningfulness of individual acts is defined by social context as shared language and customs) and historical development (referring to 'humanity's struggle to emancipate itself, to universalise its species characteristics , to realise its potential, to fulfil all human need') (see Dean, 2010, pp 21, 22).

Whether the stance adopted positions human needs as individualistic or related to the functioning of society and the development of humanity, it is noticeable that some degree of interaction with others seems likely to be required. This might position social interaction as a primary or 'meta' need – the route to meeting others. Needs are instrumental to promoting participation, though the converse might also apply, that is, participation might engender other needs. To access the goods (tangible and intangible) required to satisfy human needs must surely necessitate participation in distributive processes.

Needs that have their origins in human physiology are frequently treated as inevitable and unavoidable. Yet it could be argued that people are capable of inducing their own physiological needs. They might even be responsible for generating avoidable harm to themselves, exercising their autonomy to become addicted to tobacco, alcohol or drugs, leading sedentary life-styles, eating fatty, sugary foods or starving themselves into anorexia. While the motivation to satisfy immediate cravings (for example) could be regarded as an urgent and powerful need, in turn this is likely to generate longer-term health needs. Satisfying one need creates another.

However, perhaps addiction and eating disorders should themselves be regarded as a form of illness. Furthermore, it is possible that such behaviours are a response to the external pressures of a culture that promotes instant gratification and unachievable aspiration. The all-pervading pressure to buy and consume tasty yet unhealthy foods may be an example of how capitalism works with the grain of human motivation to generate profit, regardless of the longer- term personal, social (and environmental) consequences. It appears that any distinction between needs that have their origins in what it means to be human, and those generated by cultural pressures are not always easy to discern.

Cultural and social needs

If human needs are generated by the human condition, where do cultural and social needs come from and how do they inter-relate?

Townsend describes a dual process through which society (particularly the state) creates and reconstitutes need while simultaneously determining how resources are to be allocated to meet those needs (1985). For example, laws and rules determine whether schooling is free and how long the school day is. Should they change, then parents might need to find additional income or childcare.

It seems plausible that this dual process is a generic phenomenon, descriptive of the way in which all societies function where a dominant group has the power to determine how other people live their lives. However, it does not follow that they are organised around the same ideological principles, or that the dominant group will always be the same (although power and material wealth are often observed to go together!). Certainly, in Western capitalist societies, it is the rich who take the lead in setting social norms. According to Townsend:

> The obligations at work, in family and community and as citizens which we feel bound to fulfil…are moulded in predominant measure by the rich through state laws and the establishment of social norms. Therefore we have to look at the influences exerted by the rich in defining and controlling the conditions and setting the fashions, which are continually redefining and reconstituting the structures of need which citizens experience in their everyday lives.' (1983, pp 13–14)

He highlights the 'proselytisation of lifestyles' (Townsend, 1979, p 366), whereby the rich create a standard of living, set fashions and styles which are then sought by the mass of the population. Others too have drawn attention to how 'the ostentatious and wasteful consumption of the rich set fashions and standards that the poor aspired to but could never achieve' (Dean, 2010, p 35, discussing Veblen, 1899).

While the increasing wealth brought about by capitalism might be a means of meeting human needs, instead the perpetuation of the system depends on the continuous creation of new needs and dissatisfaction with whatever is already possessed (see Dean, 2010). Furthermore, another slant is offered on positional goods (see Chapter Two), whereby the advantage conferred on those who first acquire them is diminished or lost altogether as more people follow suit (Hirsch, 1977). Need satisfaction – and equality – are both rendered unattainable.

In order to have the money with which to strive to meet socially and culturally generated needs, for all but the fortuitously wealthy paid work becomes essential. It also becomes requisite for self-esteem and a conveyor of status in its own right. It is through paid work that needs for belonging and – if fortunate – self-actualisation can be met. Such needs become re-engineered and incentives to meet them are funnelled towards paid work as the culturally designated vehicle for need-satisfaction. It could be argued that capitalism (and maybe other social systems) bind people in by acquisitioning, integrating and exploiting 'inherent motivations' in ways that promote the perpetuation of that system (Marx saw it as a distortion of human need). Paid work can be viewed as a dominant good; the dominant form of social contribution and the dominant need. As different types of dominance converge, to be without it results in hugely disproportionate disadvantage – although to have paid work is no guarantee that needs will be met: low wages, job insecurity, long hours and poor working conditions being the reality for many.

In our extreme, unchecked brand of capitalism, it is not just a matter of high levels of poverty and unemployment. The middle classes also struggle to maintain living standards in the face of escalating costs for essential services owned by profit-seeking private companies (gas, electricity, train operators, and so on) and new costs are introduced (tuition fees, congestion charges and the like). According to Sandel (writing on the situation in the US), in what has become a market society (rather than merely market economy), 'the logic of buying and selling no longer applies to material goods alone, but increasingly governs the whole of life' (2012, p 6). He maintains that market values have usurped other norms even down to family life and personal relations – with what Miller (2001) might term instrumental association predominating. Almost anything can be bought or sold (Sandel, 2012). One implication of this phenomenon is that the power and freedoms of the wealthy expand while those of the poor shrink exponentially. We might reasonably conclude that Rawls' difference principle (1973) has been thrown out the window.

To be immersed in a culture can make it hard to see it objectively (another instance of over-proximity). It is difficult to avoid being caught up in: 'the web of beliefs which convinces many individuals within capitalist societies that the market is a natural and fair mechanism for the organisation of production, consumption, exchange and distribution' (Williams, 1979, pp 31–49, cited in Doyal and Gough, 1991, p 87). We may well be oblivious to the unwritten contract that compels us, even covertly coerces us, to 'sell' our labour – if we possibly can – in order to respond to culturally-created needs for commodities, thereby generating profit for others. While earning income through paid work might increase our liberty to consume, we sacrifice our liberty to spend our time how we might otherwise choose. Those who cannot work are culturally devalued; those who are perceived to have chosen to reject it are subject to moral condemnation.

The survival of capitalism is contingent on the continuing acceptance of that 'web of beliefs'. However, when the predicament of the majority is thrown into stark relief against a backdrop of extreme wealth and privilege enjoyed by the few, the nature of the arrangement underpinning capitalism's survival becomes increasingly blatant and, once exposed, increasingly questionable.

Universal needs

From discussion so far, we might conclude that human needs are inseparable from socio-cultural context and therefore all needs vary according to the latter. Conversely, Doyal and Gough's acclaimed theory of human need (1991) separates basic needs (the avoidance of serious harm in terms of physical health and autonomy), intermediate needs (universal satisfiers) and 'societal preconditions' and brands all of them universal.

The resulting framework sets out what always has to be in place for basic needs to be met. As a universal framework it is claimed to allow for cross-country and cross-context comparisons and rankings, which can be empirically demonstrated by a range of indicators.

Without wishing to deny the usefulness of their achievement, there are some potential difficulties with their approach to basic needs. Advocating a 'biomedical model' as the basis for their definition, Doyal and Gough draw on the WHO International classification of impairments, disabilities and handicaps (1980)[3] for detailed comparisons of degrees of impairment and associated functional limitation, which (allegedly) compromise participation and autonomy. They claim to have shown that:

> certain conditions must be met before humans can assume the mantle of persons. Logically speaking, they have to be able to participate in a cultural form of life. In practice, this means that they must have the physical, intellectual and emotional capacity to interact with fellow actors over sustained periods in ways which are valued and reinforced in some way. Loss of health or autonomy entails disablement in this respect and an inability to create or share in the good things of life, however they may be defined.' (1991, p 69)

So much for the fate of sick and/or disabled people. Even the 'mantle of personhood' is denied them. Doomed to a piteous existence, they are excluded from cultural life, from positive interaction with others, and from all the good things of life.

Of course, there is a distinction between mere subsistence and full participation in society (presumably what Doyal and Gough meant by their unfortunate turn of phrase). Sick and/or disabled people do disproportionately experience poverty. The proposition that avoidance of harm and the enablement of autonomy are basic needs is not necessarily erroneous, though avoidable harm might also include misrecognition, inequality and (as will be argued) exclusion. Neither is this to argue that indicators like malnutrition or preventable disease have no part to play in defining 'avoidable harm', although as discussed this can be a consequence of apparently autonomous action, associated with over-indulgence as well as insufficiency, as the current epidemic of obesity in the US (and, increasingly, Great Britain) testifies.[4] Instead the argument put forward here is that a set of indicators to quantify the prevalence and degree of bodily impairment cannot provide an adequate account of avoidable harm and its implications for loss of liberty.

Doyal and Gough's 11 intermediate needs cover physiological needs, safety and security needs, needs for relationships (belonging), and for education (self-actualisation), although needs for self-esteem do not appear to feature. The first five are linked to physical ill-health, while the next four concern the emotional component of autonomy. Education is added as a tenth, to 'enhance the cognitive component of autonomy' (1991, p 193). Finally, due to women's biological difference, they add one 'for them and them alone: the need for safe birth control and safe child-bearing' (1991, p 193),[5] though the spread of HIV (not to mention shared responsibility for unwanted pregnancy) suggests that this might cause men, too, to experience avoidable harm and loss of autonomy.

As for their four societal preconditions, they first take the form of a means of economic production and distribution: 'to create the food, shelter and other satisfiers required for (what are defined as) 'normal' levels of health to be achieved collectively' (1991, p 81). 'Reproduction', as in 'procreation, and infant care and socialisation' (1991, p 83) is another, along with cultural transmission – a means of communicating and promoting shared values and beliefs to create normative patterns, and finally political authority to ensure that the rules securing the success of the collective are taught and enforced.

Doyal and Gough's assertion that women and 'groups subject to racial oppression' require '*additional* and *specific satisfiers* and procedures' to address and correct '*additional* threats to their health and autonomy' (1991, p 74, emphasis in original) is particularly telling in that this 'special' provision positions them outside the social mainstream. Similarly, as discussed, Doyal and Gough appear to assume an inevitable association between functional or cognitive limitation and lack of participation or incapacity to exercise autonomy. Yet, the extent to which additional measures are required to meet the needs of particular groups, or to which a person with any form of impairment is able to participate, exercise autonomy and 'share in the good things of life', might depend on the nature of cultural and societal preconditions (to use Doyal and Gough's terminology) rather than on inherent physiological characteristics. Indeed, those preconditions might be responsible for generating needs and creating group identities as well (a proposition that will be developed in Chapter Four).

While an interconnection is usefully forged between individual (basic) needs and the intermediate 'satisfiers' and societal preconditions necessary to meet them, there appears to be a great deal more to say, both regarding the impact of each on the other, and the nature of societal preconditions in particular. Surely it is not just the existence of a means of production or mechanisms for the transmission of cultural rules and values, but how this operates and what is transmitted that matters when it comes to need formation and/or satisfaction. Whatever the undisputed value of Doyal and Gough's framework, given the variability in the way cultural and societal conditions can be expressed, once again we appear to be heading away from a universal approach towards a relative one.

Defining poverty

Whatever the potential differences in their agendas, the overall aim of those concerned to define poverty is to ascertain the degree of disadvantage arising from unmet need that is – or should be – regarded as socially unacceptable. Inherent in the concept is some form of benchmark (or benchmarks) of the deprivations that no fellow citizen should have to endure (casting aside for the moment the question of who should take action to address it). Clearly, not all types and forms of unmet needs can be expected to cause significant harm, although previous discussion has indicated some of the challenges to disentangling and prioritising them. Certain themes will resurface and be reworked in the differing approaches taken to defining poverty. Moreover, as we shall see, there are fresh challenges waiting to be unearthed.

Overall poverty

To chart a pathway through the complexities that defining poverty would seem to entail it could make sense to start with an overall definition. It might then be possible to unpack themes and issues meriting further investigation.

In 1995, the United Nations World Summit for Social Development agreed the following description of the various manifestations of poverty:

> lack of income and productive resources to ensure sustainable livelihoods; hunger and malnutrition; ill health; limited or lack of access to education and other basic services; increased morbidity and mortality from illness; homelessness and inadequate housing; unsafe environments and social discrimination and exclusion. It [poverty] is also characterised by lack of participation in decision making and in civil, social and cultural life. It occurs in all countries: as mass poverty in many developing countries, pockets of poverty amid wealth in developed countries, loss of livelihoods as a result of economic recession, sudden poverty as a result of disaster or conflict, the poverty of low-wage workers, and the utter destitution of people who fall outside family support systems, social institutions and safety nets. (United Nations, 2000, p 41)

It proceeds to list groups who are disproportionately likely to experience poverty, including women, older people, people with disabilities and refugees.

From the superficial manifestations of poverty we can start to hypothesise about causes, consequences and interconnections:

- Sustainable livelihoods seem to be contingent on the possession of an adequate amount of income and 'productive resources'.
- Unmet physical needs for adequate nutrition can be a consequence of poverty.
- Ill-health might also be a physical consequence of poverty, as might increased morbidity and mortality; but could ill-health also be a cause of poverty?

- Education and basic services seem to have a role to play, though whether they prevent, mitigate or lift people out of poverty is unclear.
- Unmet (physically or socially defined?) needs for 'adequate' shelter and safe environments can be features of poverty.
- Discrimination and exclusion are associated with poverty but, again, whether as a cause or a consequence (or both) is unclear.
- Poverty can find expression as a lack of participation, politically, socially and/or culturally. Is this the meaning of exclusion?
- Although poverty occurs in all countries, the incidence and causes of it do not necessarily look the same.
- Poverty can result from external events rather than physiological factors.
- Being in work does not necessarily mean being out of poverty.
- Support to keep people out of poverty can come from different sources – family and state.

As a definition this description seems to pose as many questions as it answers. While attempts can be made to interpret what lies beneath superficial manifestations, it requires more substantial theoretical underpinning and it is hard to see how such a definition could be operationalised. Moreover, it tells us little about what it takes to achieve inclusion, or how broad or narrow access routes are.

Many of these themes, along with others concerning the nature of needs, find expression in debates around 'absolute' and 'relative' poverty, and the implications arising from them. We will look at each of these in turn, before briefly reviewing approaches to measuring poverty and what all this tells us about inclusive equality.

Absolute poverty

Absolute poverty has been defined as a condition 'characterised by severe deprivation of basic human needs, including food, safe drinking water, sanitation facilities, health, shelter, education and information. It depends not only on income but also on access to services' (United Nations, 2000, p 41).

These 'basic human needs' appear to be defined by what it takes to secure physical, bodily survival. If so, they must be experienced by everyone and therefore in that respect they can accurately be described as universal. However, before moving too swiftly to proclaim this as a universal definition of poverty, applicable in any context at any time, even within this concise, apparently unambiguous account, there are a number of in-built assumptions that could be subject to challenge:

- Does each person need each of the designated items to an equal extent? For example, do babies need the same amount of food as adults? Is the same amount of shelter equally necessary in all climates?
- Could such needs always each be met by the same amount of income or service provision?
- Could there be circumstances where they cannot be met by any amount of income or even the widest possible access to services?
- Even if they are equally needed, could that equal need always be met by the same type of food, healthcare, shelter, education and so on?
- Although the meeting of certain basic human needs are clearly necessary for survival, are all basic human needs always equally necessary?
- Can we safely equate poverty with failure adequately to meet needs for bodily survival, or is this an incomplete account of basic human needs? It is noticeable that needs described by others as universal or 'human' do not feature, such as autonomy (Doyal and Gough, 1991), belonging and self-esteem (Maslow, 1943).

It seems that even if the 'basic human needs' listed in the definition of absolute poverty are of a universal type, to identify what is necessary to meet them must unavoidably mean engaging with many variables originating from the physiological make-up of individuals and from their environment.

Relative poverty

Reconceptualising poverty in relative terms might be necessary to address some, if not all, of these issues. A much-quoted definition of relative poverty is provided by Peter Townsend's seminal work on the subject:

> Individuals, families, and groups in the population can be said to be in poverty when they lack the resources to obtain the types of diet, participate in the activities and have the living conditions and amenities which are customary, or at least widely encouraged or approved, in societies to which they belong. Their resources are so seriously below those commanded by the average individual or family that they are, in effect, excluded from ordinary living patterns, customs and activities. (Townsend, 1979, p 31)

With its focus on participation in what is customary or approved, this definition seems directly apposite to the aim of this project; to explore how inclusion into mainstream society can be maximised. It also resonates with earlier emerging themes concerning the importance of social participation as the route to meeting needs of all kinds.

Townsend's definition unambiguously links doing with having: what people are able to do is contingent on them having sufficient resources (not necessarily just income). A connection also appears to be made between being able to participate and having average resources, or rather the existence of a band below the average within which participation remains possible. Townsend argued that below a particular threshold of resources – or poverty line – deprivation increased disproportionately to the rate of resource reduction, resulting in social withdrawal – what in a later era might be termed social exclusion.

Others broadly chime with Townsend's approach to defining poverty with reference to the standards of the society in question and the resources required to conform to them. For example, the European Commission's definition adopted in 1984 equates 'the poor' with: 'persons, families and groups of persons whose resources (material, cultural and social) are so limited as to exclude them from the minimum acceptable way of life in the Member State in which they live' (EEC, 1985). Similarly, according to a World Bank economist, '"Poverty" can be said to exist in a given society when one or more persons do not attain a level of material well-being deemed to constitute a reasonable minimum by the standards of that society' (Ravallion, 1992, p 4). Lister proposes that poverty is defined as 'an inability to participate in society, involving both a low income and a low standard of living' (2004, p 15).

While the emphasis is often on material resources, it seems that there are different approaches to defining 'resources' and that forms of 'capital' are also important. Townsend (1979) argued that cash income is just one form of resource that contributes towards living standards; others being the value of capital assets (housing, living facilities, other assets and savings), employment benefits in kind, public services in kind (health, education and so on), and private income in kind (smallholdings, gifts, personal supporting services).

Bourdieu's definition of three types of capital seems to fit well with the terms of the European Commission's definition of poverty. He suggests that capital can be understood as:

> *economic capital*, which is immediately and directly convertible into money and may be institutionalized in the form of property rights; as *cultural capital*, which is convertible,

> in certain conditions, into economic capital and may be institutionalized in the form of educational qualifications; and as *social capital*, made up of social obligations ('connections'), which is convertible, in certain conditions, into economic capital and may be institutionalized in the form of a title of nobility. (1997, p 47)

Interestingly, all forms appear to lead back to, or contribute towards economic capital. Presumably this is not inevitable, in circumstances where complex equality (Walzer, 1983) applies and material wealth ceases to be the route to all else.

Whereas the definition of absolute poverty took as its starting point the physiological requirements of human beings, definitions of relative poverty focus on the demands generated by the customary norms of the societies in which they are located. In order to comply with these it is necessary to possess the requisite resources (of whatever type). If societies have different customary norms, presumably different amounts and types of resource will be necessary to participate in culturally approved ways. However, those norms and standards first require definition before it is possible to identify resources needs. The challenges of achieving consensus on norms and standards, resource needs and consistent measurement of either seem somewhat daunting, to say the least. The more culturally diverse the society, the greater those challenges are likely to be.

As with the definition of absolute poverty, it may prove helpful to unpack a few more challenges that relative approaches might imply:

- Can a given level or type of resource consistently be converted into equal participation in whatever customary norms are agreed, or do assorted variables intervene to skew that relationship? If so, how is a consistent basis for measurement to be established?
- Should, as implied, the aim be to equalise resources sufficiently so that more, and more diverse, people can be included? Can inclusion into the social mainstream always be achieved by possessing the right quantity and type of resources?
- What is the relationship between relative poverty and inequality? While they are not the same (inequality can exist without necessarily resulting in poverty), the location of 'the average' could be affected by the span of inequality and the distribution of resources between the extremes.

Absolute and relative

There are numerous ways of conceptualising the relationship between absolute and relative poverty, between 'basic human needs' and those generated by conformity with social norms – if, as previously discussed, the two can be so neatly separated.

It could (and has) been argued that survival needs should take priority over social participation needs. The distinction between absolute and relative poverty has previously opened the door to the claim that poverty does not exist in Britain (see the speech by the Rt Hon John Moore, 1989). By this is meant, broadly, that poverty is not of the order seen in famine regions of Africa (as an example of absolute poverty). In Britain, according to such claims, all is in place for physical survival (though statistics reveal a clear-cut relationship between income levels and morbidity and mortality rates). In a wealthy society like Britain, so the argument runs, relative poverty could mean a household only having one car when the average has two. This is a classic example of confusion between inequality and relative poverty – unless the claim is that two cars are an essential requirement for participation in mainstream society, without which deprivation and social withdrawal are the result.

It remains unclear whether we are dealing with two distinct sets of needs (or wants); in the form of the physiological needs associated with absolute poverty and the social needs that participation in customary norms implies. However, closer inspection reveals a number of difficulties with such a proposition. There is no obvious reason to suppose (and previous discussion would support) that human needs for positive social interaction are not as universal and basic as needs to satiate hunger, to have access to shelter, and so on. Conversely, bodily survival needs can be generated by external environmental factors. For example, the need for food might arise due to crop failures, inefficient food delivery systems, or unaffordability attributable to economic mismanagement. Another way of conceptualising this is that needs of all kinds are generated by the interface between personal and environmental factors.

A further possibility is that both physical and social needs – human needs of all types – are socially constructed. Hunger may be satiated by stale bread or a three-course meal; by a curry and rice or a ham sandwich. It seems reasonable to assume that, where need is greatest, choices about the way in which it is met become less important. Perhaps it is possible to separate and prioritise the need for food of any kind as opposed to mere wants or preferences for food of a particular sort. In this scenario, 'need' might be regarded as absolute whereas 'want' is relative to the socio-cultural context (discussed in Dean, 2010). However, the importance of cultural conformity and the force of cultural taboos should not be under-estimated. People may be prepared to suffer gross deprivation in order not to violate them (discussed in Doyal and Gough, 1991, p 70). The inherent need to eat can be over-ridden by cultural imperatives concerning what food is acceptable to eat. The tangible value of food as a means of allaying hunger takes second place to its intangible symbolism. Certainly, it would seem mistaken to assume that the importance of cultural conformity is less worthy of attention than an 'inherent' physiological need. This may anyway be a false distinction if inherent needs can only be met by adhering to culturally determined norms, because being able to conform to those norms is itself an inherent need – and a particularly powerful one.

The notion that necessities (as opposed to wants or preferences) cannot be established in isolation from social context has a long track record. An early manifestation is to be found in Adam Smith's much-cited discussion of the clothing necessary to appear in public without shame (1776), and how this can vary subject to location and gender. The social context might dictate that this could be easily achieved, at little cost and in many ways. Alternatively, as earlier debate implies, requirements could be more narrowly drawn and ever-changing, necessitating on-going expense. It is interesting to note the importance accorded to public interaction, and to the personally destructive, emotional consequences of being unable to do so on a culturally approved basis. This adds weight to the proposition that it is not just the fact of social interaction but the quality of it – how it is experienced – that matters.

If gross deprivation results without it, is access to culturally acceptable food a need or just a preference? Similarly, if it can be culturally engineered so that possessing an expensive luxury is critical to appearing in public without shame, does a person need or merely want that item? The distinction between needs and wants is far less clear-cut than may at first appear.

Absolute capabilities

Before moving to abandon the concept of absolute need (as advocated by Townsend), we need to engage with the different approach taken by Sen in the context of his 'capability theory' (1983). Their divergence of view was the source of heated and detailed exchanges between the two back in the 1980s, not all of which need detain us here.

Sen defines poverty as 'poor living'; the 'lack of capability to live a minimally decent life' (2000, p 4). Instead of a focus on resource needs, he turns the question on its head, beginning by defining what people should be able, or have the option, to do – providing 'an account of equality based on the distribution of substantive freedom' (Burchardt, 2008, p 205). Without going into detail, and taking a bicycle as an example: 'There is, as it were, a *sequence* from a commodity (in this case a bike), to characteristics (in this case, transportation), to capability to function (in this case, the ability to move), to utility (in this case, pleasure from moving)' (1983, p 160, emphasis in original).

The person's capability of moving in a certain way is attributable to the transportation characteristic of the bike. 'Capability' refers to what a person can, or has the option, to do or be. Ownership of commodities (or income or resources) is the wrong focus for determining living standards, because it does not necessarily mean that a person is able to make use of them (though not owning them would presumably ensure that they cannot!). Utility, mental reaction to usage or consumption, is unreliable in that it may depend on an individual's temperament. Instead, Sen argues, the focus for defining living standards should be capabilities.

According to Sen, 'poverty is an absolute notion in the space of capabilities but very often it will take a relative form in the space of commodities or characteristics' (1983, p 161). He cites the capability of being able to appear in public without shame (drawing on Adam Smith's example) as an absolute need. It is not a matter of being relatively less ashamed than others, but of not being ashamed at all – an absolute achievement. There could, though, be thorough-going relativity with regard to commodities (the clothes required to appear without shame in different societies, at different times). Moreover, he argued, if starvation and hunger existed, then poverty must exist, regardless of the relative picture (Sen, 1983).

In a poor community, commodity and resource requirements for participation might be very little; mostly concerned with nutritional and physical requirements. In richer communities, where those needs are more typically met, participation would make greater demands on the possession of commodities or resources. The capability remains the same (and absolute). Yet Sen accepted that capabilities, too, could vary in importance. Needs may be absolute but they are not necessarily universal: which ones are prioritised, as well as how they are to be met, will be context-specific, and the process of prioritisation should be participatory (Burchardt, 2008). Sen is vague about how capability theory might be operationalised, suggesting that it might take the form of 'some kind of efficiency-adjusted level of income with "income" units reflecting command over capabilities rather than commodities', and (not altogether helpfully), that this would be 'a rewarding field of research' (1983, p 165). According to him, what Townsend was doing in his detailed, scientific work on measuring relative deprivation was estimating the varying resource requirements necessary to fulfil the absolute need of participation in community activities.

Unsurprisingly to anyone familiar with Townsend's 1979 *magnum opus*, Townsend took a dim view of Sen's remarks on numerous grounds. Many of his objections have their roots in the case for objective, scientific measurement, the limitations of subjective approaches and the associated risk of opening the door to suggestions that, even in developed industrial societies, all the poor require are meagre, subsistence-level benefits (a well-founded fear, as previously illustrated). He objects to the imprecision of capabilities (far from being 'absolute', degrees of meeting them are surely possible). Even the drive to overcome 'starvation and hunger' is ambiguous (hunger being a less severe condition than starvation and much more widely experienced, sometimes or often). He highlights the difficulty of reconciling the (alleged) absolute nature of needs with the proposition that they, as well as how they are met, can both vary. Townsend also challenges Sen's focus on commodities and individual states or wants, condemning this as an adaptation of individualism that cannot explain the social construction of need.

Whatever their evident differences, the two approaches both have implications for the project in hand:

- The focus in capability theory on what people are actually able to do might offer a route through the tricky adjustments that otherwise have to be made to equivalise incomes, and the possible intervention of other forms of social barrier that could distort the conversion of resources into action and/or consumption.
- Capability theory might offer a way of defining the parameters of the social 'space': the freedoms that should be available to all.
- Are capabilities and associated needs really 'absolute', or (as Townsend queries) are degrees of achievement possible? For example, depending on the context and the clothing, the experience of appearing in public could be abject humiliation, neutral indifference or positive affirmation of superior status.

- Sen rejects utility as an appropriate benchmark due to the variability of individual temperament and mental reaction; yet surely 'shame' is just such a reaction. Individuals may be more, or less, sensitive to what others think of them.
- How is scientific objectivity to be reconciled with equal voice? Do not people with experience of poverty have more authority to describe that experience than people who never have?
- With the best will in the world, if we all are to some extent prisoners of our own culture, personal experience and interests, is objectivity ever going to be possible, and will claims to it be credible?
- Both Sen and Townsend appear to accept that more resources will be required for participation in richer societies than in poorer ones; but is this inevitable?

Objective and subjective

One of the major tensions emerging from previous discussion (first flagged in Chapter Two) concerns the respective value of objective versus subjective accounts. There are risks that focusing down onto individuals, their motivations and feelings could mean sight is lost of the socially constructed barriers that cut across, disadvantage and define swathes of the population. Yet, to remove subjective perceptions and experiences from the equation could mean that valuable knowledge and insights are foregone, that scientifically-derived benchmarks have no basis in reality, and that the disempowerment of poor people is compounded. Conversely, to base measurement on subjective accounts could be to place undue reliance on 'individual temperament', unfounded or ill-informed perceptions: 'It is surely impossible to assess the importance of subjective deprivation as an explanatory variable independent of assessing actual deprivation' (Townsend, 1979, p 48). Moreover, to attempt to introduce subjective views into scientific measurement would presumably destroy objectivity and with it the authority of such endeavours.

It is self-evident that the challenges of measuring poverty are significant, no matter how conceptualised – though any distinction between measuring and conceptualising is debatable; ways of measuring being themselves conceptualisations. The case for objectivity versus subjectivity has to be located within the context of the wider goal of developing definitions that are fit for purpose. According to Townsend, 'a good definition should be comprehensive, should depend as much as possible on independent or external criteria of evaluation, should involve the ordering of a mass of factual data in a rational, orderly and informative fashion, and should limit, though not conceal, the part played by the value judgement' (1979, p 38). That is not to say all would agree.

In many ways, an obvious place to start would seem to be to measure income distribution. As discussed, in capitalist societies, where markets predominate, income (as well as the means of acquiring it) is a 'dominant' or 'primary' good which provides the route to many others (Walzer, 1983; Rawls, 1973). In a marketised society where almost anything can be bought or sold (Sandel, 2012), income might reasonably be expected to play a major role as a determinant of deprivation and of liberty. Money also appears to offer a precise, objective and consistent basis for establishing value and making comparisons. Given that income can be easily redistributed there should be practical reasons for focusing attention on it.

A widely used measurement in research, for cross-Europe comparisons and tracking changes over time, is 60 per cent of median household income (with equal numbers of households above and below). Fifty per cent of the mean has also been used. The households below average income (HBAI) datasets are one source of information on income distribution that is frequently used to plot trends in Britain. Another approach (used in the past by the UK government) is to use social assistance benefit[6] levels as the criterion of income adequacy, and benefit take-up as a measure of the prevalence of poverty. Instead of income adequacy determining benefit levels, benefit levels define income adequacy. Of course, as Sen (1983) points out, this implies that the most effective way to reduce poverty is to cut benefit levels!

One further difficulty with income-based measures is how to account for the fact that not every person in every situation requires the same amount of income to achieve the same living standard. Even if indisputably a dominant good in our culture, cash income is not always a reliable indicator of command over resources and of outcomes (Piachaud, 2008). Some experience extra costs, for example due to expensive medical needs or disability (Dworkin, 2000), while larger households might achieve economies of scale. It also depends on other factors, such as local variations in price or the availability of family or community support, consistent with Townsend's definition of resources (1979).

Thus, whatever the illusion of objectivity that income-based measures might promise, assertions that those below a certain percentile in the income distribution are 'in poverty', or that the level of social assistance benefits represents a poverty line 'have no status as poverty measures; they reflect nothing more than power holders' or theoreticians' subjective opinion' (Veit-Wilson, 1998, p 12). It means that benefit levels could be grossly inadequate and underlines the importance of objective, scientifically-derived data on actual living standards and their relationship to income levels.

It was the latter that Townsend sought to supply. In essence, his approach entailed identifying indicators relevant to or determining a 'national style of living', covering 'diet, clothing, fuel and light, home amenities, housing and housing facilities, the immediate environment of the home, the characteristics, security, general conditions and welfare benefits of work, family support, recreation, education and social relations' (1979, pp 249–51). Surveys were then carried out, scores for different forms of deprivation were calculated and comparisons made with household income, in order to identify the point where social withdrawal escalated at a disproportionate rate. Although Townsend was clearly acutely aware of the need to account for differing lifestyles of minority groups, it is less evident how well his methodology was able to accomplish this.

In fact, since Townsend's development of deprivation indices, methods of measuring poverty have become increasingly participatory. Building on his approach, Mack and Lansley pioneered a 'consensual approach' (1985) in their Breadline Britain survey in 1983, which was then revisited and refined in 1990. These used 'consensual methods' to establish majority public perceptions of necessities and attitudes towards poor people (1985, 1992), and to reveal the living standards of the latter. The survey was designed to get a representative view from the general population and to include a large enough sub-set of poor people to be able to examine their living standards (Mack and Lansley, 1985). These studies in turn formed the starting point for the Poverty and Social Exclusion in Britain survey (Gordon et al, 2000), which extended the scope of study to encompass 'four dimensions of social exclusion', from adequate income or resources, the labour market, services and social relations. It also explored movements in and out of poverty. Of particular relevance to our purpose is the fact that the survey questionnaire included subjective measures to find out how many people considered themselves to be in absolute or overall poverty (see UN definitions cited above). This sophisticated study also allowed for international comparisons and investigation into the circumstances and responses of particular groups.

Other methodologies have also sought to include the views of the public and/or particular groups, using surveys or focus group discussion. The calculation of minimum budget standards involves identifying (and costing) a basket of goods and services judged necessary to meet minimum standards, whether founded on expert or public opinion, or a combination of the two (for example, see Bradshaw et al, 2008). Such budgets can be (and have been) developed for different households (with and without children, lone parents, single or partnered pensioners, and so on), and to some extent for other groups, such as disabled people. In each case, the budget for a particular household or group is developed with people from the group in question.

The challenge of operationalising capability theory was picked up in quite different ways by Nussbaum (2000) and Burchardt and Vizard (2007). Unlike Sen, who emphasised the importance of a context-specific participative approach, Nussbaum's approach was to reason from ethical and philosophical first principles to identify universal components of human flourishing[7] (Nussbaum, 2000). Burchardt and Vizard (2007) did a bit of both, using a combination of human rights frameworks and workshop discussions involving people with differing characteristics. Human rights provide a very helpful universal benchmark although, again, what it takes to implement them will be specific to the social and cultural context (see Mandle, 2006). The resulting ten 'domains of central and valuable capabilities' provide a framework for monitoring progress on equalities. Starting with the rather important capability of 'being alive', they cover physical security, health, skills to participate in society, a comfortable standard of living, engagement in productive and valued activities, enjoyment of individual, family and social life, participation in decision-making (having voice and influence), expressing yourself and having self-respect, protection and fair treatment by the law.

One of the difficulties of any approach that is concerned to define the average or majority is that the scope for, or range of, diversity risks being overlooked. In effect, the primary focus is often on defining sameness rather than on outlining the parameters within which there is space for difference. Burchardt and Vizard's capabilities provide a focus on sameness, shared commonalities that cross-sect groups defined by age, disability, sexual orientation, gender, race and religion or belief, although they also allow space for differences and for different strategies to achieve equality accordingly. The authors do, though, acknowledge that some capabilities will be more salient to certain groups than others, even if all capabilities need to be secured for everyone. Moreover, while it would be quite wrong to suggest that approaches to developing deprivation indices or minimum budget standards fail to acknowledge that different groups may make different choices or have different requirements, their primary aim is to define (relative) poverty, not to ascertain how wide or narrow the mainstream 'national style of living' is.

It would be interesting to explore whether any of these methodologies could be adapted for such a purpose.

Subjective accounts

There are clearly many parties with an interest in defining poverty. It is also the case that their voices are far from equal. Politicians can (and do) use their power to define poverty (or deny its existence) and to set wherever they please the benefit rates that many have no choice but to live on. They also have the power, via a compliant media, to influence public opinion of poor people, to brand them as feckless, idle scroungers; as members of an underclass, 'distinguished by high rates of illegitimacy and violent crime and by drop-out from the labour market' (Murray, 1996). Meanwhile, the possibility that impoverishment is a consequence of the economic restructuring generated by the activities of a super-rich overclass (Townsend, 1993) is rather less frequently heard, as are any counter-arguments from poor people themselves.

Academics and campaigning organisations comprised of people without personal experience of poverty have sometimes been accused of compounding the disempowerment of poor people; of being part of the problem rather than the solution (for example, see Beresford et al, 1999). However, as discussed, it is clear that poverty researchers have found various ways, allowing for differing degrees of involvement, of tapping into public opinion and/or that of designated groups where their circumstances are the topic for investigation. Moreover, the right of 'poor people'[8] to speak for themselves, and the importance of hearing their voices, is increasingly gaining acceptance (Lister, 2004). The case seems partly based on matters of principle and partly the acknowledgement that lived experience of a situation engenders expertise about it, with much to contribute towards developing strategies for action (see also Dean, 2010).

Participatory approaches to research with people who have experience of poverty reveal that they tend to give priority to intangible, relational matters such as loss of autonomy, powerlessness, disrespect, shame and stigma (Lister, 2004). It is noticeable that even where the practical constraints of very low incomes are discussed by 'poor people', it is the associated emotional toll that dominates; anxiety at being unable to meet supermarket bills, anger that elderly people sit in the dark because they cannot afford electricity bills, and 'being unable to cope' if shoes get holes in them (Beresford et al, 1999). The experience of applying for benefits was described as 'degrading' (Beresford et al, 1999). Officials treated claimants 'like dirt', behaving 'like they own you'; 'as soon as you are on income support everybody officially knows your business'. The process was experienced as adversarial, not supportive. According to Lister, 'What people living in poverty want is the universalist recognition of their common humanity and citizenship and of the equal worth that flows from that' (2008, p 111). It is clear that misrecognition in the form of 'sameness-blindness' goes hand in hand with material hardship. While poverty has long been seen as a concern for distributive justice, this suggests that recognition and voice are just as relevant (Lister, 2008).

The focus of much (even consensual) poverty research, on goods, access to services, activities and incomes, may not readily capture the sorts of issues that 'poor people' have been shown to prioritise. It is interesting to note that, in developing their Equality Measurement Framework, workshops wanted to include 'hope, joy and celebration', capabilities concerned with emotions and affiliation, which had featured on Nussbaum's list and which Burchardt and Vizard (2007) had initially rejected as too remote from daily life. This reinforces the importance of emotional response and the quality of interaction. It may even be possible to sustain an argument that emotional response lies at the root of all else; that the quality of interaction is judged by it, that engagement or disengagement is driven by it and that material resources, human rights and recognition matter because they prevent emotionally costly experiences like oppression, humiliation and unjust exclusion. This would suggest a rather different ordering to Maslow's hierarchy of need.

Implications for inclusive equality

The poverty literature clearly has much to contribute towards the development of a vision for social justice as inclusive equality, building on and refining themes from Chapter Two. Much has focused on cultural norms and the lower echelons of the income distribution, rather than on the full span of inequality. However, the latter continues to play a key role. It was argued that it is the rich who set the (aspirational) norms and clearly the location of median income is determined by the pattern of distribution between extremes. Exploration in this chapter also revealed some additional areas that merit further consideration.

Despite the emphasis on the socio-cultural environment in which people are located as the determinant of resource needs, much of this debate appears to remain primarily within a distributive paradigm, although there was evidence that the impact of misrecognition was of particular concern to people experiencing poverty. It is as if poverty assumes the form of an attributed personal characteristic, such as gender, race or disability. Like these, it can convey symbolic misinformation about a person's incapacity or inferiority, in accordance with prevailing socio-cultural stereotypes. This might suggest another way to position distribution and recognition paradigms; not only can misrecognition contribute to distributive injustice, misrecognition can be a consequence *of* distributive injustice.

Generally, though, the ultimate goal is to equip people with the resources they need to participate, such as redistribution of income and wealth via tax and benefit systems, and targeted capacity-building. Of course, it is quite possible for social policies concerned with such matters to result in changes to the sociological structures and values (as Townsend argued, social policy and sociology should not be treated as separate disciplines (1975, 1981) – see Chapter One). However, it could be argued that such strategies, important though they are to levelling the playing field, do not essentially change the nature of the game. It is possible that changes to the environment could both reduce resource requirements and expand access to participation for those with less, or different, capacity/ies. Changes to the way society operates can increase or decrease needs for income, and hence for its redistribution. Sometimes they can remove at source the underlying inequalities that create 'conversion' issues and increase the income needs of certain groups. Sometimes it concerns redistribution in other guises.

In our very unequal capitalist system, ever-shifting goal-posts of needs and aspirations ensure that they never can be met by the majority of us. Rawls' primary goods become conflated. Liberty, opportunity and power all become contingent on income and wealth. The economic sphere and market principles of distribution invade all others (see Walzer, 1983). People become defined by the resources and commodities that they possess, and the intangible qualities they convey about status – or lack of it.

Social justice, as it refers to the way in which society operates to frame needs and set values, would seem obviously incompatible with the artificial creation of needs that people cannot meet and the blaming of them for their failure to do so. It must surely mean reducing needs where possible, and offering people many routes to meet them, including for status and self-esteem. This does not just apply to needs for income and wealth, or even resources as more widely defined by Townsend (1979). It also applies to the other 'primary goods' of power, liberty and opportunity. It implies 'complex equality'; the separation of spheres (Walzer, 1983) and the equal valuing of different forms of contribution. This begins to sketch out in universal terms the cultural and societal conditions that minimise need, widen social norms and expand the social mainstream to accommodate diversity. To do so should simultaneously reduce the role of potentially stigmatising, separatist measures targeted at otherwise excluded groups.

A universal goal

This chapter has explored some very different answers to the question of what people need to have and be able to do if they are to participate in mainstream society. A key difficulty concerns the fact that what is regarded as customary is a movable benchmark, and therefore so, too, are requirements for having and doing. A further consideration is that needs have an emotional dimension, and that how people feel, expect to feel or are made to feel can override other forms of need. That is not to deny the existence of structural factors, or to suggest that there is nothing universal or generic to be said about human motivation. We may indeed all be unique individuals, but our emotional needs are surely as much a part of the human condition as our needs for bodily survival. The need to participate in mainstream society would seem to arise from both sources.

With this in mind, it is possible to start (tentatively) sketching out a proposal on the liberties that all should equally have and the human needs that all should be able to meet; perhaps what could be described as the outer parameters for social realisation (see Chapter Two). Given the aim of maximising scope for diversity, and minimising the oppression of difference, Doyal and Gough's focus on autonomy would seem to be a good place to start. The promotion of well-being might be a more positive take on the avoidance of harm. Both these could be taken as guiding principles, though they are clearly interconnected – scope to exercise autonomy might be considered an essential aspect of well-being. Maslow's (1943) identification of human motivations (though not his ordering of them) expands on the personal needs, both pragmatic and emotional, that have to be met for well-being to be achieved. These are elaborated further by the capabilities framework developed by Burchardt and Vizard (2007). This was informed by a human rights framework – and human rights, as set out in European law and assorted United Nations Conventions, are obvious and necessary components of the overall picture. Rawls' primary goods (1973) and Baker et al's dimensions of equality (2004) might also be positioned as general enablers: requirements for well-being or autonomous action that do not prescribe a purpose or an outcome.

Individual well-being can be seen as intimately interwoven with that of the wider collective. Marx's essential characteristics of the human species and of its 'species being' move towards what is required for the well-being of society, or could be seen as bridging individual and societal needs. For our purposes, the aim of encompassing as much diversity as possible while sustaining social cohesion would also be a key feature of societal well-being and of social justice. To achieve this, inequalities of many types need to be addressed, given their impact on emotional (for example, empathy, status and self-esteem) as well as pragmatic considerations and their implications for well-being.

None of this is to suggest that all societies should look the same, or that the same actions would need to be taken in each case, if the goal set out is to be achieved. There may be many different routes towards promoting inclusive equality and what is required to promote it will be relative to each society. It is also the case that the way in which society operates to frame and create needs, and the barriers to meeting them, must be addressed.

Reducing resource needs

What factors have an impact on resource needs and/or access to resources? Bearing in mind Townsend's definition of resources, it is possible to suggest a few (this is not intended as an exhaustive list):

- Geographical or area-based variations: climate, terrain, rurality, the quality of local infrastructure, proximity to essential services, and the availability of support from local communities.
- The quality, availability and design of housing.
- Needs related to physiological characteristics, such as the needs of people with particular health or age-related conditions for extra heating or special diets.
- Needs related to roles, like child-rearing.
- The accessibility of mainstream goods and services (for example, public transport), and whether it is necessary to pay for private alternatives (such as taxis).
- Funding regimes, whether essential services are free at the point of use, subsidised or neither.
- Macro-level factors, such as the efficiency of distribution networks.
- Scope to recycle and re-use, sustainable design and energy generation.
- Cultural values and expectations.
- The interface of all the above.

Some of these might be mitigated at source by changing the way society creates and reconstitutes needs; others by the targeting of additional resources to mitigate their impact. Of course, unlike the former, the latter does not reduce personal resource needs (as would be ideal, where it can be done); they remain disproportionately high.

Inasmuch as everyone is not equally affected by such factors, they can also be causes of inequality. Reducing resource needs should thus reduce resource inequalities or the impact of resource inequalities and promote inclusion. Policy responses include rethinking the design of mainstream, standard goods and services, capacity-building areas (rather than, or as well as, groups or individuals), redistribution through tax and benefit systems and funding services centrally via taxation rather than via personal income. Of course, where the dominant ideology revolves around cutting taxes and reducing the size of the public purse, scope to do much of this diminishes and the need for cash upfront increases. Far from reducing personal resource needs, new costs are introduced to pay for the private provision of previously publicly funded goods and services.

Equalising power and voice

It is clear that there are a variety of parties with an interest in defining poverty and that not all of them share the same power to do so. Voices are far from equal, both in framing definitions and in shaping attitudes towards poor people. While poverty researchers have increasingly brought the voices of the public and 'poor people' into the debate, it is with politicians that the power lies. If the aim is to influence their actions, credibility and persuasiveness might be contingent on demonstrating objectivity – an absence of subjective perceptions and agendas. However, it is questionable whether, despite best efforts, subjectivity can ever be truly eliminated, or unequivocally demonstrated to those with no desire to accept its conclusions. Alternatively, it might be more persuasive to engage in a process of 'public reasoning' (Sen, 2010), to promote dialogue between all parties, to brook the social distance of inequality, to hear each other's voices on an equal basis and thereby come to understand each other – and ourselves – better. We are all to some extent, often unwittingly, creatures of our own experience and culture. None of us is objective, but perhaps we can gain sufficient distance by interacting with people who are differently placed, to see ourselves and our views through their eyes.

To engage with subjective feelings and perceptions of individuals is not necessarily to descend into a disorientating world without benchmarks or comparators. Of course, surveys that reveal the views of the majority are one approach of extracting the order residing within apparent chaos. However, an alternative might be to explore whether universal, generic approaches could apply. If as human beings we share features in common, that may extend to how we are likely to feel about differing qualities of social relationships and interaction (explored further in Chapter Seven). To discount how people feel, or expect to feel, about engaging with an institution or each other, risks failure to understand how to promote inclusion. Structures and people, rigorous data and subjective experience, all have roles to play.

If empowerment is to be more than 'a chameleon "feel-good" term that means different things to different people in different contexts' (Lister, 2004, p 173) it suggests that study would be worthwhile of how power operates more generally in social processes, and whether power shifts can be achieved within them. If needs for autonomy, self-esteem and respect are important (among others relating to how people feel), there is a case to develop a better understanding of how social processes are structured and of the nature of the relationships through which they are enacted. It follows that relationships with welfare institutions whose role is to address poverty and disadvantage are likely to be of particular importance.

Towards the end of the previous chapter it was proposed that distributive and recognition paradigms of social justice could be combined. A conceptualisation of a staged process of distribution was envisaged, during the course of which there was scope for misrecognition to intervene at various points. Given the aim of building a framework comprised of themes from different literatures, if such a process is to form its outline we need to ascertain where themes from the poverty literature best fit. In essence it seems mostly concerned with inputs, outputs and outcomes, the relationship between them and factors in the external environment which exert influence over them. Themes from the literature on need explore why a person might choose to engage in the process: what output or outcome they seek to gain from it.

The difficulty of recognising barriers (or conversion factors) that we have not experienced ourselves along with the aim of equalising power and voice both add weight to the case for involving recipients at different stages of the distributive process, enabling them to influence the design of the product, access criteria and delivery methods. Without that perspective, products may be inaccessible; even if they can be accessed they cannot necessarily be made use of. This is consistent with a goal of promoting inclusion – if inclusion is a process as much as an outcome. It confirms that inclusive equality does not just have implications for the substance of social policy but for the way in which it is developed and delivered.

Limitations of resources

While poverty research often focuses on the personal resources necessary to avoid deprivation and enable participation, it is possible that deprivations cannot be overcome and lack of participation cannot be addressed by any amount of personal income or type of material resources. For example, malnutrition may be caused by macro-level failure to produce or distribute food or by lack of awareness about what constitutes a balanced diet. Lack of access to services may be due to the unavailability of services or of transport to reach them, or the nature of criteria to access them. The role of personal income and material resources in addressing unsafe environments is far from clear. Instead these may be attributable to inadequate policing, pollution, domestic violence and so on.

Possessing resources, particularly income, may certainly provide an individual with more options, particularly in a society where almost anything can be bought and sold (Sandel, 2012). Barriers presented by inaccessible public transport may be circumvented by a privately owned car, personal security may be enhanced by employing a bodyguard, and so on. However, there are limits to what money can buy (of a different sort to those discussed by Sandel, 2012), or indeed what can be overcome by any form of capital. A racist employer is unlikely to be persuaded of a black candidate's competency to do a job on the grounds that said candidate is well-off, and the extent of candidates' income and wealth would anyway be a highly questionable criterion for identifying suitability for most jobs! No amount of personal income will enable a wheelchair user to get up stairs to enter a public building, shop or place of work. Conversely, a non-disabled person may be penniless, but have no difficulty gaining access. Even if we take a wider definition of resources, it makes no difference. The wheelchair user and the black person might have any amount of assets, access to services, and family support. They might be educated to PhD level or have valuable practical skills (the two not necessarily going together!) and be on first-name terms with the Prime Minister. The wheelchair user remains stuck at the bottom of the stairs and the black person without a job.

The universal goal for inclusive equality (and the primary goods of liberty, power and opportunity) cannot be delivered by resources alone (even if income is accurately equivalised to account for potential variables). Discrimination can restrict access to acquiring resources, increase resource needs or render having resources redundant. It is to the literature on discrimination that we now turn.

Notes

[1] While 75 per cent agree that the income gap between rich and poor is too large only 35 per cent believe the answer is for government to redistribute more (Park et al, 2011).

[2] Maslow later added two more to the list after self-actualisation: 'cognitive needs' to acquire knowledge and understanding and 'aesthetic needs' for creativity and the appreciation of beauty and structure (1970, discussed in Dean, 2010).

[3] The World Health Organisation classification sees disease leading to impairment which in turn leads to disability and handicap. Impairment is defined as 'any loss or abnormality of psychological, physiological, or anatomical structure or function' representing a deviation from the norm in the individual's biomedical status; disability refers to the 'consequent restriction or lack of ability to perform an activity in the manner or within the range considered normal for a human being'; handicap is defined as any social consequence of disability 'that limits or prevents fulfilment of a role that is normal (depending on age, sex, and social and cultural factors) for that individual' (1980, p 29, cited in Doyal and Gough, 1991, p 174). The classification was updated in 2001 with one that took account of environmental factors.

[4] The obesity rate in the US is 34 per cent, compared to an OECD average of 17 per cent (OECD, 2011). Life expectancy in the US is lower than the OECD average, despite having the highest expenditure on health (OECD, 2011), although perhaps it is not so straightforward. Heart disease, stroke and obesity, once the 'diseases of affluence', have become the diseases of the poor in affluent societies (Wilkinson and Pickett, 2010).

[5] Doyal and Gough list intermediate needs as: 1) adequate nutritional food and clean water, 2) adequate protective housing, 3) a non-hazardous work environment, 4) a non-hazardous physical environment, 5) appropriate health care, 6) security in childhood, 7) significant primary relationships, 8) physical security, 9) economic security, 10) appropriate education, 11) safe birth control and child-bearing.

[6] Social assistance benefit is the means-tested safety net (income support, formerly supplementary benefit).

[7] Nussbaum's list of 10 central human functional capabilities (2000, pp78–80) can be summarised as follows: 1. Life (normal length); 2. Bodily health (including reproductive health, adequate nourishment and shelter); 3. Bodily integrity (including freedom to move from place to place, security against assault, opportunities for sexual satisfaction, choice over reproductive matters); 4. Senses, imagination and thought (including an adequate education, freedom of expression respecting political and artistic speech and religious exercise) 5. Emotions (to love, grieve, experience longing, gratitude, justified anger, emotional development unblighted by fear, anxiety, abuse or neglect); 6. Practical reason (able to form a conception of the good, engage in critical reflection about planning one's life, liberty of conscience); 7. Affiliation (including being able to engage in social interaction, imagine and have compassion for others' situations, to be treated as a dignified being of worth equal to others, protections against discrimination); 8. Other species (live with concern for and in relation to animals, plants, the world of nature); 9. Play (able to laugh, play, enjoy recreational activities); 10. Control over one's environment (able to participate in political choices that govern one's life, the right to political participation, to hold property, have equal property rights, seek employment on an equal basis, freedom from unwarranted search and seizure).

[8] People may have income levels that lead objective measurement to categorise them as 'poor' yet they may reject that label, hence the use of inverted commas.

FOUR

Discrimination

Defining discrimination

What exactly is discrimination? Its specific role in generating disadvantage requires clarification: 'it is essential to distinguish discrimination from the larger phenomenon of disadvantage, as this can be seen in patterns of gender and racial inequality. These patterns are the products of a great variety of causes, of which discrimination is but one' (Banton, 1994, p 19). This general point does, of course, apply to patterns of inequality pertaining to other groups as well. Moreover, if patterns of inequality are the outcome, it implies that it is necessary to explore where discrimination intervenes in the processes that give rise to them.

In this chapter we move on from exploring how to define 'what' is needed for inclusion to questions about 'who'; how identity is defined and its implications for inclusion. In Chapter Two it was proposed that the purpose of the distribution, closely linked to the social meaning of the good to be distributed, should be reflected in the criteria for assessing who should receive it. It would follow that how identity is constructed, conveyed and understood, must be of critical importance to achieving socially just distribution. Further implications flow from recognising the identity of prospective recipients, including an appreciation of their needs and what would (and would not) meet them, of different ways in which criteria could be met, and how to conduct the process so that it is accessible to them and promotes their engagement (assuming the overall goal is for inclusion). However, there are many reasons why identity might not be accurately recognised and, consequently, why the treatment that a person, or group of people, receives can be unjustifiably inequitable.

Discussion in Chapter Three indicated that there were some situations where the possession of any amount or type of resources would make no difference to exclusion. It was also apparent that poor people experience disadvantage beyond the practical consequences of insufficient resources, such as lack of respect. Of course, this may reflect the narrow way status is conveyed in capitalist societies via the intangible qualities of goods and position in the production hierarchy. There is, however, more to it. Important though resources undoubtedly are to enabling participation in 'customary activities', in certain situations and for certain people they are not what bar, or grant, access; neither does having an abundance of material resources of any type necessarily guarantee respectful treatment.

As with the multiple interpretations of social justice and poverty, discrimination, too, might have different meanings. Unlike those topics, the definition of discrimination has not been subjected to debate in quite the same way. However, there is a vast literature emanating from many sources. This describes and theorises inequality, discrimination and oppression as experienced by particular groups; focusing on gender, race, disability, sexual orientation and so on. There is surprisingly little cross-fertilisation between theories and approaches, although those developed within each silo *are* often fiercely contested. Nonetheless, even a cursory glance across the silos reveals the recurrence of common themes. They may use different language, but authors' preoccupations are often similar. Where they differ, they often cast fresh and relevant light on others. This might suggest that a generic, universal approach is possible. However, it is not immediately obvious that black people, old people, gay and lesbian people, disabled people and so on must necessarily have anything in common with each other. The reasons for discrimination, the form/s it takes and the types of inequality that ensue might all differ.

At its most neutral, discrimination can be defined as 'simply a matter of identifying differences' (Thompson, 1998, p 9). To say a wine-taster had a 'discriminating palate' would be to applaud their ability to minutely distinguish subtle variations of flavour. It is thus ironic that so much discrimination would appear to originate from inaccurate stereotyping, failure to identify the barriers confronting people who are different to ourselves or to appreciate where we have things in common with people who appear different. It seems that normative discrimination, that is, in the latter sense, has a great deal to do with misrecognition, whether deliberate or incidental.

One of the apparently few generic definitions of discrimination to be found in the academic arena describes it as 'the process (or set of processes) by which people are allocated to particular social categories with an unequal distribution of rights, resources, opportunities and power. It is a process through which certain groups and individuals are disadvantaged and oppressed' (Thompson, 1998, p 78). This is helpful up to a point. It is a little unclear whether the intention is to position discrimination as something that particular social categories experience or whether it is the very process of allocating people to those categories that is branded discriminatory. It does, though, signal that the reason for disadvantage and oppression is attributable to how and if personal identity is recognised and categorised. To draw on Walzer's observation that 'distributive justice has as much to do with being and doing as with having' (1983, p 3), the emphasis is on 'being' – who a person is, or is perceived to be – notwithstanding that what they have and do may be highly relevant to conclusions about identity. The assessment process might indeed be crude and inaccurate, even in formal settings. However, contrary to the objective, considered approach that the word 'process' might imply, when it comes to hate crime, and perhaps discrimination more generally, it takes the form of an emotionally-charged response. It is a direct expression of attitude, of contempt or fear, of failure to recognise and empathise.

On this occasion, moves towards a more comprehensive, generic approach appear to have been largely driven by developments in the policy rather than the academic arena, in particular by European initiatives and subsequent developments in national policy. A total of nine separate pieces of legislation covering particular groups or aspects of discrimination[1] were brought together by the British government with the introduction of the Equality Act 2010. The aim was to simplify the legislation and harmonise protection for people with 'protected characteristics', of age, disability, gender reassignment, marriage and civil partnership, pregnancy and maternity, race, sex, religion and belief, sex, and sexual orientation. The Act broadly defined direct discrimination as occurring where the reason for a person being treated less favourably than another is a protected characteristic. It had considerably more to say on generic forms of discrimination and specific applications, as will be explored.

None of this necessarily tells us what causes 'an unequal distribution of rights, resources, opportunities and power' (Thompson, 1998, p78) or why disadvantage is unjust – if it is. Whether disadvantageous outcomes are attributable to external factors or to the inherent qualities of individuals has been a recurrent theme. If external socio-cultural factors are to blame, something must be occurring that prevents certain people from acquiring and consuming goods on an equal basis. If attributed to the inherent and immutable inferiority of certain individuals and social categories then disadvantageous outcomes are regarded as a natural consequence – although whether justice entails acceptance of such naturally occurring inequality or its redress is another matter. Questions also remain concerning the justice of the (inevitably external) basis or benchmark for judgements of another person's worth.

Another way of approaching this is to ask where identity comes from; whether characteristics are externally created and attributed, or physiological (biological or genetic) facts. If (as discussed in Chapter Two) some forms of difference and ensuing group definitions are not amenable to erasure by changes to the socio-cultural context, there must be something inherent to group members that persists, regardless. Of course, the significance imputed to any such inherent factors and their social and personal impact will be a consequence of the prevailing culture, and this may have the capacity for change.

To maximise social inclusion, we need to understand what gets in the way of accurate recognition of identity. We need to explore where change is possible, through recognising scope to remove artificially created impediments to inclusion. If, as proposed, the strengthening and sustainability of society is an essential goal for social justice, it should be helpful to consider the commonalities that people share as well as responses to difference. Given that the paradigm of social justice as cultural recognition was largely developed by authors working in the gender field it is reasonable to expect that themes around recognition will feature in discussions of discrimination. Misrecognition and discrimination seems to be very closely associated. They may even transpire to be one and the same thing.

The task is to explore the implications of a model of social justice as inclusive equality and what themes from the literature on discrimination can add. The aim is to see if anything universal can be extracted about an approach consistent with such a goal. The chapter begins with an exploration of attitudes; where they come from and how they can skew understanding. It then considers issues around social categorisation and how identity is formed and conveyed. It proceeds to examine emerging cross-cutting themes relating to the location and cause of inequality, before moving on to explore what this means for distributive processes and for social policy.

Negative attitudes

Responding to difference

The description of misrecognition as it might occur within a model distributive process implies a degree of conscious, rational awareness that may be far from the reality. Within the context of public sector distributions, criteria for access are often explicitly defined in legislation and statutory guidance. For many social processes they are much more nebulous. In all cases, they entail human action and interaction.

No matter how formally constituted, the attitudes of all parties, their assumptions, past experience, expectations, emotions and sense of self, will inevitably come into play. Along with imbued cultural norms, these constitute the lens through which we view the world and each other.

As discussed in Chapter Two, attitudes towards people perceived as 'different' are critical in driving how processes are conducted and their ensuing outcomes. A desire for what Giddens terms 'ontological security' (1984) – for a sense of order, stability and continuity – would seem to predispose us to respond more positively to whatever is familiar to us. It may be a need rather than a desire: there are strong echoes of Maslow's description of 'safety needs', second in his ranking only to physiological needs, and Doyal and Gough's designation of safety and security as an intermediate need or 'universal satisfier' (see Chapter Three).

According to Wharton, writing on the sociology of gender:

> people are drawn to those whose attitudes, values, and beliefs are similar to their own. People who share our views affirm us... We may also feel that people who are like us in these ways are easier to communicate with... We may trust them more and feel a greater sense of kinship with them. Conversely, when people are different to us, we may feel threatened and find communication difficult. (2005, p 59)

However, the logical consequence of such an approach is that social divisions are entrenched when engagement might instead erode them. Misplaced assumptions remain untested and opportunities for expanding horizons are foregone. The territory covered by the familiar is and remains small and insular. Understanding – not only of each other but of ourselves – is built on narrow, shallow and hence insecure foundations.

Perhaps another approach is possible:

> On meeting antipodal man one could marvel at his fundamental likeness to oneself or one could gasp at his immediately striking differences. One could regard these differences as of degree or of kind, as products of changing environment or immutable heredity, as dynamic or static, as relative or absolute, as inconsequential or hierarchical. (Stocking, 1982, p 45)

This suggests that there are choices to be made concerning how difference is understood and hence ways of responding to it. It is not inevitable that difference is seen as immutable or significant, or that difference rather than similarity should be the focus. There is no obvious reason why difference could not be positively received as enriching, exciting and promoting creativity. Engaging with it might be necessary to meet the need for self-actualisation. Perhaps it is only through moving out of our comfort zone that we can develop skills, increase learning, fulfil potential and acquire self-esteem (see Chapter Three).

This discussion has to a considerable extent equated difference with the unknown. It stands to reason, to the point of tautology, that without adequate information assumptions have to be made. The issue is whether or not assumptions are recognised as such and are provisional and revisable in the light of evidence to the contrary. However, assumptions do not just revolve around understandings of the identity of people who appear different in unfamiliar ways but, as Stocking observed, from where that difference is understood to arise.

A recurrent theme in recent social theory (postmodernism, social constructionism and related developments), and a major preoccupation across the group-based literature, is the challenge to 'essentialism'. This can be summarised as the view that the 'essence' of each individual, or individual characteristic around which groups are founded, is natural, unalterable and unique. Generally, this is taken to mean rooted in genetic or biological make-up. Essentialism may be accompanied by reductionism: 'the process of reducing a complex, multifaceted reality to a simple, single-level explanation' (Thompson, 1998, p 145), in effect stereotyping. Often this will take the form of biological reductionism. One implication of reducing individuals to genetic or biological entities is to increase the power of experts working in such fields, in particular the medical profession.

There is no obvious reason why reductionism could not apply to understandings of the social environment as much as the appreciation of individual identity. The notion that cultures are uniquely and inherently different is suggested by Malik's assertion that 'Cultures are sealed compartments which separate 'us' from 'them'. Cultures impose upon us (even from before birth) ways of being and modes of thinking from which we cannot escape' (Malik, 1996, p 164). This suggests that societies and cultures, too, are susceptible to reductionist stereotyping (not to mention essentialism).

Any of these approaches can be exacerbated by dogmatism – a refusal to engage with alternative views, a rejection of evidence and rational argument in favour of prejudice. It may stem from insecurity, lack of experience or an inability to engage with complexity. It may be a defensive response, or a requirement of faith-based or political creeds. Dogmatism effectively shuts down debate on the possibility of change, whether of individuals or their environment, denying the existence of room for manoeuvre.

Such attitudes both promote the likelihood of inappropriate in/action and constitute justifications for it. They are testaments to immobility, to fixity, affirming the inevitability of the status quo. Yet, it may prove possible to challenge apparent fixity by diffusing defensiveness, relieve insecurity through education and capacity building and find accessible ways to communicate complexity. Even so, there are reasons why fixity may endure, not because of anything to do with the people subject to assessment but instead because it suits assessors to insist on the immutable inferiority of the assessed: 'it is simply not in the interests of the dominant groups, who have benefits without actually paying for them, readily to give up those benefits without a struggle' (Grosz, 1994, p 135).

Impact of negative attitudes

We now move on to consider the ways in which negative attitudes might find expression and be experienced by those on the receiving end. A useful starting point is to be found in Thompson's typology of processes of discrimination (1998), in the form of stereotyping, marginalisation, invisibilisation, infantilisation, welfarism, dehumanisation and trivialisation. These all minimise significance. They diminish the person, their power and their voice. People may consequently be ignored, over-protected, patronised and not taken seriously. At the extreme, they are treated as less than human.

Conversely, it could be argued that demonisation, the exaggeration of power or threat, is another form of misrecognition. Here the rationale is to stoke fears and promote emphatic rejection, justify aggressive acts or legitimise the enforced assimilation of those deemed dangerously different. Yet, as demonstrated through hate crime, aggression can also be perpetrated on people who are powerless. Far from being invisible and ignored, people whose difference is deemed to be inferior can find themselves the focus of very unwelcome attention, in the form of bullying, harassment or worse.

A further, more insidious distortion of identity assumes the guise of something more positive. The 'personal tragedy' model (Swain and French, 2000) portrays disabled people as tragic victims, or as heroic survivors of personal tragedy. While pity and admiration are not always negative or inappropriate responses, in this context they can convey 'better dead than disabled' (Swain and French, 2000; see also Crow, 1996).

All of these are distorted and disproportionate responses to difference. Both under- and over-statement create distance between 'the mainstream' and particular groups, caused by and exacerbating misunderstanding and misrecognition. They skew the relationship between victim and perpetrator by reinforcing, exaggerating or inventing differentials in capacity, power and/or moral superiority. The social distance this creates can fracture society in much the same way as divergence in income and wealth.

Sources and victims

So far, discussion has been based on the premise that there are two parties, one of whom (the more powerful) holds negative attitudes which give rise to their misrecognition of the identity of the other, to the detriment of the latter. However, there are other possibilities regarding the source of negative attitudes, how they are made manifest through discriminatory practices and who is adversely affected by them.

There is a distinction to be drawn between direct and indirect discrimination. As previously mentioned, the Equality Act 2010 defines the former as occurring where the reason for a person being treated less favourably is a protected characteristic. This encompasses situations where it is not the person who has the protected characteristic who is the victim, but someone who receives less favourable treatment because of their association with a person who does. It also allows for the possibility that the victim is wrongly assumed to have a protected characteristic when in fact they do not. Indirect discrimination occurs when a policy that applies in the same way to everybody has an effect that disproportionately disadvantages people with a protected characteristic.

It is possible that the people enforcing a discriminatory policy are not the people responsible for developing it. Indirect discrimination would appear to be closely linked to institutional discrimination, inasmuch as institutions are usually the source of policies affecting swathes of people. Each institution may have its own structures, culture, policies and processes that create distinct sets of barriers for those wishing or needing to engage with them. Institutional discrimination (discussed in race and feminist literatures) is a by-product of the ideology, assumptions, wants and needs of the powerful within that setting. Yet, the difficulty of viewing objectively the culture of which one is a part can pervade throughout institutional hierarchy. Even those at the top become 'institutionalised' – unquestioningly accepting institutional norms. Discriminatory practices might, therefore, originate from an earlier era, become embedded – or institutionalised – into culture, and be unwittingly reproduced. Thus institutional racism can mean 'circumstances where exclusionary practices arise from, and therefore embody, a racist discourse but which may no longer be explicitly justified by such a discourse' (Miles and Brown, 2003, p 109). This emphasises the importance of taking an historical view. Given that the operations of society (discussed in Chapter Three) will generally be designed and enacted via its institutions, if they harbour unacknowledged exclusionary practices there is a risk they will be replicated and imposed on external parties with whom they interact.

It is not automatically obvious why indirect discrimination could not also describe actions of an individual that are inadvertently disadvantageous to someone with a protected characteristic. It is also not inevitable that discrimination resulting from institutional policies is inadvertent. This suggests that a further distinction can be drawn; between deliberate and inadvertent discrimination. Negative attitudes are not necessarily consciously held – indeed over-protection, misplaced pity and admiration may arise from wholly positive intentions. Buildings are unlikely to be designed with the explicit goal of keeping wheelchair users out. Whether deliberate or otherwise, ignorance has a major role to play in the formation of negative attitudes. This once again underlines the critical importance of equal voice and of willingness to learn from people who may appear unlike ourselves.

Defining identity

Discussion so far has suggested that negative attitudes lead to the misrecognition of identity and unjust, discriminatory treatment. Along with the nascent typology of discrimination that has begun to take shape, this constitutes a generic, universal approach to discrimination as misrecognition, which nonetheless allows for very different experiences. It is therefore not a matter of choosing between a generic- and a group- (or protected characteristic) based approach, but of understanding how a generic approach applies to different social categories. Nonetheless, it is important to delve more deeply to ensure that this does not simply reduce all experiences of discrimination to a lowest common denominator. Different experiences need to be acknowledged, as do the different causes to experiences that may, superficially, appear much the same. Policy solutions based on such misrecognition are unlikely to succeed, instead exacerbating disadvantage and exclusion. It therefore should be helpful to examine more closely how identity can be defined.

Academic study has frequently been concerned with discrimination and associated inequalities as they affect particular groups, sometimes taking the form of separate disciplines, as in Women's Studies or Disability Studies. An exploration of, and comparisons between, group-based theories may prompt fresh insights into the nature of discrimination experienced by each. It could enable deeper, more complete theoretical conceptualisation of discrimination, oppression and their relationship to exclusion. This might also reveal cross-cutting themes that could form a shared platform for challenging discrimination and chart a clear steer for action. An appreciation of both differences and sameness is required for accurate recognition.

Oppression

The impact of enforced identity distortions is often described in terms of oppression. This seems to denote the serious and longstanding negative impact of power on those without it (Thompson, 1998; Grosz, 1994). It is less clear, other than in broad terms, what form that impact may take. It could represent the enforced limitation of the expression of identity or the development of potential, or the reshaping of behaviours into an approved mould, as defined by those with power. It might deny or inhibit autonomy, awarding control over people's lives to others, or affirming that control. The characteristics and behaviours which are oppressed (or perhaps more accurately repressed) are those which do not conform to the 'norm of the homogenous public' (Young, 1990, p 179), which places 'unassimilated' persons or groups at a disadvantage in the competition for scarce resources and requires them to transform their sense of identity in order to assimilate. However, oppression could be socially just, such as where it prevents behaviours that would threaten the human rights of others and provoke social disintegration.

While oppression might well be a cause of exclusion, it might also be a requirement of the terms of inclusion. There could be advantages to existing outside mainstream society, where its parameters are narrowly drawn and the personal cost of conformity is high. Queerness is, by definition, in opposition to 'the mainstream'; eternally the alternative (Grosz, 1994). People working in the affirmative model of disability draw attention to the advantages of the superior education that (some) disabled people (may allegedly) receive in 'special' schools, the avoidance of usual social pressures to form heterosexual relationships and get married, and a heightened awareness of the oppressions endured by others (Swain and French, 2000).

It would certainly be consistent with previous observations to argue that distance from a culture is necessary in order to challenge it and that marginalised groups might thus be better placed to see its norms and their impact. Yet 'the mainstream' does not have to be homogenous or static. Norms do not have to be narrow – it could be normal for a variety of equally valid alternatives to co-exist. If the mainstream were indeed wide enough to accommodate alternatives, perspective could be acquired, not by alienating social distance, but by immediate and well-informed comparison. Challenges to the status quo could be made from inside the tent, rather than outside. Moreover, such a status quo might be expected to be less subject to challenge, except, of course, by those wishing to promote and justify inequality and exclusion.

Oppressive constraints to identity might not just arise from misrecognition of entirely valid and feasible alternatives – of social contribution, life-styles and so on – but as a direct consequence of a lack of the material resources required to express identity and fulfil potential. Certainly the incentive to repress characteristics and behaviours deemed negative and exhibit those contrived to be necessary to access resources may be particularly acute, if failure to do so results in material deprivation. However, it may be helpful to disentangle material hardship from identity distortions. While each may well lead to the other (remembering the testimonies of 'poor people' concerning the discrimination that results from poverty), each independently can result in oppression.

Practical limitations

Although the ignorance that spawns negative attitudes can be addressed by measures to raise awareness and increase familiarity, there remain serious practical obstacles to accurate recognition, no matter how hard we strive for it. It is particularly so in situations where we need to gauge other people's identity and probable behaviour accurately and speedily. In such circumstances, allocating people to social categories on the basis of visual and verbal clues (such as accent) is an unavoidable, if short-cut, means of working out with whom we are dealing: 'We use…visible and accessible characteristics as 'proxies' for qualities that would be time-consuming to determine, such as values, attitudes and beliefs' (Wharton, 2005, p 60). Reductionism might not necessarily reflect an assumption that there is nothing more worth knowing about a person, so much as a lack of information with which to make a more rounded judgement.

When it comes to socially just distribution, indicators, markers (Wharton, 2005, writing on gender) or significators (Miles and Brown, 2003, writing on 'race') – of need and desert are required. If being, doing and having are relevant to distributive justice (Walzer, 1983), indicators of all three will be required. As with goods, significance may be relevant. As with goods, their significance may be determined by the wider socio-cultural environment and/or the immediate setting. Wearing a white coat in a hospital might indicate that you are a doctor. In a school canteen it might suggest that you are a dinner lady! In one context killing another human being results in a life-sentence of imprisonment; in another in being awarded a medal.

It is not just that indicators of identity are superficial and unreliable, and that their meaning can change subject to external context, people do not necessarily fit neatly into categories, even where based on one (apparently) readily-discernible characteristic.

At the extreme, postmodernists envisage the breaking up of all social groupings, leaving identity free-floating, detached from the bases of social structure. This chimes with the approach taken by queer theory where, as previously flagged, the basic tenet is indeterminacy. The focus is on disassembling norms and rejecting categorisations (Kirsch, 2000; also Grosz, 1994; Butler, 1990). This 'leads to the rejection of all categorizations as limiting and labeled by dominant power structures' (Kirsch, 2000, p 33). Queerness defies categorisation; it is 'eternally the alternative…What's queer now may not be queer in five year's time' (female-to-male transsexual Jasper Laybutt, cited in Grosz, 1994, p 133).

Authors writing on gender and sexuality have both identified as problematic the use of binary oppositions, such as male/female or black/white (Fraser, 1997; Butler, 1990). These are seen as precluding variation and suggesting mutual incompatibility – a person must be one or the other and cannot be both, or comprised of elements of both. It assumes the existence of clearly defined, unique features possessed by each category. Even where essential difference is proclaimed by group members themselves it can be problematic, erroneously suggesting that all group members subscribe to one unified voice (Phillips, 1997). Instead, Fraser has argued for the destabilisation of all identities and affiliations, with binary oppositions replaced by 'networks of multiple intersecting differences that are demassified and shifting' (Fraser, 1997, p 31; also Butler, 1990).

The meaningfulness of race as a social category has similarly been challenged: 'Race exists only as a statistical correlation, not as an objective fact. The distinction we make between different races is not naturally given but is socially defined' (Malik, 1996, pp 4, 5). This again poses the question of whether the origins of social categories lie in biological fact or cultural or procedural construct; whether it is a matter of self or externally-imposed identification. According to Butler 'it becomes impossible to separate out "gender" from the political and cultural intersections in which it is invariably produced and maintained' (1990, p 3). Yet, even when conceived as having biological origins, contrary to essentialist claims it is not necessarily the case that characteristics are fixed for all time; the ageing process being the obvious example. In the disability literature Zola (1989), argues for the 'universalisation of disability' on various grounds, including that impairments can fluctuate and can affect anyone, at any time.

Multiple characteristics

The fact that everyone has multiple characteristics (ascribed or otherwise) and the implications for social categories formed around just one characteristic, has sometimes, but not always, been subject to theoretical analysis: 'Class, race, sex, and gender are all categories that receive acknowledgement in the queer literature, but they are rarely fully analyzed' (Kirsch, 2000, p 11). The boundaries of a group may be expanded or, arguably, new groups created by defining identities and experiences based on more than one characteristic. It is possible to work outwards from one group to link with another, or inwards on segmentation within a group. For example, the contrasting experiences of the impact of sexism and racism within the disability population have been discussed by various authors (Begum et al, 1994; Killin, 1993; Morris, 1991; Stuart, 1992).

Identities can certainly be highly complex, and different aspects will have social significance subject to context. An individual can have a proliferation of identities – female, lone parent, working class, African-Caribbean, disabled, and so on. Both Bradley (1996) and Zappone (2003) look at the interaction of two categories/sets of lived relationships. The latter identifies new distinct social groupings of people with two combined characteristics, while acknowledging that respondents had additional characteristics which they considered just as (sometimes more) important. The logical implication of this (which she does not pursue) is the emergence of a plethora of social groupings, with ever more restricted membership. Given the uniqueness of each individual, it could be argued that each social category would ultimately have a membership of just one.

Social categorisation has, therefore, been challenged from all sides. It seems possible that any act of social categorisation is discriminatory and oppressive, in that characteristics must always be overlooked in the simplification (or reductionism) that grouping people entails. If those unrecognised characteristics are important to the person's sense of self, and/or would meet the criteria for distribution, then psychologically and/or practically damaging restrictions to identity and potential can ensue. Moreover, social categorisation may not just be undesirable, but impossible in any meaningful sense. If identity is eternally fluid and indicators inherently untrustworthy, the best that could be hoped for would be a snapshot taken at a particular time and in a particular context.

The case for social categorisation

Before abandoning all attempts at social categorisation as inherently undesirable, discriminatory and oppressive, not to mention unfeasible in practical terms, it is worth pausing to reflect on its possible advantages. One place to start is with an exploration of the implications of a world without social categorisation. First, it necessitates that distributive policy takes a personalised, individualised approach. Every individual has to be assessed without recourse to any common benchmark, because no such thing exists. In a world comprised of uniquely different individuals, there are no comparators. The justice of how a person is treated cannot be relative to, and equitable with, the treatment of others who share the same characteristics and circumstances, because nobody does. Just treatment can only be relative to the needs and goals of the individual her/his behaviour and the impact on other individuals. Social justice becomes individual justice. Equality becomes a meaningless concept.

Second, the arena for action and scope for change is localised down to the environment surrounding each individual. Any shared, collective platform for action at a higher level becomes difficult to construct and will be built on shifting sands. It is not to say that alliances cannot be forged, that commonalities do not exist, but that a focus downwards on each person's uniqueness can make them hard to discern, and they can be easily destabilised by constant change. If disadvantage is attributed to socio-cultural factors, it would also make it very difficult to see structural barriers that originate at a higher societal level. Moreover, to focus solely on what makes each of us an individual, on what is different about each person, is to leave each of us isolated. We are each on our own.

The reality is that there is meaning and relevance to social categorisation. To deny this is to leave the door wide open to discriminatory practice and undermine the scope for social change. As discussed in Chapter One, it is an empirical fact that certain social categories are disproportionately poor, unemployed and/or subject to hate crime. That is not to say that everyone in that group will be adversely affected (or affected in exactly the same way) but that there is an increased probability that they will be. As has long been acknowledged, not least of all by Beveridge,[2] certain characteristics (such as old age, sickness and disability) are correlated to an increased risk of poverty. This being so, to recognise the significance of those characteristics, categorise people and target resources accordingly, would be entirely appropriate; so, too, would action to ensure equitable treatment between group members where sameness is shared.

The nature of the social category – how broad or narrow; who defines and labels it, whether chosen or imposed – will impact on how social categorisation is experienced. Where being forced to conform to unnecessarily narrow, externally imposed social categories requires the distortion of identity, loss of autonomy, and the denial of aspects of identity that are important to the individual, oppression is experienced. Conversely, where group membership is chosen, it can be a positive affirmation of identity, removing feelings of isolation, building confidence and strengthening platforms for challenge, as necessary to achieve social (as opposed to personal) change.

Of course, it could still be argued that social categorisation, even where chosen, serves to segregate, to create social distance, thereby working against social cohesion. Essentialism, reductionism and dogmatism can be exhibited by group members themselves, generating separatist, oppositional dynamics. Certainly, it would be naïve to imagine that the interests of different groups will always coincide, and to assume so risks misrecognition through 'difference-blindness' (Taylor, 1992). As noted in Chapter Two, 'The culture, perspective, and relations of privilege and oppression of these various groups…may not cohere' (Young, 1990, p 48). Conversely, to assume that they never do could be just as inaccurate. While group (and hence personal) identity may be consolidated by drawing attention to shared experience, an inward focus could ultimately prove counterproductive. If social categories are created by inequalities arising from the socio-cultural environment, to reinforce their boundary walls from within seems an unlikely strategy for achieving wider social change.

It is inevitable that group members formed around a shared characteristic will also have many characteristics that are not shared. The diversity within groups could be an important factor in the creation of alliances across groups. Young claims that it is widely recognised that 'None of the social movements asserting positive group specificity is in fact a unity. All have group differences within them' (1990, p 162). She adds that the development of sub-groups and cross-subgroups offers: 'some beginning models for the development of a heterogenous public. Each of the other social movements has also generated discussion of group differences that cut across their identities, leading to other possibilities of coalition and alliance' (1990, p 163). As is true of any two individuals: 'Different groups are always similar in some respects, and always potentially share some attributes, experiences and goals' (Young, 1990, p 171; see also Zappone, 2003).

The importance of going beyond individual characteristic-specific understandings of discrimination and oppression is forcibly articulated by Grosz, writing in the context of queer theory:

> For notions like oppression, discrimination or social positioning to have any meaning, they must be grasped outside any particular form (whether racist, imperialist, sexual, class, religious.)...even though we recognise that oppressions have massive historical and cultural variations, something must be shared by all the different forms of oppression, if they are to be described by the same term. Both this core, or perhaps even 'essence', and the range and variability of the term need to be addressed if one is to come to a clear understanding of the relations and interactions between different forms of social domination, and their concrete differences and specificities. Our understanding of the term must be precise if it is to be used not only to cover a wide variety of different types of oppression, but also to articulate the interlockings and transformations effected by the congruences, convergences, points of reinforcement and/or tensions among these different types. (1994, p 134)

Some have stressed the need to join together on political rather than theoretical grounds: 'In the harsh and uncertain welfare world of the late twentieth century we need to go beyond the fragmentation of post-modern political radicalism and forge new alliances across bodies, experiences and socio-economic structures' (Williams, 1996, p 210).

A focus on commonalities between distinct social categories is clearly important in strengthening voices in order to achieve social change, and never more so than at a time of soaring inequality and austerity.

There is always a risk that groups of disadvantaged people are played off against each other in the competition for scarce resources. Energy is diverted into challenging other groups of disadvantaged people, rather than focusing on shared experience of the real injustice – avoidable and damaging inequality – and its perpetrators.

It seems that alliances between groups might be built on two grounds: some forms of inequality are shared across groups; everyone has multiple group memberships. As observed in Chapter Two, it is not inevitable that the latter brings any inherent tension or contradiction – any more than having multiple aspects to your identity necessarily poses challenges to personality integration. It may instead be a means of promoting social cohesion of a complex kind, around multiple possible points of commonality.

Much as a strategy of personalisation promises advantages to people who use services by tailoring provision to their specific needs and goals, it could also be beneficial to those in power. It deflects attention away from their actions and dismantles the collective power that could successfully challenge them. The bigger picture fades from view as attention is diverted to the creation of millions of miniatures.

The notion that a person is either a unique individual or a member of one or more social categories is clearly a false dichotomy. We are each both, and there is no reason why policy should not reflect this. More than one lens is required for accurate recognition. Both too much distance and too close a proximity carry risks of misrecognition and disempowerment. It is important to avoid the construction of over-broad social categories that lose sight of relevant differences, or of individualising to the extent that inequitable treatment becomes impossible to discern. Whichever lens is used by external parties, and even if both are, only a partial view will be obtainable. Accurate recognition demands the direct involvement of whoever is being assessed and information that only they possess.

Understanding our own identity

So far, discussion has explored how identity is recognised from an external perspective. At its core, identity concerns how we understand and feel about ourselves. While this will obviously be affected by the quality of relationships – whether experienced as empowering or disempowering, humiliating or ego-boosting – we may need a reasonable level of self-esteem to interact socially in the first place. Discussion in Chapter Three began to indicate that whether or not we choose to interact (where we have a choice) critically depends on our expectations of how it will make us feel; whether we are confident that we know what to do and can do what it takes to engage successfully.

Once again, there are questions concerning where notions of appropriate behaviours come from. Are they biologically or genetically driven? Or do they result from internalising cultural messages about expectations of people with a particular make up?

There are a variety of theories from the field of psychology that assorted authors draw upon to answer such questions. The socialisation process through which people take on gendered qualities and characteristics can be conceptualised as moving towards environmental factors as an explanation (see Wharton, 2005). Theories of social learning tend to view people (particularly children) as lumps of clay, moulded by their environment and the reinforcements received for gender-appropriate or -inappropriate behaviours. In contrast, cognitive approaches are more concerned with the internal motivations of children to understand themselves, and how gender meanings are internalised and used to construct identity. Identification theorists argue that unconscious psychological processes account for at least some aspects of gender. For example, to summarise crudely, in societies where women are typically the primary carers, it is with them that both male and female children form their primary initial attachment (Chodorow 1978). However, their sense of gendered self is informed by identification with a same-sex parent or adult, bringing different implications for each; the maintenance of that initial connection predisposing female children to comfort with empathetic connection, while the identification of male children with more distant adult male figures not only reinforces separateness, but can prompt a need to 'prove' masculinity (Chodorow 1978, discussed in Wharton 2003).

In a similar vein, Llewelyn and Hogan (2000) discuss the use of systems analysis – 'process–person–context' – in studying children with physical disabilities. They explore 'the dynamics that can drive and accelerate the course of development by examining the synergistic influence of the characteristics of the person and of the environment that produces the behaviour' (2000, p 160). Very much like theories of social learning described by Wharton, they discuss how a negative response from others can provoke negative self-belief, and avoidance. Their focus on process is potentially a third element to add to the mix of biological and social factors as contributors to the formation of identity.

The biopsychosocial (BPS) model is a further approach incorporating a psychological component. This has been used to explain the nature of incapacity for work and in steering approaches to rehabilitation. Broadly, it aims to address the fact that it is not possible to assess impairment in isolation from the person with that impairment (Waddell et al, 2002). Experiences of physical pain and responses to it will always be filtered through a person's beliefs and expectations about their situation:

> The extent to which psychological and social processes can influence physical activity should not be under-estimated, and vice versa…Disability is not only a question of physical impairment, but of behaviour and performance, too. Performance depends on anatomical and physiological capacities, but also on psychological and social resources… ability may be set by physiological limits but performance is set by psychological limits. (Waddell et al, 2002, p 12)

Despite what the 'social' part of its name might suggest, the analysis of environmental impacts is rarely accounted for by purveyors of this model, even where acknowledged (Williams, 1996). It appears to question disabled people's own assessment of their capacity and to imply that they can overcome barriers of all types simply by building their confidence. While acknowledging how important confidence can be to decisions to engage, and that how we feel about ourselves and our situation could be a determinant in steering action, to fail to tackle very real barriers like employer discrimination, inaccessible buildings and transport risks raising expectations only to dash them, destroying confidence in the process.

Locating the problem

Throughout the preceding discussion, questions have arisen concerning the cause of unequal outcomes; whether they reflect inequalities of capacity or merit arising from innate physiological or psychological make up, or external factors arising from the socio-cultural environment; how society operates and its prevailing cultural norms and values. In addition, literature on identity formation drew attention to the qualities of interaction and their implications. These are recurrent themes within and across the literatures and they each require further exploration.

Socio-cultural context

In Chapter Three, there was considerable discussion of the nature and operation of socio-cultural context and the literature on discrimination has more to add. Thompson (1998) argues that discrimination operates at structural, cultural and personal levels, with the former underpinning the latter two. The structural level is comprised of 'the constraints of the various social, political and economic aspects of the contemporary social order' (1998, p 16). These are interwoven with cultural patterns – the values and norms of a society, institution or group. The personal is embedded into the cultural level, so that an individual's beliefs and values reflect those that prevail more widely.

The question remains of what generates 'the contemporary social order' and the cultural patterns that ensue. To take a historical perspective (as advocated by Miles and Brown, 2003, writing on race), Western culture clearly has roots in Christianity. As societies become increasingly multicultural, so the value-bases of other religions come into play. However, for most commentators, it is capitalism that is the focus of attention as the dominant ideology. Explanations that attribute inequalities to socio-cultural context might well start by exploring how ideology is reflected in social structures and culture. One way of construing where social categories come from, and for explaining why people with certain characteristics are accorded less value, rights or power, is to consider the relationship of those characteristics to the goals and consequences of capitalism. Obviously, categorisations of socio-economic class explicitly reflect roles in production. However, it is possible that the predominance of economic imperatives and relationships in Western society not only generates categorisations of socio-economic class, they also drive the formation of 'cultural' or characteristic-based groupings and the values attributed to them.

This point has been made by various commentators from different fields (for example, Oliver, 1990, on disability; Malik, 1996, and Miles and Brown, 2003, on race; Young, 1990, on gender; Kirsch, 2000, on queer theory). There are differences, though, in how the impact of capitalism is understood. For example, Oliver (1990) relates the oppression experienced by disabled people to how capitalist society treats those considered economically unproductive. Malik (1996) locates the rise of racism within the context of the divisions created by capitalist society. Kirsch (2000) links queer theory's promotion of the self as an alternative to wider social interaction with the development of late capitalist ideology and its disassembling of the social ties binding communities together. Despite their differences, what unites these authors (apart from their negative account of capitalism) is the view that the dominant ideology has a direct impact on how identities are construed, the nature of social categorisation, and subsequent disadvantage. Building on discussion in Chapter Three, the way in which society operates not only creates and reconstitutes need, it does much the same to identity.

Demands for 'cultural' equality could, therefore, to some extent be interpreted as challenges to the consequences of capitalism and its goals. However, this does not adequately explain why groups who could be economically productive are prevented from fulfilling such a role, and consequently experience disproportionate economic inequality. Neither does it account for why lesbian and gay people, who do not experience disproportionate economic inequality, nonetheless experience negative attitudes. Clearly, the historical (and in some cases contemporary) influence of religious views which condemn certain behaviour and/or accord lower status to certain groups may have a role to play, even in modern-day secular societies.

In addition, it may be fruitful to consider who holds the power within each ideological construct. If to be part of a culture means being so subsumed into it as to be oblivious to it (Thompson, 1998) there is potential for ethnocentrism: 'the tendency to see the world from within the narrow confines of one culture, to project one set of norms and values onto other groups of people' (Thompson, 1998, p 16). It would follow that ethnocentrism, too, can be unconscious; perhaps only apparent to those who are not part of the dominant culture or dominant group that created it. This echoes earlier observations that people who do not experience barriers are not always easily able to recognise them. The resulting inequalities experienced by people from subordinate groups are variously attributed to eurocentrism, 'the authoritative construction of norms that privilege traits associated with "whiteness"' (Fraser, 1997, p 22); 'androcentrism' or 'phallogocentrism', both meaning that social structure and values are determined by men, to the disadvantage of women.

There is still more to clarify regarding just what these socio-cultural barriers are that can intervene to create inequality and prevent inclusion. Those working in the disability field offer a way forward. Originally defined as 'the disadvantage or restriction of activity caused by a contemporary social organisation which takes no or little account of people who have physical impairments and thus excludes them from the mainstream of social activities' (UPIAS, 1976, cited in Oliver, 1990, p 11), the social model has since been extended to cover people with learning disabilities, (Oliver, 1996). Barriers can be attitudinal (negative assumptions, fear, hostility), environmental (inaccessible buildings and public spaces) and organisational (inflexible processes and policies). This list could be elaborated to cover communication barriers (inaccessible language and negative imagery), mobility (inaccessible transport) and financial barriers (failure to accommodate extra costs and restricted access to earnings) (Witcher, 2005).

The social model decouples the causal link between 'impairment' and 'disability', instead attributing the cause of disability to the impact of socio-cultural context on people who have impairments. In a barrier-free environment, a person with even a severe impairment can participate on an equal basis. Alternatively, a person with a slight impairment could be seriously disabled by the barriers created through the way in which society operates.

There is no obvious reason why the social model should not have wider application (Shakespeare, 1996). Environmental barriers can obviously exist for people with children in pushchairs, but they may also take the form of no-go public spaces for women, gay or lesbian people or black people, due to fears for personal safety. Sexist imagery, jargon and failure to translate essential materials into other languages can all constitute communication barriers. All betray discriminatory attitudes of one sort or another, even if rooted in ignorance rather than intent.

Clearly the impact of social barriers will differ subject to the person's characteristics, but the types of barrier are common to all. Alternatively, it could be argued that social barriers can create characteristics (such as disability) and their social meaning. Although not all forms of barrier will necessarily be experienced in every case, such barriers could intervene to create inequality, generate group differentiation and thwart the achievement of social or personal goals.

These social barriers constitute a generic, universal taxonomy of the fundamental social conditions that are required for inclusion. They could be conceptualised as transactional or relationship infrastructure, and perhaps as an elaboration of Doyal and Gough's societal preconditions (1991) discussed in Chapter Three. Similarly, in any setting, the existence of such social barriers can create avoidable harm (in its wider sense) and prevent flourishing. To explore them more closely might suggest that they can interact, and that some may take priority. In effect, attitudes of dominant groups underpin and give birth to all the rest. Attitudes, as previously discussed, are primarily what spawn misrecognition – of people outside the dominant group, for whom the world created by that group can be a very poor fit.

It might also be the case that failure to address one set of barriers can be expressed by the creation of others – particularly financial. Extra costs may be imposed, for example to make built environments accessible, to get documents translated or to take taxis for journeys through areas where safety is a concern. Simultaneously, such barriers can intervene to curtail access to earned income.

Biological and genetic explanations

Not all subscribe to the view that inequality and social categorisation emanate from socio-cultural context, if such a possibility occurs to them at all. Instead, these are seen as arising from qualities within individuals, often deemed to be biological or genetic in origin. This might be taken to infer that the allocation of people to social categories with inferior rights and resources appropriately reflects the inferiority of people with particular personal characteristics: that this is not 'normative' discrimination but accurate recognition (reminiscent of arguments justifying slavery). Alternatively, it might be argued that they should receive superior rights and resources in order to level the playing field. Debates on biological or genetic explanations for inequalities, and justifications for differential treatment are to be found in race, disability, gender and queer theory literature. This approach even made a guest appearance in Doyal and Gough's theory of human need (1991), in the form of a 'biomedical model'.

Much revolves around concepts of health, and the role of the medical profession. Their influence can extend far beyond medical matters: 'The medicalization of life can be seen as a form of social control. Because important moral and political decisions (about the allocation of resources, for example) are redesignated as matters of professional decision-making, the power to influence, or even control, moral and political issues is given to doctors' (Thompson, 1998, p 135).

The tag 'unhealthy' similarly extends far beyond allusion to disease or illness. Instead it assumes wider social, even ideological significance: 'older people, disabled people or gays, lesbians and bisexuals are often presented ideologically as ill or sick' (Thompson, 1998, p 110; see also Bradley, 1996; Kirsch, 2000). Barnes and Mercer (1996) remark on the distinction between the medical concern with disease and sociological portrayals of sickness as a social state. It can be social norms, not personal physiology, that determine the meaning of healthy.

While many have forcefully resisted the case that inequality is a natural and inevitable consequence of biological or genetic composition, where does this leave people for whom such issues are an undisputed reality? Of all groups, disabled people have probably found themselves most exposed to medical intervention and disempowerment. According to Crow 'we have one fundamental difference from other movements… There is nothing inherently unpleasant or difficult about other groups' embodiment: sexuality, sex and skin colour are neutral facts. In contrast, impairment means our experiences of our bodies *can* be unpleasant or difficult' (1996, p 58).

The medical model of disability: 'takes the biological reality of impairment as its fundamental starting point' (Williams, 1996, p 196), with medical discourse used to present disability as a form of individual pathology (Thompson, 1998; Llewellyn and Hogan, 2000). In contrast to the social model, which casts social barriers as the source of disablement, impairment and disability are viewed as one and the same. Instead of social barriers being removed to neutralise the impact of impairments, the aim is to adjust (cure or treat) the person. The way society operates is implicitly assumed to be unalterable (Llewellyn and Hogan, 2000). Of course, there may be occasions when, despite positive external adjustments, incapacity persists. Yet, in such a situation it remains a question of attitude (a potential social barrier), separating caring from policing and transforming paternalism into capacity building.

It is not just disabled people who can experience disproportionate medicalisation. People from BME communities have higher rates of admission for psychiatric care, are more likely to be compulsorily admitted to hospital and to be diagnosed schizophrenic (Skellington, 1996). However, we should take care to ensure this is not just another reflection of discriminatory practice or evidence of the toll that repeated exposure to discrimination might reasonably be expected to take on mental health.

Evidence of racial discrimination is certainly abundant – even in academic study. Some have attributed inferior IQ levels and 'socially undesirable' behaviours like lone parenthood and welfare dependency to ethnicity (Herrnstein and Murray, 1994). The long history of anti-semitism, the development of myths about Jewish conspiracy and behaviours, right down to the Nazi's measurement of facial features in order to determine Jewishness, similarly attribute much to genetic make-up. Yet, 'Geneticists have shown that 85 per cent of all genetic variation is between individuals within the same local population… Just 7 per cent of genetic variation is between major races' (Malik, 1996, p 4); or, to put it even more emphatically: 'as far as the biological and genetic sciences are concerned, 'races' do not exist' (Miles and Brown, 2003, p 88).[3]

In other fields, too, a genetic root has been sought to 'explain' difference or confirm alleged inferiority. It might seem reasonable to point out that men and women are distinguishable by rather obvious biological differences. Yet even here we are not on safe ground. Certainly for transgender people there is a mismatch between gender identity and the biological features with which they were born. Moreover, an estimated 2 per cent of live births are of infants who cannot be easily categorised as male or female (Blackless et al, 2000).

Perhaps unsurprisingly, 'More than any other group...the medical profession has defined the issue of intersexuality and societal responses to it...intersexuality has come to be defined as a condition requiring medical intervention' (Wharton, 2005, p 19).

Aside from questions of whether genetics define who we are, others have sought to demonstrate that they are responsible for generating behaviour. The search for a 'gay gene' or 'neural anomalies' that supposedly afflict lesbians, are features of an ongoing quest to explain homosexuality in medical terms (Kirsch, 2000). Others have highlighted the importance accorded to women's 'biological role' as a mother, confusing childbearing with rearing (Gittins, 1993). Yet, the notion that behaviours of men and women must be intrinsically different, reflecting their biological differences has been comprehensively challenged (Wharton, 2005). While this does not rule out the possibility that some behaviours are more common among men than women (or vice versa), purist notions of biological essentialism cannot be sustained.

Essentialism is a common feature of this approach; explaining behaviour and unequal outcomes as a natural and inevitable consequence of the biological, physiological or genetic 'essence' of each individual or group. However, it seems to be very clear that some 'essential' characteristics are in fact viewed as unnatural and alterable. It is assumed that medical intervention can (and by implication should) 'correct' unnatural, unhealthy (in both senses) and undesirable abnormalities of these sorts. Far from being unalterable, it is *only* biological, physiological or genetic features that offer scope for positive change. Where the limits of medical (including genetic) science make such alteration impossible, the aim is to change, contain and control behaviour by such means as segregation, hospitalisation, oppression and social stigma. A further strategy is to prevent 'abnormal' people from being born, by testing foetuses and aborting those who fail to make the (medically-defined) grade. Another concerns proposals to relax the laws against killing disabled people.[4]

It is important to make clear that arguing in favour of adjusting and widening socio-cultural norms to accommodate diversity is not to make essentialist claims denying the scope for individuals to adjust or to assert that there is never any need for them to do so. Capacity-building, the acquisition of new skills and learning, constitute positive means of change. Where behaviours threaten other people's human rights or social cohesion, they do need to change or be contained. Neither is it to deny any place for medical intervention but to challenge the power of such professionals and the disempowerment of their patients or clients. Instead, it is to recognise the key role that socio-cultural norms play when it comes to defining 'healthy' and 'natural', the value of diversity, and how changes in the way society operates can accommodate it, promote empowerment, inclusion and equality.

Systems and interactive processes

As with social and individual explanations, interactionist or process-based approaches are to be found in different group-based literatures. Queer theory could be seen as interactionist in as much as it often casts identity as 'performative'. A person's identity is not freestanding, it is constructed through actions and interactions (Butler, 1990) or discourse (Butler, 2002; Lyotard, 1984). To return briefly to Walzer's formulation (1983), the key indicator of identity here is what people do, rather than the messages about status conveyed by what goods they have, or by physical characteristics giving visual clues as to who they are. Indeed, Grosz argues that the oppression of lesbian and gay people is distinctive in that the oppressions experienced by other groups are 'based primarily on what a person *is*, quite independently of what they do…In the case of homosexuals…it is less a matter of who they *are* than what they *do* that is considered offensive' (1994, p 150).[5]

A very different tack is taken in the development of interactive models in the disability field, which focuses on the process of interaction between an individual and their environment:

> As the interaction between the individual and their environment is a *social process*, this implies that disability is dynamic, occurring over time and within a particular social context. The problem is not *located* either in the individual or the social alone, so dynamics could be altered through elements of both individual and social change…Problems can arise at a systems level; hence the solutions concern changes that need to be made to the functioning of a system as a whole. (Howard, 2003, p 5, emphasis in original)

This signals three possible sites where adjustments might be possible to achieve a smoother fit: the social environment, the individual (for example, in terms of capacity, awareness or behaviour) and the processes through which they interact. It may be that some social barriers are immovable, some characteristics are immutable (or there is no socially necessary reason why they should change) and some features of process cannot be made more flexible without dissolving into incoherence. Both socio-cultural context and the way in which process is enacted (or performed) may be important in defining identity. Exploration of these three areas would seem to be critical to establishing the scope for increasing social inclusion, not just for disabled people but in general. If social justice requires the removal of artificial barriers to the inclusion of diversity without jeopardising the integrity of the whole, room for manoeuvre needs to be explored.

Implications for inclusive equality

The literature on discrimination provides explanations of why having resources is not necessarily enough to enable participation and why a straightforward connection between 'having' and 'being able to do' cannot safely be made. It fleshes out some further requirements for the fulfilment of the universal goal for inclusive equality that was sketched out towards the end of the previous chapter. The removal of social barriers is clearly imperative. Action to expose and address the negative assumptions and attitudes (often rooted in ignorance) that spawn other such barriers is likely to be of particular importance.

It tells us a great deal about the nature of misrecognition, its causes and range of possible impacts. However, there are not only limits to what resources can achieve. There are also unavoidable limits to accurate recognition of something as complex and fluid as another person's identity. That is not to say nothing can be done to increase the chances of accurate recognition. There is much that can be done to raise awareness of unconscious assumptions, the inadvertently discriminatory consequences of actions, and how to disentangle sameness from difference. Once again, this underlines the importance of dialogue, empathy and equal voice.

The key role played by process is once again indicated (see Chapter Two in particular). Social (including distributive) processes combine socio-cultural and personal factors. Indeed, it could be argued that it is through them that such factors take form or find expression. For processes to be socially just the infrastructure (or preconditions) for distributive processes must be in place if people are to have equal opportunity to participate, if the resources and potential they possess are to receive equal treatment in assessment procedures, and if they are able to take delivery and make use of the good in question. Social barriers, and/or unjustifiable oppression (because viable diverse alternatives exist that are consistent with the purpose of the distribution), can arise at any stage of a distributive process. This is why a focus on social categorisation at the point of assessment is insufficient. For example, to get that far you have to be able to access communication about the existence of the process in the first place and the timing of the assessment needs to take account of childcare commitments. It is no good being able to purchase a cinema ticket if you then cannot see the film because the cinema is inaccessible. In effect, an environmental (as in built environment) barrier has intervened to prevent you from realising a 'capability'.

While the types of barriers that may intervene are universal, their impact will vary, as will the action required to prevent or remove them. Yet a focus on the uniqueness of individuals means that there are no comparators, equitable treatment is a meaningless concept and social justice becomes individual justice. However, people are both members of social categories and unique individuals. It implies that different lenses are required, to identify the barriers that will have an impact on all with a particular characteristic (comparisons can be made with regard to others in that social category) and on the particular combination of barriers experienced by each individual.

The removal of social barriers is thus indicated as a key focus for social policy, in terms of its substance, its development and delivery. For this to be achieved, the voices of those on the wrong side of barriers – who are consequently best placed to see them and propose what would remove them – need to be heard throughout. It underlines why a capabilities approach is appropriate, on the basis that barriers of all kinds must be overcome if freedoms are to be equally exercised. It also adds weight to the proposition that adjustments to the design and delivery of distributive processes are of paramount importance to achieving social justice as inclusive equality.

Notes

[1] The legislation was: the Equal Pay Act 1970; the Sex Discrimination Act 1975; the Race Relations Act 1976; the Disability Discrimination Act 1995; the Employment Equality (Religion or Belief) Regulations 2003; the Employment Equality (Sexual Orientation) Regulations 2003; the Employment Equality (Age) Regulations 2006; the Equality Act 2006, Part 2 and the Equality Act (Sexual Orientation) Regulations 2007.

[2] William Beveridge was the founder of the British welfare state.

[3] Arguments concerning genetic similarities between 'races' should not be overplayed: a high proportion of our genetic make-up is also the same as other species.

[4] See the 'Not Dead Yet UK Campaign': www.notdeadyetuk.org/

[5] That queer politics should just be about the right to 'do' or commit certain acts has been challenged; some arguing that gay and lesbian people should also have the right to look gay and lesbian (Wilchins, 2004).

FIVE

Social exclusion

Defining social exclusion

At the beginning of the millennium social exclusion was described as 'the single dominant issue on the current political agenda in contemporary Europe' (Ratcliffe, 2000, p 169). According to the European Commission (a source of much activity on the subject) in their 1992 Communication 'Towards a Europe of solidarity' (COM (92) 542), social exclusion results from: 'mechanisms whereby individuals and groups are excluded from taking part in the social exchanges, from the component practices and rights of social integration and identity. Social exclusion goes beyond participation in working life; it is felt and shown in the fields of housing, education, health and access to services.'

What are those mechanisms? What social exchanges, component practices and rights? What have they got to do with social integration and identity? Just what that issue is – the meaning of social exclusion – has been, and remains, far from apparent. All that can be said with confidence is that social exclusion is not a single issue. Indeed, a persuasive case could be made that a defining feature of the concept is that it encompasses so many issues and contradictory interpretations of them that it becomes near meaningless. Nonetheless, beneath the myriad superficial manifestations are to be found distinct bodies of thought with clear historical and ideological foundations (see Byrne, 2005). That is not to say it is necessarily obvious which is being referred to at any one time. The power of the concept (as well as much confusion) arises from the way social exclusion can, 'almost unnoticed, mobilise a redistributive argument behind a cultural or integrationist one – or represent cultural or integrationist arguments as redistributive' (Levitas, 2005, p 27). Byrne contends that the 'babbling' of political elites about social exclusion is a kind of 'linguistic trick to assert a continued commitment to the values of order liberalism/reformist social democracy, whilst the actual tenor of policy supports globalization and neo-liberalism' (2005, p 60).

The difficulties in pinpointing meaning are nowhere more acute than when it comes to social exclusion. Helpfully, commentators have flushed out into the light the ways in which it can elude capture.

They have also suggested that sometimes there can be advantages to leaving it in darkness. Politicians and those seeking to exert pressure on them have both taken advantage of the conceptual slipperiness of social exclusion. In the late 1980s/early 1990s, when Conservative politicians denied the existence of poverty in Britain, it enabled dialogue on disadvantage to continue (Walker, 1995; Veit-Wilson, 1998; Berghman, 1995; Room, 1995). It was enthusiastically adopted by what had evolved into 'New Labour', off the back of the report from the Commission on Social Justice (instigated by John Smith, then Labour Party leader). The themes of this report (1994) meld imperceptibly into the discourses of social exclusion developed by Silver (1994) and Levitas (2005), among others. All are derived from long-established strands of social theory, mostly (though not exclusively) emanating from differing responses to capitalism (see Byrne, 2005). Whatever its historical roots, in its latest guise social exclusion was proclaimed to offer 'a way of reconceptualizing and understanding social disadvantage as the globalization of economic relations occurs' (Gore et al, 1995, p 9).

Perhaps in keeping with postmodernism, multiplicity of approaches and fragmentation of thought reflect the complexity and fragmentation arising from globalisation, indicating the futility – or worse – of the quest for a metanarrative of social exclusion (Lyotard, 1984, branded the quest for metanarratives as an act of terrorism). Perhaps it is only fitting that social inclusion should include 'a wide diversity of conceptions or discourses' (Stewart, 2000, p 3; also Gore et al, 1995; Silver, 1994; Hills, 2002).

Whether social exclusion is nothing more than a rehashing of assorted other discourses or a new concept with which to make sense of globalisation, our task is to identify what its particular contribution may be regarding the development of a theory of social justice as inclusive equality. Attempting to synthesise them all into a coherent whole may not be a fruitful way to spend the time. However, there may be some new and helpful tidbits worth selecting from the discourse smorgasbord. To that end, this chapter briefly reviews the relationship of social exclusion to poverty and inequality before proceeding to explore what else it has to offer towards our goal. It is noticeable (and unsurprising) that numerous themes from other literatures reappear here.

Poverty and inequality

Social exclusion and poverty

Is social exclusion anything more than a politically convenient euphemism for poverty as numerous authors suggest (Lister, 2000; Room, 1995)? Certainly, there are obvious synergies between definitions of relative poverty in terms of not being able to participate in customary norms and the consequence of social exclusion that this would logically seem to imply. The concept has also been discussed with reference to social rights to basic living standards and participation in social and occupational activities (Observatory on National Policies to Combat Social Exclusion, cited in Gore, 1995). Again, this is remarkably similar to notions of relative poverty, though the distinction drawn between social and occupational might prove helpful.

Others claim that social exclusion is multi-dimensional rather than purely about financial disadvantage, leading to the accusation that it takes the focus off poverty as income inadequacy, diffusing pressure to increase benefit levels (which may indeed have been part of the New Labour agenda). However, it is clear that concepts of poverty have progressed a long way from a narrow focus on income, even if the implications for income adequacy feature as a key part of other methodologies (see Chapter Three). It has been suggested that social exclusion is a dynamic process rather than an outcome, or that poverty (as in lack of income or resources) is a specific form of the wider deprivation represented by social exclusion (Berghman, 1995) (though the converse seems just as plausible: social exclusion could be one aspect of a wider definition of poverty). Although an emphasis on the dynamic nature of processes arguably adds a new slant, it does not follow that a new concept called social exclusion has emerged; a multidimensional dynamic view is needed to understand poverty properly (Hills, 2002).

Another suggestion is that social exclusion can take the form of 'increased social isolation, reduced morale, deviant behaviours' (Walker, 1995, p 116). The social withdrawal of those below the poverty line (Townsend, 1979) would seem to account for the first of these. However, just how poverty erodes social relationships and connections may merit further exploration. Certainly issues concerning the quality of social interaction and how it is experienced have surfaced before. Room (1999) suggests that one new element to the 'reconfiguration' that constitutes social security is a shift from distributional to relational dimensions of stratification and disadvantage. The citation of 'reduced morale' draws attention to the impact of poverty on how a person feels, again as discussed in Chapter Three. As for 'deviant behaviours', this is consistent with the designation (some might say invention) of an 'underclass', comprised of culturally alien beings – again a phenomenon that emerged in the context of discussion of poverty.

Some have argued that the defining feature of social exclusion is that it 'allows the phenomenon of interest to extend beyond non-participation due to lack of material resources' (Burchardt et al 2002a, p 5), with factors like discrimination, chronic ill-health, geographical location or cultural identification also relevant. Perhaps social exclusion's contribution is to encompass all causes and manifestations of poverty and discrimination within the one concept, although how that differs from the UN definition of overall poverty is far from apparent (see Chapter Three). As with that definition, without some theoretical underpinning this does not take us very far forward.

Social exclusion and inequality

We have previously come across the notion that inequality of income and wealth (Wilkinson and Pickett, 2010) can create social divisions that threaten social cohesion. At the extreme, all connection breaks down, as sight is lost of people on the other side of the chasm. This may indeed be what Room (1999, p 167) describes as 'catastrophic rupture', casting groups adrift from the social mainstream to lead 'parallel lives' (Cantle, 2001).

This raises questions about the components of the social fabric that weave us together and what can be done to prevent inequalities from stretching it so thin that it becomes threadbare and finally rips asunder. Just where the tears occur, and their subsequent implications, might be significant. As evidenced in Chapter One, elongation of the income distribution has occurred most dramatically in an upward direction. Even back in 1999, Room observed that the gap between the new breed of super-rich and people on benefit 'belies the notion that people share a common citizenship' (1999, p 173), or of any consensus around criteria for the distribution of rewards. Decoupling from the mainstream can occur at the top as much as it can at the bottom: 'the revolt of the elites is as much a problem as welfare dependency' (Gray, 2000, p 23; also Giddens, 1998; Hutton, 1996; Barry, 2002). Other points of separation might occur between the middle classes and the poor, the middle classes and the rich (as appears to be happening) and, as some would have it, between the honest poor and a disreputable underclass (Murray, 1996).

It is clear, as Levitas contends, that society needs to be understood in its entirety, comprised of the unequal included as well as the detached 'underclass' existing outside its notional parameters (see Levitas, 2005). Moreover, to fail to look upwards risks losing sight of the potential detachment of what Townsend termed the overclass (1993). Gray argues that 'The ideal of inclusion…is distinct from any ideal of equality; but it acts as a constraint on inequalities at both the bottom and the top' (2000, p 31). If the 'elite' opt out they will take with them disproportionate wealth that might in theory be redistributed, but which these days could easily be relocated to a less progressive tax environment. If newly wealthy middle classes choose to replace public services with private provision, support for the former to be funded via their taxes may be expected to evaporate, leaving poor services for poor people. Finally, with the demise of all solidarity with the poor, proclamations of the existence of a morally deviant 'underclass' gather strength.

So far, this implies a rather two-dimensional view of equality as referring to socio-economic classes and the distribution of income and wealth. However, it is not just the warp but the weft of the social fabric that can break; it is not just a matter of the vertical distance between socio-economic classes but the horizontal separation of particular groups, like older people, black people and so on. Axes of inequality can transect societies at any angle. Fault-lines around cultural recognition, or recognition more widely, can be just as catastrophic, and the duration of inequality may entrench and exacerbate divisions. We need to look from side to side as well as up and down to take in society in its entirety.

None of this is to argue that degrees of exclusion neatly reflect degrees of inequality: 'Exclusion is not about graduations of inequality, but about mechanisms that act to detach groups of people from the social mainstream' (Giddens, 1998, p 104). However, quite what is intended by inequality requires further elaboration. As previously discussed, it can take various forms. It can mean sameness, equivalence or equilibrium. It can be complex or simple (Walzer, 1983). It can refer to primary goods like resources, power and voice (Rawls, 1973), Baker et al's five dimensions (2004), and to a raft of capabilities (Burchardt and Vizard, 2007). Yet, that aside, there is no obvious reason why the social distance created by inequalities might not be the cause of fragmentation that the mechanisms holding society together can no longer prevent. Exclusion might indeed not be about graduations of inequality, as Giddens claims, but this does not preclude the possibility that inequalities of various forms and types are what detach groups of people from the social mainstream.

Reframing the debate

It seems that, to explore poverty and inequality through the lens of social exclusion prompts particular themes to come to the fore. The central questions seem to be 'What binds us together?' and, conversely, 'What pulls us apart?' The arising challenges could be construed in various ways. It may be a matter of preventing avoidable harm to the social fabric, strengthening social bonds or increasing their type and number. We need to explore what it is that we share in common, what causes us to engage or disengage. We need to understand more about the mechanisms – the social glue – that holds society together. It seems very likely that inequality (potentially of different forms and types) is at least part of the story. Social relationships seem to be pivotal, suggesting that discrimination (or misrecognition) is also implicated.

Discourses of exclusion

As previously discussed, disadvantage is expressed and created, and needs are framed by the way a society operates, as steered by its dominant ideology and groups, and associated social norms and values. While myriad authors drew connections between poverty and discrimination and features of capitalism, discourses of social exclusion can be seen to have their roots in differing responses to capitalism (Byrne, 2005). One argues that 'market capitalism will work well and the only role of political systems of the collectivity is to ensure that the recalcitrance of the idle is overcome by appropriate discipline'. In contrast, a raft of others (including Catholic 'solidarism', non-transformational socialism and Keynesianism): 'accept the need for collective regulation and management of capitalism in order to ameliorate excesses of inequality and maintain stability in an inherently unstable system'. While these do not challenge the long-term viability of capitalism, so long as it is appropriately managed, Marxist socialism takes the view that 'capitalism is not a long-term option and that the future sustainability of human societies depends on its transformation into something else' (Byrne, 2005, p 34).

While positioning capitalism as the centrepiece is an entirely sustainable approach, it is possible to argue that discourses have their roots in different cultural heritages and hinterlands. It may well be that capitalism is viewed differently from the perspective of each. However, discourse formation could feasibly have been initiated and shaped by other systems of social organisation and associated social theory.

Silver (1994) traced the implications of different social theories for understandings of inclusion and exclusion in her development of 'three paradigms'. The 'solidarity paradigm', founded on French Republican tradition, centres on the social bond between individuals and society expressed as 'a national consensus, collective conscience, or general will' (Silver, 1994, p 541). Exclusion is 'inherent in the solidarity of nation, race, ethnicity, locality and other cultural or primordial ties' (Silver, 1994, p 542). Her 'specialisation paradigm', emanating from Anglo-American liberalism, starts from the premise that the difference in individuals gives rise to specialisation and differentiation. Integration occurs through exchange, both networks of voluntary exchanges between autonomous individuals and contractual exchange of rights and obligations. Social structures are specialised, comprised of separate, competing social spheres. Exclusion arises from 'an inadequate separation of social spheres, from the application of rules inappropriate to a given sphere, or from barriers to free movement and exchange between spheres' (1994, pp 542, 543). It can take the form of discrimination: 'the inappropriate exercise of personal tastes or the enforcement of group boundaries that individuals are not free to cross' (Silver, 1994, p 556). Finally, the 'monopoly paradigm', concerning the formation of group monopolies over scarce resources, is based on social democratic notions of citizenship and is inherently conflictual (Silver, 1994). The social order is coercive, 'imposed through a set of hierarchical power relations (Silver, 1994, p 543). Monopoly 'creates a bond of common interest' (Silver, 1994, p 543) among insiders. Exclusion occurs where 'closure' is exerted to preserve and maximise advantage.

People are brought together through the fellowship of a cultural collective, as 'specialised' individuals who consequently need to engage in exchanges with each other, or by force, necessitated and sustained by the need to preserve advantage. While each paints a distinct picture, there is no obvious reason why they cannot co-exist to differing degrees, in different places at different times. Neither is it entirely obvious why discrimination (even in Silver's narrow terms), or monopoly-style closure might not apply more widely. The second is most obviously associated with capitalism, though it could certainly find a place for the other two. Collective solidarity might be a means of meeting needs that are essential but unprofitable. Hierarchical power relations and the preservation of advantage are, of course, familiar features of contemporary capitalism.

Levitas's highly influential three discourses of social exclusion (2005) draw upon Silver's paradigms but they appear more obviously situated within the context of modern-day capitalism. 'RED' is a redistributionist discourse, closely intertwined with approaches to poverty, inequality and citizenship, the latter encompassing not just economic but also social, political and cultural dimensions. This discourse 'implies a radical reduction of inequalities, and a redistribution of resources and power' (2005, p14) along with a central role for citizenship rights. In opposition to this, the 'New Right', drawing on arguments emanating from the US, employed a discourse of the underclass and a culture of dependency, which Levitas refers to as 'MUD'. While state support, particularly in the form of benefits, was accepted (or at least tolerated) for the so-called 'deserving poor', others, were branded as scroungers, 'exploiting an overgenerous and insufficiently-policed system' (2005, p 15). This misplaced munificence created dependency, 'sapping personal initiative, independence and self-respect' (Levitas, 2005, p 15). Exclusion is attributed to the 'recalcitrance of the idle' (Byrne, 2005) – and certainly not the operation of capitalism.

Finally, 'SID' is a social integrationist discourse, with its origins in French republican tradition and Durkheimian notions of solidarity, (as per Silver's solidarity paradigm): 'Exclusion is understood as the breakdown of structural, cultural and moral ties which bind the individual to society' (Levitas, 2005, p 21). However, despite the broadening out of French discourses of exclusion to encompass groups marginalised 'economically, socially, culturally and even spatially' (2005, p 21), within the European Union, social integration, cohesion and solidarity have acquired a narrow focus on paid work. Inclusion comes to mean being a worker; in paid work. Yet, Levitas observes that all three discourses posit paid work as a major factor in social integration/inclusion, and all three have a moral content.

Together, these discourses indicate that the causes and effects of disadvantage are not just attributable to how society is structured, but how structure is viewed and articulated from different perspectives. The more unequal the society, the more divergent those perspectives seem likely to be. Each implies different 'terms of inclusion', causes of exclusion and remedies to it. Familiar themes are evident, if reframed: libertarianism versus egalitarianism, the role of the market versus state, the importance of paid work and the case for redistribution. The structure versus agency debate is clearly evident in Levitas's MUD discourse. Misrecognition surfaces to a limited extent (explicitly anyway) in the reference to discrimination in Silver's 'specialization paradigm' (which appears to cast difference as inherent to individuals – see Chapter Four) and in Levitas's account of the treatment of gender. Lone parents are singled out for blame by underclass proponents (MUD), while women are overlooked by SID. The scope for inclusion through the valuing of unpaid work is not acknowledged (Levitas, 2005).

While to a considerable extent these discourses reflect and give shape to the dynamics of contemporary debates, particularly in Silver's paradigms it is possible to identify some more generic themes concerning the structure of society, and the nature of social bonds. For example, her reference to 'an inadequate separation of social spheres, from the application of rules inappropriate to a given sphere' (1994, pp 542, 543) has strong echoes of Walzer's case for complex equality (1983 – discussed in Chapter 2).

To continue our exploration of how to widen access to the social mainstream to maximise the inclusion of diversity on an equal/equivalent basis, it should be helpful to take a step back to consider how to conceptualise society in generic terms. At a more abstract theoretical level, there are different ways in which the phenomenon known as society can be conceptualised. There is much to be found on the subject within the social exclusion literature, often informed by more general social theory – and there may be more to add from such sources.

Conceptualising society

Drawing on discussion from previous chapters, we might deduce that there is an entity known as society, though its parameters are hazy, to say the least, in the wake of globalisation and mass migration. Mainstream society is comprised of social norms and cultural values about lifestyles, living standards and customary activities. These emerge from historical and cultural heritage, ideology and the imprint of dominant groups. People can be compelled to participate in the arising socio-cultural edifice through direct enforcement and/or through the more subtle harnessing and reconstitution of their needs and motivations in ways which strengthen and perpetuate the status quo. The manner of its operations, and the associated nature of its value-base, will generate unequal social divisions and categorisations, some of whom will experience disadvantage and exclusion.

The social exclusion literature does much to flesh this out, though the focus for its inquiry differs. Those that will be discussed here are less obviously concerned with explaining such matters as unmet needs, misrecognition and socially just distributive processes. They focus more explicitly on conceptualising the construction and operations of society and mechanisms for engagement. However, as we will see, these converge to form a comprehensive, nuanced account of social exclusion, revealing the role of inequality in its various guises, and some clear signposts for policy.

General approaches

There are different ways of conceptualising the boundary (or boundaries) between inclusion and exclusion, perhaps the simplest being to think of it in terms of being inside or outside a circle depicting mainstream society (Touraine, 1991, cited in Burchardt et al, 2002a, p 3). Quite what that boundary (or boundaries) consists of needs clarification. It might be defined by the 'norm of the homogenous public' (Young, 1990, p 179, discussed in Chapter 4), which suggests cultural consensus among a uniform population. As such, it might be expected to set a rigid boundary with clear-cut access criteria. If heterogeneous, the boundary may be more permeable, allowing for various access routes. Or there may be many interconnecting boundaries with no one included in all.

To think of 'society' as 'containing' a homogenous set of activities, having a single boundary or a single gateway to inclusion would clearly be wildly over-simplistic. Perhaps society should be thought of as spherical, rather than a linear circle, three dimensional rather than two. Perhaps its shape, and social positions, are not fixed, but might fluctuate over time, making the structure (which starts to resemble an organism) four dimensional rather than three.

Along with structural and cultural approaches to delineating boundaries, a further possibility is to focus on the 'mechanisms for engagement'. Mainstream society can be conceptualised not as accessed by such mechanisms but as comprised *of* mechanisms for engagement. Echoing Giddens' structuration theory (1984), Room suggests that it could be construed as: 'the product of active human agency over time, in which different social groups continuously contest and assert their relationship to each other' (1999, p 171). Yet it may not just be a question of how groups relate to each other, but to institutions and collective structures operating at different levels – supranational, national or local. These may be conceptualised as defined by the nature of mechanisms for engagement with them. In this scenario, social exclusion might be understood to result from inaccessible or inadequate systems, processes and relationship networks.

Levels of society

It is a familiar notion that societies are composed of interacting levels, variously cast as macro, meso and micro, systems and social, or as supranational, national, regional and local, down to family/household and individual. According to Byrne, 'The real issue for social science is understanding how there is a complex and recursive relationship among all of the social levels of macro, meso and micro' (2005, p 65). A primary feature of social exclusion is that it highlights 'the relationships and processes, between micro and macro mechanisms, between individual and collective dimensions' (Yépez del Castillo, 1994, p 15, cited in Gore, 1995, p 6). When it comes to inclusion and cohesion, the question concerns the interface and interaction between systems and 'actors' (otherwise known as people) at and between social levels. It requires consideration of the relationships and processes between 'collective dimensions' and between actors.

According to Lockwood's classic theory, 'the problem of social integration focuses upon the orderly or conflictual relationships between *actors*, the problem of system integration focuses on the orderly or conflictual relationships between the *parts* of a social system' (1992, p 400). Each can have an impact on the other (Mouzelis, 1991). Dysfunctions or incoherence in the way institutions (economic, bureaucratic, legal, political and so on) relate to each other, and in the structures and processes of each separately will be replicated in the positions and resources consequently accorded to 'actors' (echoing discussion in Chapter Four of the impact of institutional discrimination). This will in turn provoke social conflict between groups of actors or between actors and institutional processes. It might even play out to create dissonances in personal identity, as different facets of identity are singled out and subjected to inconsistent categorisation and unequal treatment.

As macro-level strategic incoherence plays out, it is left to those further down the delivery chain – right down to the people who use the services being delivered – to make sense of it. Examples of this are rife in the field of state welfare delivery, where the multiple agencies involved fail to communicate with each other, where the interplay between benefits can be fiendishly complex and service users undergo repeated assessments. Systems integration has both vertical and horizontal dimensions. There may be a disconnect between a policy strategy defined at a higher level and its delivery on the ground (vertical). It could also apply to the interface between several policy areas at any level (horizonal); between institutions established for different purposes and the systems they administer.

Exactly how levels interact still remains unclear. Mouzelis proposes that micro- and macro-level phenomena are linked through social hierarchies (1991). Macro-actors (decision-makers representing collectivities, or individuals with power to make their decisions felt) have a key role to play in social integration. Presumably they may also be critical to systems integration, where they have powers to change institutional rules. However, inequalities in power can be a cause of detachment, as when political action appears to be impervious to democratically determined direction or accountability. The imbalance created by the globalised economy as it diminishes the powers of national political subsystems can be characterised as a systems-level crisis (Anderson, 1999). The way to redress this power imbalance is through 'the creation of multiple actor networks' (Anderson, 1999, p 139), first to integrate actors at the bottom and then enable them to operate across different levels in order to create new types of governance. This points to the need for institutional infrastructure through which relationship networks can connect micro- to macro-actors, bringing levels closer together and equalising powers in the process. For example, the disconnect between international organisations and the citizens of the countries their actions affect requires democratic infrastructure to knit them together.

It seems that the phenomenon of 'catastrophic rupture' may not just detach particular social categories of actor, it can also occur vertically and horizontally, creating structural barriers that divide one level from another, or create dissonances between different systems or sub-systems operating at the same level. It can be generated by inadequate institutional infrastructure through which to enact relationship networks and by strategic incoherence between sub-systems, policies and their delivery. It can also be expressed in geographical form, in the isolation of countries from supranational institutions, or local areas from wider communities. Neighbourhoods might become detached by the intersection of different forms of inequality. Inadequate resources, and perhaps racism, are compounded by the intervention of social barriers (negative attitudes, lack of transport, inadequate information or communication, and so on) eroding the physical infrastructure and the relationship networks connecting inhabitants to jobs, resources and opportunities. Inequalities – in rates of unemployment, lone parent households and crime, in educational and health outcomes and in quality of housing stock, public services and poor environmental conditions (see for example Lupton and Power 2005, Lupton 2003) – are concentrated in the resulting spatial segregation and entrenched by the length of time the situation endures.

However, spatial segregation is not just a feature of poor neighbourhoods. Wealthy people may choose to live in gated communities. The difficulties of seeing and recognising others across social distance are reinforced by walls that literally block the view. Of course, the implications for the rich are very different. Their networks enable them to tap into far-flung resources and opportunities (Perri 6, 1997). It seems that access to relationship networks and their spread is an important determinant of social inclusion. Inequalities in power, voice, resources and opportunities might both close down access to such networks and be the consequence of failure to access them – not that the infrastructure for requisite networks necessarily exists.

There are clearly numerous ways in which ruptures originating elsewhere can result in the detachment of particular social categories and individuals. If access to relationship networks is key, whether formally constituted and enacted via institutions or informal social contacts and friendships, there is scope for the social barriers discussed in Chapter Four to intervene.

Spheres and systems

Social exclusion is often described as multi-dimensional, reflecting 'inequalities in many dimensions – economic, social, political, cultural' (Rodgers, 1995a, p 50). The relationship of dimensions to spheres (Walzer, 1983) and of both to systems (and sub-systems), and the nature of their boundaries is far from obvious to the uninitiated. Certainly, 'dimension' and 'sphere' appear to be used interchangeably. These rather abstract concepts might be thought of in terms of areas of public life, or aspects of citizenship. Each will have institutions that oversee and implement systems through which interactions and distributions occur, via the relationship networks linking people to wider collectives and purposes. In this scenario, exclusion can be said to occur when people become detached from the systems emanating from major social institutions (Berghman, 1995, citing Poverty 3 researchers).

While other formulations of key institutions and their purposes are possible, Berghman characterises the democratic and legal system as promoting civic integration while the labour market promotes economic integration, the welfare state system social integration, and the family and community system interpersonal integration. Together these systems are seen as guaranteeing full citizenship (Berghman, 1995). It might follow that citizenship rights (civil, political, social) are the key systems through which inclusion occurs (see Powell, 1995; Marshall, 1950). Yet, not all systems of attachment appear necessarily rights-based, or concerned principally with citizenship. Economic systems can be rather more concerned with consumers than citizens – as discussed earlier, income and wealth rather than rights seem increasingly to be the way to gain access to most things. It is also entirely possible that informal community-based interaction has other goals – support from that source can be an important resource (Townsend, 1979). As previously discussed, citizenship is just one discourse among others of marketisation and solidarity.

Systems integration would appear to concern how these fit together. For example, how does the economic system interface with the political system? Does the economic system support the social system, or vice versa? It seems unlikely that the relationship between them will necessarily be static or equally balanced. Indeed, the scope for different arrangements may be what distinguishes societies in different times and places. In his classic work *The Great Transformation* (originally published in 1944), Polanyi provides an illustration of how shifts might occur (1957). He argues that at one time production and distribution were 'embedded' indistinguishably into local neighbourhoods, family settings, religious and political affiliations (discussed in Olofsson 1999). Then, with the birth of liberal markets, the economy became 'disembedded' to form a separate sphere. This in turn spawned the development of distinct social systems to protect people from the impact of economic downturn (Olofsson, 1999, Mouzelis, 1999).

While this illustrates the possibility of different configurations of spheres and their capacity for realignment, it is unclear in this instance whether movement indicates that spheres have become better balanced, so that economic objectives are moderated by social concerns, or whether this represents a more sophisticated understanding of the conditions needed for profit, such as a healthy, work-ready reserve workforce to draw upon, as required. In the latter scenario, the dominant economic sphere somehow colonises others, re-engineering their objectives to become compatible with its own, thereby achieving better systems integration. This resonates thunderously with Walzer's concerns about dominant spheres and goods (discussed in Chapter Two).

Dynamics between spheres and their systems at a macro-level, whether separate, inter-connected or subsumed, may find expression at micro-level. If one sphere dominates others, then disadvantage in relation to that one can be expected to bring wider repercussions. It may also begin to explain why forms of disadvantage and advantage can be accumulative, and the need for policy to take a holistic approach. Certainly there is some empirical evidence of interconnections between different forms of disadvantage, broadly related to different spheres. For example, using the British Household Panel Survey (BHPS), Burchardt et al (2002b) explored interconnections between consumption, production, political engagement, and social interaction (see also Gordon et al, 2000). This could be represented as an exploration of interconnections between economic, political and social spheres. The clustering of different forms of disadvantage might indicate that systems are integrated. However, it could also show that one sphere has colonised or dominated others – that complex equality does not apply. This suggests that better systems integration may still undermine social justice where it occurs through the inappropriate colonisation of one sphere by another. It is the nature of systems integration that is significant, not the fact or it. This further suggests that the separation of spheres, to prevent accumulations and achieve equilibrium between them could be a feature of social justice as inclusion.

Social relationships

Social exclusion can be defined as 'the result of a gradual breakdown of the social and symbolic bonds – economic, institutional, and individually significant – that normally tie the individual to society' (Xiberras, 1993, cited in Silver, 1994, pp 533, 534). At macro level, social relations refer to the social positions and roles of different social categories. At micro level, social relationships are the 'mechanisms for engagement' through which individuals are 'attached' to society, its institutions and each other. The types of relationships, how they are accessed, what cements them and what causes them to break down therefore require further examination. In this context, it is worth recalling earlier discussion about human motivations (Maslow, 1943), distinctions between objective and subjective perspectives, the importance of the quality of interaction and how people feel, or expect to feel, about engagement (see Chapter Three).

With some echoes of Miller's definition of three types of distributional relationships (2001 – see Chapter Two), it seems that types of relationship, too, may be associated with particular spheres and their functions, although whether such association reflects our contemporary situation (and configuration) or is of a generic, inevitable nature is very questionable. The 'contract' model of relationship is basically a market model, and related discourse is much in evidence. Inclusion is seen to depend on individual capacity rather than structural factors (Stewart, 2000). 'Contract' relationships are described as impersonal, pragmatic and goal driven. In contrast, 'compact' relationships might be associated with the social sphere and a discourse of solidarity. They concern 'the recognition of social relationships of *interdependence* and *mutuality* and prioritise solidarity and collective empowerment' (Stewart, 2000, p 59, emphasis in original). It is about a sense of fellow-feeling extending beyond immediate contacts (Barry, 2002). It might also entail integration into a 'moral community' (Rodgers, 1995b) – perhaps indicating an overlap, or integration, of social with cultural spheres. We could speculate about other types of relationship, around persuasion and resource mobilisation towards goals (collective, explicit or otherwise) in the political sphere, and perhaps another typical of a legal setting, where objective, formal judgement is required.

It would seem that there are different access requirements associated with relationship types, and/or related discourses, and that each can be associated with different distributive principles, purposes and values. Contract relationships require the objective assessment of what is useful to achieve a goal. To participate means both having those resources, and that they are recognised. However, it is individualistic, acknowledging only agency and oblivious to structural or social barriers. It has previously been discussed in terms of 'commodification' – a concept that appears to extend to people themselves, who are valued according to their resources and/or their economic productivity, rather than their intrinsic worth as human beings.

In contrast, access to compact-type relationships are contingent on being recognised to be part of a collective community of mutual support. Relationships are held together by concern for the well-being of others rather than the quest for personal profit. If the source of mutuality and interdependence is not the pragmatic need for others' resources to meet personal goals, it implies that support, solidarity, unconditionality and trust arise from emotional drivers. Interdependence, group loyalty and shared moral values are the hallmarks of relationships in the social sphere. However, it is important to note that interdependence is not always desirable, if unchosen or unequal so that one party is more dependent on the other. This can lower self-esteem, compromise autonomy and provoke disempowerment (discussed further in Chapter Seven). Moreover, trust seems likely to be a key ingredient of social bonds of all types (Sennett, 2000).

Meanwhile, a discourse of citizenship frames social exclusion as '*incomplete citizenship*, which is due to deficiencies in the possession of citizenship rights … and inequalities in the status of citizenship' (Gore, 1995, p 19, emphasis in original). The having and exercising of rights necessitates relationships with state institutions and these become the route to inclusion. This signposts the significance of criteria for accessing rights, what exactly they give rights to, and the ways in which institutional processes are structured and delivered.

If it is possible for different spheres to dominate at different times and places, it would follow that participation in a particular type of relationship will be critical for inclusion into others. It is possible to illustrate this phenomenon and its implications with reference to the operation of contemporary Western society, as discussed in Chapters One and Three. It was shown that successful relationships in the market-place can become the route to political power and preferable treatment by health, education and even justice systems (the possibility of purchasing a prison-cell upgrade in some American states is cited by Sandel, 2012). Prioritised relationships are those with (and within) the market economy, particularly the labour market. According to some, the predominant relationship of the workplace is purely contractual in nature – the antithesis of solidarity: 'Bonds and partnerships are viewed...as things to be *consumed*, not produced; they are subject to the same criteria of evaluation as all other objects of consumption' (Bauman, 2000, p 78). Yet, for Levitas, the SID discourse positions paid work as the (unduly narrow) locus for solidarity and social integration. This echoes earlier discussion concerning the harnessing of needs of all kinds and their channelling into activities conducive to the perpetuation and reinforcement of the dominant system. It might illustrate how one sphere (here the economic sphere) can subsume others.

Further implications include the invasion of the dominant value-base into relationships of all kinds. The demise of any collective, or even personal, sense of responsibility to or for others, the commodification of people and the failure to connect with or value their humanity that this implies, might be a factor in the appalling treatment of older people in some hospital or care settings or the rise in hate crimes against disabled people. It might be discernible in the behaviour of bankers who mis-sell products to increase their commission, MPs who fiddle their expenses and young people who engage in wanton looting (see Chapter One). The ongoing political push towards greater marketisation also serves to weaken solidarity founded on the justification of universal public services on the grounds of 'the human needs they meet and the role these services have in cementing a common life' (Gray, 2000, p 28). Education, healthcare and so on, along with the people who need them, come to have value only to the extent that profits can be made from them.

A few words of caution are in order. It is important not to assume that the designation of particular spheres and their associated functions, values and so on are somehow pre-ordained. They are nothing more than ideal, simplified models that broadly distinguish the different facets that may be discerned in any society, to a greater of lesser extent, though they can take very different forms (there are some passing similarities with Doyal and Gough's universal societal preconditions – 1991). While conjuring such entities might create a helpful theoretical device with which to explore alternative scenarios, to conceptualise and describe how societies are constructed and evolve, the picture described here is not inevitable. The configuration of spheres, their associated purposes, systems and values are all emergent: they are outcomes rather than starting points.

Simplification extends to descriptions of behaviour. People are complex and not always rational beings and we should take care not to oversimplify the causes of behaviour (as economists, particularly public-choice advocates, have been known to do). Not everyone responds in the same way to the same stimulus. Happily, not all will take opportunities for their own advancement at the expense of others. Simplified models have their uses but also their limitations and, if misused or misunderstood, could promote unhelpful reductionism. There are many reasons why people behave as they do and many different attitudes and behaviours among politicians, medical staff, young people and, of course, any other group. Thus there may be many reasons why people fail to engage empathetically with each other. There will also be situations where emotional engagement might be costly, or even regarded as unwanted, inappropriate and disrespectful by those on the receiving end (explored further in Chapter Seven).

Finally, it is worth noting that while relationships are here characterised in 'instrumental' terms, as the means of acquiring something through distributive processes (formal or informal), relationships can have 'constitutive importance' (Sen, 2000). Being excluded from social relations can be a deprivation in its own right, as well as provoking other deprivations. Consistent with earlier remarks, this also signals that the outcome of one social relation can have implications for others. These may not be immediate: 'The relationships in which a person is involved today may have implications for his or her capacity to manage relationships in subsequent phases of life' (Room, 1999, p 171). This is yet another angle on the time dimension of social exclusion and how disadvantage accumulates.

Relationship networks

It was previously suggested that access to relationship networks is likely to be of critical importance to social inclusion. In fact, the structure of society can be envisioned as comprised of social networks: 'the social environment can be expressed as patterns or regularities in relationships between interacting units' (Wasserman and Faust, 1994, p 3). Network models 'conceptualise structure (social, economic, political, and so forth) as lasting patterns of relations among actors' (Wasserman and Faust, 1994, p 4). As Bourdieu (1997) suggests, 'more or less institutionalized' relationships form networks, through which acts of mutual recognition occur. Relationship ties serve as channels for the transfer or 'flow' of resources, whether material or non-material (discussed in Wasserman and Faust, 1994). However, networks can also be informal, fluid and transient, forming around a particular issue or area of interest, then dissipating (see Rhodes, 1981; Smith, 1993 on 'policy communities' and networks). Interestingly, both social justice themes of recognition and distribution are evident here.

If society is comprised of networks, inclusion might depend on having access to differing numbers, types and combinations. Membership of one might grant, or possibly prevent, membership of others – networks, too, can be construed in terms of dominance. Cohesion might depend on crossovers between memberships, or different memberships forming discrete clusters. Society thus becomes conceptualised as a mish-mash of intersecting networks, some fluid, some more structured and formal. Individuals might be 'connected' to each other via participation in the distributive processes emanating from economic, political, social and civic institutions. They might be connected through shared membership of communities, geographically-defined, situation-specific (such as workplace, school, church, prison, and so on), or virtual (like Facebook). Whatever the points of commonality within multi-faceted identities may be, they provide scope for multiple corresponding relationship networks. That is not to say points of commonality will always be recognised (sameness blindness may intervene), or that all relationship networks will be of equal value (however defined). Clearly, not all are members of all networks, but the crossovers between them are tight enough to form a coherent, cohesive whole.

Relationship networks may converge on particular institutions, spanning across them where processes do likewise. If such networks are necessary for distribution, access to resources will be contingent on membership. A series of discontinuous memberships (or denials of them) and their consequences – can thus come to be expressed in terms of continuous spectrums of inequality. While networks can be conceptualised as creating social structures they can also be understood as tying component parts of society together (spheres, levels, institutions, communities and individuals), the extent to which they intermesh determining social cohesion.

For network analysts, the units of analysis include households, social categories, and neighbourhoods. Individuals are 'included' through attachment to social networks via relationship ties. These include friendship, liking, or respect; transfer of resources, behavioural interaction (talking together, sending messages); mobility (migration, social, or physical); physical connection (road, river, bridge), formal or biological relationships (Wasserman and Faust, 1994). It is noticeable that some of these (friendship, formal, biological) seem to refer to the type of relationship. Some (behavioural interaction, physical connection) describe mechanisms or infrastructure requirements for relationship enactment. Social barriers and misrecognition (discussed in Chapter Four) can intervene to prevent relationship ties and render inaccessible the infrastructure necessary for connection and enactment .

Relationship networks may not only converge on institutions, but on events. 'Occasions' (rallies, cruises, hunts, parties, and so on) can be a means of bringing together 'individuals as homogenous as possible in all the pertinent respects in terms of the existence and persistence of the group' (Bourdieu, 1997, p 52). Ceremonies associated with these are 'mechanisms which allow the participants to affirm their affiliation and commitment to their collectivities' (Goffman, 1983, p 9). According to Sennett, 'ritual is society's strongest cement, its very chemistry of inclusion' (2000, p 279).[1] While events might indeed serve to reinforce sameness (and in ritualised form this seems particularly likely), there is no obvious reason why they have to be devices for reinforcing peer group boundaries, or why peer groups cannot accommodate considerable diversity. Events could equally serve to bring together disparate groups or networks to facilitate mutually beneficial exchanges.

If networks are composed of people (or other units) who share something in common, the strength of the network and of social cohesion would presumably be proportionate to the degree of commonality: 'the strength of a tie is a (probably linear) combination of the amount of time, the emotional intensity, the intimacy (mutual confiding), and the reciprocal services which characterize the tie' (Granovetter, 1973, p 1361). Such ties will be weaker with people who are unknown: 'Weak ties are more likely to link members of *different* small groups than are strong ones, which tend to be concentrated within particular groups' (Granovetter, 1973, p 1376, emphasis in original). Yet, to achieve an objective may require the input of different characteristics (skills, goods, and so on) to those already possessed within the group. This suggests that networks can be held together by commonality or mutually enriching difference; by ties based on emotion or pragmatism.

Whether it is to build a customer-base, locate resources required for production, to learn about innovative approaches, or identify new opportunities for any form of transaction, to stimulate creativity by exposure to alternatives, there are many reasons to engage with new networks: 'those to whom we are weakly tied are more likely to move in circles different from our own and will thus have access to information different from that we receive' (Granovetter, 1973, p 1371). Engaging with people who are, or appear, 'different' might also build emotional connections, as the unfamiliar becomes familiar and formerly obscured commonalities start to shine through. As a means of improving recognition and opportunities for participation, the forging of new networks is likely to be critical for promoting inclusion and cohesion. There is therefore much to be gained by building relationship networks on grounds of difference as well as on shared commonalities.

However, if as Sennett alleges, trust is a key ingredient of social bonds of all types (2000), to trust people we do not know could be risky. It might suggest a time dimension to relationships: 'the exchanges which lie at the heart of social inclusion have a time dimension: they require duration in social relationship – not permanence, but sufficient time for unfolding, repeated interaction to give an experiential meaning to formal commitments' (Sennett, 2000, p 283). If so, this could pose challenges to some forms of relationship between welfare providers and recipients, where brief interaction or lack of continuity feature. However, it is possible that trust might be engendered in other ways, such as through evidence of specialist knowledge or scope for legal enforcement, should it be required. It is also possible that trust is created by shared expectations concerning the nature of the process, or the balance of power within it.

Limits to inclusion and cohesion

What is there to stop everyone from being included in mainstream society, if social barriers were removed and access to relationship networks were forged? Some have argued that social exclusion may be inevitable, whether because it is 'a normal and integral part of the power dynamics of modern society' (Room, 1999, p 172) or because 'throughout history, all the main axes of inclusion have been simultaneously axes of exclusion' (Stewart, 2000, p 55). Perhaps there must always be exclusion if there is to be clarity about inclusion, and if it is to be meaningful.

However, the boundaries between inclusion and exclusion are more subtle than this might imply, even when people have citizenship rights and paid employment. Neither are necessarily guarantees of inclusion, though not having them could be an indicator of increased likelihood of exclusion. Rights can grant access but cannot guarantee outcomes.

However, if they are too complex people will fail to exercise them. If rights-based services are inappropriate, or delivered in stigmatising ways, again, rights may not be exercised. People may have political rights to vote but, as previously discussed, it takes more than this to make democracy meaningful. And people may be in paid work but still be living in poverty. Terms of employment may be exploitative (Sen, 2000). People may struggle to reconcile work with family responsibilities. They may also experience considerable loss of personal autonomy (Silver, 1994).

It may be possible to be objectively included yet subjectively to feel excluded, or to be technically included and still experience significant disadvantage. People may be members but unable to benefit from their membership. For example, it is open to anyone who fulfils residency criteria to apply for jobs, but people who live in areas of high unemployment will nonetheless struggle to find work. A disabled person may 'count' as a citizen but, because of social barriers, be unable to express citizenship.

In some cases, the desirability of inclusion becomes questionable. As Gore points out, discussing the African literature, it is the terms of 'incorporation' that can be problematic: 'People are not suffering from poverty owing to exclusion. Rather they are excluding themselves from the wider economy and society, from the burdensome and unequal obligations of citizenship, in order to survive' (1995, p104). Sen refers to 'unfavourable inclusion': 'many problems of deprivation arise from unfavourable terms of inclusion and adverse participation, rather than what can be sensibly seen primarily as a case of exclusion as such' (2000, p 28). As he observes, being 'kept out' and being included on unfavourable terms are different problems.

While cautioning against accepting too readily that apparently chosen self-exclusion is in fact voluntary, Barry (2002) also queries whether social exclusion must always be seen as a 'bad thing'. If terms of inclusion are oppressive, exclusion may indeed be preferable, as was argued in Chapter Four by proponents of the affirmative model of disability who highlighted the (alleged) positive advantages to life outside the mainstream. Meanwhile queer theory appeared to reject any terms of inclusion as inherently limiting. This underlines the importance of diversity being included on terms which respect and value difference by removing unnecessary limitations and oppression. Just what 'necessary' constitutes in this context also requires clarification.

There may be other social and personal costs to inclusion. The resource implications of according membership to 'unproductive' people would need to be addressed – or perhaps it is notions of 'productive' that need to be widened. Personal costs may take the form of the need to compromise or be tolerant of others. How time is spent, the activities undertaken or company kept may not be what an individual would ideally choose, but if it means toleration of difference and acceptance that preferences cannot always be realised, oppression could be a positive force. There may also be good (as in theoretically inevitable) reasons why an individual or behaviour cannot, or should not, be included. Their inclusion might compromise rather than enrich the integrity of the whole, because two alternatives must be confronted and are mutually incompatible in a major way. There may be other positive advantages to oppression or repression. Some firmness of boundaries and expectations are necessary to provide social and personal security, and this is necessary for social cohesion: 'If security without freedom feels like repulsive oppression, freedom without security prompts one to dream of oppression as the miraculous cure for the pains of vulnerability' (Bauman, 2000 p 86).

Social cohesion

It is commonly assumed in social exclusion discourse that social inclusion automatically engenders social cohesion: 'An inclusive society is a cohesive society' (Gray, 2000, p 23). Yet, very different actions may be justified in the name of cohesion, not all of them inclusive in any meaningful sense. Indeed, there are times when cohesion is achieved by the purposeful exclusion of those deemed different. If discriminatory attitudes can take the form of distancing through the demonisation of others (Chapter Four), fear, threat and contempt can similarly be used to shore up group boundaries, strengthening the cohesion between those included – and perhaps those excluded too – into discrete strata (reminiscent of the 'closure' that featured as part of Silver's monopoloy paradigm). In such instances, group cohesion is achieved through opposition, not collaboration.

Cohesive societies are not necessarily the result of cosmopolitan tolerance. They may achieve stability through repression, enforced subordination and hierarchy (Gray, 2000). If inclusion is enforced rather than voluntary, cohesion depends on society's ability to repress dissent or oppress difference: 'Such societies remain cohesive by disabling individual autonomy' (Gray, 2000, p 25). Nonetheless, their overall integrity may be weakened by ongoing internal pressures generated by the force required to 'reshape' individuals so they conform to a narrowly drawn norm, and the resistance that those individuals might well be expected to express.

The existence of different cultures within one and the same society might be thought of as a possible source of rupture, subject to degrees of compatibility and mutual tolerance. This depends on degrees of compatibility and mutual tolerance. Conversely, it should not be assumed that cohesion will always result from all subscribing to the same set of cultural values and goals. Indeed there is no logical reason why divergent behaviours may not arise where goals, such as, for example, economic prosperity, are shared but the extent of obstacles to fulfilling them is unequally distributed. These may be beyond the power of individuals to address, hence the scope for agency and choice is curtailed. People may then find socially destructive ways like burglary, drug-dealing or looting, of achieving that still-shared goal for economic prosperity. Such behaviours do not necessarily indicate that the perpetrators are part of a culturally distinct underclass; they may fully subscribe to the values of a mainstream culture that measures status by income and possessions.

The underlying premise seems to be that social cohesion depends on social stability, whether by fair means or foul, negotiation of differences or their oppression. Even if so, stability may be unattainable: 'the day-to-day workings of deregulated world markets impose a degree of economic insecurity on all countries exposed to them that is inimical to cohesion and, therefore, to inclusion' (Gray, 2000, p 34). In such circumstances 'social cohesion cannot mean stabilizing the positions of people in an immobile or stationary condition of society. It can only refer to a particular way of coping with change' (Gray, 2000, p 25). A further possibility is that instability is deliberately created: 'Once the basic cause of poverty is removed…this must be replaced by the development of an artificially created and subjective sense of insufficiency, for nothing could be more menacing to industrial society than that people should declare themselves satisfied with what they have' (Seabrook, 1988, cited in Bauman, 2000, p 75).

The incapacity of rigidly oppressive societies to absorb ever-changing pressures generated both internally and externally, deliberately or otherwise, suggests that looser, more fluid forms of attachment may be desirable, if the social cohesion of a diverse, mobile populace is to be sustained. To maximise inclusion, strategies to accommodate diversity and diffuse conflict will be of critical importance. Most importantly, what this section shows is that social inclusion and social cohesion are not always desirable any more than oppression is always undesirable. The terms of inclusion, and the means of achieving social cohesion, are what matter. Within the limitations described, the wider those terms of inclusion can be, the more choice, mobility, autonomy, they permit, the less rigid and oppressive (de facto) that society will be. If people are members of many intersecting relationship networks, the social fabric – and social cohesion – is strengthened as they weave together.

The implications for inclusive equality

This chapter began by highlighting the apparent difficulties in defining social exclusion. Authors appear concerned (not always explicitly) with exclusion from different things: societal spheres; public services; the approved moral code; the labour market or the market in general; citizenship, or social relationships and relationship networks. Exclusion is variously attributed to state failure, economic failure or personal failure. Policy implications are contradictory. The benefit system should be strengthened, restructured or cut back; unemployed people should be protected from, or pressurised into, engagement with the market.

However, over the course of discussion, it has become possible to find coherence amidst the confusion, and to extract some clear signposts for policy. The role of inequality in its various forms can be shown to be both cause and consequence of 'catastrophic ruptures' of many kinds. This is not just a matter of unequal resources detaching those at the bottom and the top of the income distribution. Neither is inequality just a matter of the detachment of particular social categories. Inequalities are what demarcate social structures; they delineate the contours of society and of social exclusion.

The separation between different levels of society is marked by inequalities of power and voice. The inadequacy (or absence) of infrastructure through which to conduct relationships between actors at different levels (that is, between micro and ever more macro actors), makes it impossible for individuals on the ground to know how power is being exercised, to exert any influence, or to hold those with it to account. Their connections with supranational structures are particularly lacking. Yet, as globalisation advances, so the powers of those structures increase and those beneath diminish. They exert increasing impact in determining ideology, the creation of social divisions, the framing of needs and resource distribution methods, the values attributed to activities, possessions and people (being, doing and having). In effect, they can spawn multiple forms of inequality. Devolution could be a means of creating a more equitable distribution of power and of enabling diversity to be expressed. The notion of an association between the size of state and degree of power distribution is not new; it can be traced back to Rousseau's Social Contract (1762). He defined democracy in terms of government put 'in the hands of the whole people, or greater part of the people' (Rousseau, 1968 translation, p110), compared to government by the few (aristocracy) or the one (monarchy). He further proposed that 'democratic government suits small states, aristocratic government suits states of intermediate size and monarchy suits large states.' (Rousseau, 1968 translation, p111).

It might follow that devolving decision-making right down to family or individual levels is the thing to do. Indeed, the ethos of privatisation is based on precisely this. Through the market, it is argued, individuals are empowered to choose the goods and services which best match their specific needs and aspirations (of course, one of many screamingly obvious flaws in the argument is that they require resources to do so). Such diversity, it continues, could never be catered for, and empowerment consequently could not be achieved, by cumbersome, bureaucratic state-run institutions. But why not? It is not automatically obvious why public sector institutions cannot support and promote autonomy and choice, and there is increasing evidence that they could (see Chapter Seven). Meanwhile, it seems hard to sustain the notion that there is anything much to choose between financial service offerings, supermarkets, and privatised utilities, and instances where no choice is possible despite privatisation, such as for railway passengers wishing to make a particular journey.

The case for complex equality, the separation of spheres as a means of defusing dynamics of accumulation (Walzer, 1983), is evident in the way that the market, in particular the possession of income and wealth and the focus on paid work as the route to acquiring them, has increasingly come to dominate all else. What, however, would greater equilibrium between spheres mean in practical policy terms? Obviously is has to mean limiting the extent to which money and associated distributive principle, can overrule all others (like need or deservingness). It should not be the route to political power, or preferential treatment by health, education and justice systems. Freedoms should not be contingent on it, and so on. However, for such measures to be taken would appear to require a change of heart from the very people who most benefit from the status quo – not something that it would seem wise to count upon.

One alternative might be to explore what can be achieved by taking a 'bottom-up' approach. This might include, for example, local 'freecycle' schemes, where goods that are serviceable but no longer needed by one party are given to another who could make use of them. Another initiative might be to establish 'time banks' – where time spent on community activities is 'banked' and can be exchanged for someone else's time. This is a means of recognising the 'invisible' work of women and the contributions of people 'for whom the market had no use' (foreword by Edgar Cahn, NEF, 2008). It entails 'rejection that money and market price is the sole acceptable measure of value…There are domains we all recognise are beyond price: family and loved ones, justice, patriotism, spirituality, the environment.' (2008, p 2). This signals the possibility that different forms of contribution can be accorded equivalent value, as can everyone's varying skills and capacities. Two hours of legal advice might be exchanged for two hours of gardening.

It is Cahn's contention is that the market has not just encroached onto public sector provision but has also colonized and undermined what he terms the 'non-market economy' (Cahn, 2000). The momentum generated by market dynamics is so powerful that it continues beyond the point where the market is strengthened and it starts undermining its starting point. Cahn's proposition is picked up by the NEF, 'Market logic applies to narrow deliverables, but misses out the crucial dimension that allows doctors to heal, teachers to teach and carers to care: the relationship with patient, pupil or client' (2008, p 8). Once again, the importance of the quality of relationships and of strong communities is indicated. A focus on community development – the creation of both physical and relationship network infrastructure is also strongly implied – in situations where communities become detached by the intersection of many forms of inequality (the importance of strong supportive communities as a form of resource was also highlighted in Chapter Three).

This debate also enables us to elaborate upon the vision for the overall goal of inclusive equality, which began to take shape in Chapter Three. In order to realise capabilities, the nature of systems and institutions in economic, political, social and civil spheres is likely to be significant. For example, 'participation in decision-making' (having voice and influence) seems obviously to point to political systems and institutions, while 'protection and fair treatment by the law' are requirements of those concerned with civil justice. However, decision-making occurs across all areas of public life, as indeed do laws and the need for fair treatment. 'Engagement in productive and valued activities' might suggest access to paid employment – or (as discussed) the importance of recognising the value of other forms of activity and generating options for participation in it.

Discussion has also drawn attention to the 'mechanisms for engagement'. Relationship networks can be construed as the routes through which exchanges of all kinds occur; as the mechanisms through which engagement with institutions and with each other is enacted. It is they that bind together, or cast adrift, the disparate components of which society is composed. This might suggest an important role for social policy in extending and/or preserving attachments to relationship networks. Yet, aside from 'welfare to work' measures specifically aimed to enhance the chances of access to the labour market, which might be conceived in such terms, this does not always appear to be a primary focus. There may be more that could be done in healthcare, community care and education policy, for example, to generate or preserve connections. Instead of prioritising economic capital, it underlines the invaluable role of social capital (Bourdieu, 1997) as the route to acquiring all else.

This once more brings as back to the nature of distributive processes and the importance of accurate recognition if social justice is to be achieved. Where networks break down, inequalities are indicated as either (or both) cause or consequence. Yet the way in which processes are designed and delivered can be pivotal to promoting or exacerbating inequalities, and to engagement or disengagement. It is through them that the terms of inclusion are expressed and experienced. The next two chapters look more closely at how distributive processes could be designed and delivered, to maximise the inclusion of diversity by minimising inequalities.

Note

[1] This is not an original claim. It can be traced back to Durkheim's theory of ritual as 'stereotyped sequences of behaviour that have the capacity to arouse emotions and reinforce symbols and, hence, social structures; or…to generate new symbols and structures' (discussed in Turner, 2002, p 20).

SIX

Inclusive policy processes

Introduction

This chapter draws on themes arising from previous discussion and explores their implications for the way in which social policy is designed and delivered, if it is to enable people to realise capabilities. This seems likely to entail removing social barriers, increasing people's resources and/or reducing their resource requirements.

It was previously suggested that the outcome of one process becomes the starting point for the next. Processes may not be best viewed as merely the means to achieving an end outcome; outcomes could be the means of engaging in more processes. It has also been proposed that participation in relationship networks is central to inclusion. The nature of the processes through which relationships are enacted therefore takes centre stage.

Individuals relate to each other and to wider society for various reasons: 'we come together to share, divide and exchange' (Walzer, 1983, p 3), all of these distributive processes oviously necessitating some form of interaction. Preceding chapters have each had something to contribute towards conceptualising how such processes might best be structured and enacted in ways that promote inclusive equality. This chapter aims to draw together and develop insights regarding process design as it pertains to the distribution of welfare goods and services. Different models are possible; some more conducive to inclusive equality than others. The chapter begins by reflecting in general terms on how an overall social goal of maximising inclusive equality and with it the scope for social realisation, could reshape the purpose and operations of institutions. It then narrows the focus down onto those involved in the design and delivery of welfare goods and services, due to their potentially pivotal roles in either facilitating inclusion or entrenching exclusion.

We examine how the process of distribution can be broken down into functions and stages and consider who might be responsible for particular aspects of the process, or contribute towards its framing and enactment. Through deconstructing processes in this way it becomes easier to pinpoint where misrecognition can intervene to undermine policy intentions – not to say social justice – leaving individuals unjustifiably disadvantaged. Social barriers, including organisational, environmental and communications barriers, can intervene at any stage. While there is much that can be done to remove such barriers and open up access, it is possible to identify a range of unavoidable limitations.

To carry out distributions can require processes and relationship networks that span different institutions, levels, spheres, their systems and sub-systems. Clearly, these days the functions and processes formed around the distribution of publicly funded social or welfare goods do not all occur in the public sector. Increasingly public funds and responsibility for delivery (or elements of it) are channelled to private sector organisations. Voluntary sector organisations, too, are often involved in competing for contracts. There are well-rehearsed debates about which type of organisation – public, private or voluntary – is to be preferred. Each traditionally has been attributed particular strengths and weaknesses. However, it is far from clear why features such as efficiency, quality, flexibility and the promotion of user choice should necessarily be the prerogative of any particular sector (or indeed that alleged associations between feature and sector can necessarily be empirically supported). This is not a debate for now. Instead our concern is to define what the best should look like, while acknowledging that conforming to it might pose different challenges for differently placed institutions.

In Chapter Four, it was suggested that maximising social inclusion might be achieved by considering the fit, and scope for 'adjustment', to socio-cultural context, individuals (their circumstances, resources, capacities and so on) and the processes through which they come together. Drawing on this approach, the chapter concludes with some thoughts on what this might mean for policy and strategy. Hopefully there are aspects of this discussion that might be of interest to those engaged in the relatively new discipline of service design, which applies design skills and techniques (including those more traditionally associated with product design, such as developing blueprints and prototypes) to generate creative and innovative approaches.[1] There is also, no doubt, much they could do to improve upon the approach set out here.

The purpose of institutions

As discussed in Chapter Two, Sen draws a distinction between social justice concerned with institutional rules and arrangements, and social justice in terms of the lives people actually manage to live – 'social realisation' – recognising that institutions can have an impact on social realisation but that other factors also play a role (2010). The former is broadly concerned to design socially just institutions that would distribute according to socially just principles, on the (shaky) presumption that this would elicit socially just behaviours. Instead, he advocated a focus on social realisation.

In accordance with this, our starting point concerns what people are able to do, their scope for autonomous social realisation and the diversity (and sustainability) of the ways in which it could be expressed. We are concerned with defining how institutions should operate but not on the assumption that this would determine how people should and would live their lives. However, by taking a bottom-up approach, tracking back from the outcome of inclusive equality to the institutions that could promote it, much is revealed about the implications for the latter.

It is necessary to reflect on what institutions are for; what role they do or could perform to support our goal. They can be conceived in terms of infrastructure through which actors operating at different levels of society communicate with each other, either vertically (macro to meso to micro; global to national, through various levels down to individual), and/or horizontally, between parties at the same level. They are the means through which evidence is assembled, decision-making processes are conducted, outputs are delivered and outcomes evaluated.

The fact that those affected by decisions are a source of vital information (as argued in Chapter Two with reference to the tricky question of who should get the flute), and the importance of equal voice in reaching a conclusion, all suggest that justice requires the process of decision-making as well as the outcome to have regard for inclusion and equality. This would be consistent with Sen's account of 'comprehensive' as opposed to 'culmination' outcomes. The former includes 'actions undertaken, agencies involved, processes used, etc., *along with* the simple outcomes seen in a way that is detached from processes, agencies and relations' (2010, p 215, emphasis in original); the focus on simple outcomes alone being the hallmark of the latter.

When it comes to social policy (though far from uniquely) processes and decisions will often concern the distribution of outputs in the form of goods and services. A bottom-up approach points towards exploration of the interaction between institutions' systems, culture and processes, and the individuals seeking to avail themselves of the goods and services they distribute. The nature of their relationship with front-line employees responsible for assessment and administration – the vehicle through which interaction occurs – is likely to be key (pursued in the next chapter). It will be important to understand the role of goods, services, distributive processes and relationships in promoting equality (of different types) and inclusion – or exclusion.

If inclusion is about processes as well as outputs and outcomes, and if it is about equalising power, we need to explore the potential role for the end user in influencing the design of the distribution process and the good or service that is to be distributed. Socially just institutional arrangements become those that enhance the involvement of prospective end users, in the development and enactment of distributional processes and relationships, in designing goods and services and in designating the outcomes that these are intended to realise.

By opening themselves up to the involvement of actual and prospective recipients, the dividing wall between institutions and social realisation starts to crumble. Institutions cease to be the means through which the decisions of the powerful are imposed on the powerless. Instead a shift in power towards greater equality enables them to become arenas where different perspectives engage with each other, where formalised 'objectivity' meets subjectivity, promoting multiway dialogue and negotiation. The dichotomy between socially just institutions and socially just social realisation dissolves; the former being contingent on the extent to which it supports the latter.

Deconstructing processes

We start by defining a theoretical 'ideal model' of a traditional distributive process. There is much to draw on from earlier discussion concerning the stages of processes, the functions and roles implied and the errors that can inadvertently occur in designing and enacting them.

Social meanings and purposes

The first step to devising a procedurally just process would seem to require clarification of the social meaning of the good to be distributed. There is clearly a great deal that social policy, and welfare goods and services specifically, could contribute towards supporting the realisation of capabilities, such as good health, skills to participate in society, a comfortable standard of living and engagement in productive and valued activities. It suggests that the broad purposes of welfare goods and services could be to increase, develop or maintain resources of all kinds, or prevent resource loss; to build and sustain capacity to participate in relationship networks and distributive processes. Ultimately their (interconnected) purposes could be characterised as to equip people to exercise autonomy, the expansion of their scope for social realisation and the promotion of their wellbeing, thereby strengthening the society in which they live.

Social security benefits, education, healthcare, community care and public housing each have the potential to contribute in different ways to such goals. Each in some way contributes to resourcing the population, or particular social categories within it. They do of course differ in terms of the type of resource they address and the type of good they deliver. For example, some take the form of tangible goods like income and housing. Intangible goods, such as healthcare services and education, become 'embodied' in the recipient, to use Bourdieu's terminology (1997). Each may have constitutive importance for individual recipients as well as serving instrumental purposes; the route to opening up access to other goods, processes and relationship networks. Through so doing, welfare goods (including services embodied in their recipients) might in turn contribute towards social goals. For example, they might support the economy and/or promote social solidarity.

While the purpose of welfare goods has been cast in positive terms, it is not inevitable that their social meaning is similarly positive. Much hinges on such factors as the design of welfare goods (including services), the manner of their delivery and the criteria for distribution. Of course, it could be argued that the quality and availability of welfare goods is simply a matter of how well they are funded and this may indeed be a key part of the picture. However, a service could be well-funded and widely available yet still fail to meet needs. The structuring and enactment of the processes concerned with the design and delivery of welfare goods could still exacerbate incapacity, inequality and exclusion rather than the reverse.

As explored in Chapter Three, human needs and motivations come in various forms, both pragmatic and emotionally-based. Failure to accommodate these could open the door to less positive social meanings becoming attached to welfare goods. While engagement might be driven by pragmatic imperatives (to pay essential bills, to treat illness, and so on), disincentives could arise from failure to take account of emotional needs, such as for self-esteem, self-respect and self-expression. At worst, neither sort of need is met. The good fails to meet pragmatic needs because it is inadequate or misconceived, perhaps because the nature of the need is not understood and so neither is what is required to meet it. Furthermore, it is delivered in ways that are experienced as disrespectful, patronising or disempowering, which undermine self-esteem. Access criteria require demonstration of incapacity, and thereby serve to underline it. The purposes of welfare goods might still be to promote well-being, to strengthen capacity, autonomy, networks and so on, but the design and delivery of welfare goods promote the opposite. The social meaning of welfare goods – and what they convey about recipients – shifts from positive to negative even if the declared purpose remains positive.

Negative messages are, of course, not only generated by factors internal to design and delivery. Politicians' demonisation of benefit recipients as feckless, idle scroungers is an obvious example of how they can be externally generated. Neither is it the case that the political aim is necessarily to promote the take-up of welfare goods, or to make the process of claiming them anything other than a deeply unpleasant experience. People may be compelled to undertake jobsearch activities (regardless of whether jobs they conceivably could do exist in their area) or to undergo humiliating medical assessments.[2] The primary agenda may well be to cut expenditure on benefits and thus to provide incentives not to claim them. Other agendas, too, could have an impact, for example the deliberate underfunding of public sector provision as an incentive to those that can to seek private sector alternatives, the transferal of public services and public funds to the private sector, where the quest for profit overrides all other goals, and so on.

It could be argued that to target welfare goods on people who are most lacking resources (of whatever kind) is the way to achieve greatest value for money and that therefore negative associations between those goods and incapacity are unavoidable. However, to intervene early, to prevent needs from becoming acute rather than waiting until they do, might be just as – even more – cost-effective as well as less costly in terms of human suffering. Positioning welfare goods as preventative diffuses associations with incapacity. Acknowledging that we all at certain times of our lives need education, healthcare and other forms of care, could provide a basis for welfare goods that strengthens social solidarity. Negative messages become less likely if recipients include the middle classes.

It is clearly important that the social meaning of welfare goods does not convey negative messages about the (low) status of recipients if they are to promote positive engagement, not just in the processes to acquire such goods in the first place but, through them, with wider society. The active cooperation and input of recipients is generally required, for example to achieve education or healthcare goals (see Cahn, 2000). Compulsion is not necessarily the route to achieving this. For example, while young people may be compelled to attend school, it does not necessarily follow that they engage with what they are taught (or 'embody it', in Bourdieu's terms). This is not to argue that compulsion is always unnecessary or undesirable, but to suggest that at best it is a precursor to engagement and at worst – where compulsory activities are judged pointless or experienced as demeaning – a reason to rebel against it.

All this suggests that welfare goods could play a pivotal role; either exacerbating exclusion and social division or the reverse. Aside from funding issues, the way in which they are designed and delivered can compound disengagement, incapacity and disempowerment or precisely the opposite. It also suggests that, whether positive or negative, it is unsafe to make assumptions that social meanings, purposes and goods must be mutually consistent and reinforcing. Even where they are positive and consistent, in keeping with the notion of widening the mainstream, there is nothing to say that they have to be narrowly and rigidly defined. Indeed, if the aim is to promote empowerment, to be prescriptive might be inherently counterproductive: power to shape the good received and to decide how to deploy it may be what empowerment is at least partly about. Yet while a good's basic social meaning and associated purpose can be broad, allowing scope for diverse applications, it must be unambiguous, if a coherent process is to be feasible and fairness assured.

Functions and roles

While different models of distributive processes would appear to exist, for any such process to occur, various functions need to be performed and associated roles are thus implied. Burchardt et al (1999) have suggested that functions can be split into financing provision, decision-making about who should get what, and delivery. Although these certainly are core functions, it is proposed that these headlines each encompass a series of sub-functions. Furthermore, as will be explored, distributive processes generally require additional functions not adequately encapsulated in any of those three. Different models might add still more to the list.

A traditional approach to distribution might be set out as follows. As proposed in social justice literature, it is first necessary to define 'a bounded society with a determinate membership, forming a universe of distribution' (Miller, 2001, p 4). In an era of globalisation, anyone could be a prospective recipient, or factors like nationality or habitual place of residence might constitute the threshold of a 'universe of distribution'. To access a good or service the prospective recipients first need information to know it exists and how to access it. Once through the door, they need to demonstrate that they meet the access criteria used to distinguish between the members of the 'universe of distribution' and assign them into social categories. Assessment occurs and the good is allocated or withheld accordingly.

Supranational, national, regional and local institutions all can play a part in the design and delivery of welfare gods. The intended broad social meaning and purposes of the goods to be distributed and the parameters of the distribution process to be followed are commonly 'framed',[3] or shaped, by what Mouzelis calls 'macro-actors' (1991) in higher-levels organisations. They might be expected to determine the social category of recipients, the criteria for access (or terms of inclusion), who is to assess and make decisions, the nature of the goods to be distributed, and delivery methods. For example, macro-actors at European Union level may set parameters within which nation-state level framers then must operate; they do likewise for framers at regional level, and so on. In this model, greater detail is filled in and room for manoeuvre diminishes as it descends towards the end user.

Often, the policy framework is set at one level, then delegated to another (with or without some residual policymaking responsibility) to be implemented by delivery agencies. These, or particular staff within them, act as gatekeepers to resources, assessing prospective recipients against the access criteria handed down, making decisions on distribution and delivering the goods accordingly. It is in these meso-level intermediary institutions that the interface occurs between macro-level policy intentions and micro-level actors; between the objectivity of the assessor and the subjectivity of the assessed (not that it is necessarily so clearcut in practice).

When it comes to publicly-funded welfare goods and services, prospective recipients may be required to demonstrate qualities such as need, capacity, risk and desert (even if cost is the overriding consideration); that they have potential to gain (in socially approved ways) from the good received, and that to distribute to them would be to the advantage of wider society, consistent with its norms. Assessing such qualities can be far from straightforward. Other forms of criteria, such as having insufficient funds to manage without support or, conversely, having sufficient funds to pay for it, may be more straightforward to measure, although in some cases when setting criteria definitions of sufficiency are likely to be heavily contested (see Chapter Three).

To ensure adherence to the process, 'witnesses' to the ritual of formal distributive processes (Sennett, 2000) are likely to be required. They may be independent institutions (like auditors) or arm's-length roles within the distributing institution itself. They are responsible for ensuring the quality of operations, the consistency with which processes are administered and the extent to which objectives for them are met.

An ideal model of this type of distributive process is summarised in Figure 6.1.

Figure 6.1 Stages, functions and roles of a distributive process

Stage 1: Framers clarify the social meanings of the goods for distribution and funding arrangements, 'frame' the objectives, process, social category of recipients and criteria/ indicators, and convey these to assessors

↓

Stage 2: Prospective recipient accesses information about the good and the process

↓

Stage 3: Prospective recipient shows to the assessor how/if they meet the criteria

↓

Stage 4: Assessor judges this against the criteria set by the 'framers'

↓

Stage 5: Assessor distributes or withholds goods accordingly

↓

Stage 6: Recipient consumes the goods, or presents them to show that the criteria for another distributive process are met, or invests/saves them for subsequent transaction

Process, and/or specific stages, are independently regulated, reviewed or witnessed

Models and variations

While this might describe a much-simplified ideal-type hierarchical distributive process, there are other possible variations. In this model, of all the parties it is the end user who has least power. This underlines the fact that inclusion in a process is not an adequate goal. It may be possible to be technically included in a process but effectively disempowered.

Even where the process is formal and regulated, it does not follow that roles will always be distinct. Functions may be discrete, carried out by different parties, or combined into a given role. Framing may be tight or loose, imposed top-down or devolved. It is possible that recipients or those charged with delivery might have an input to framing the policy or to designing the product to be delivered. Furthermore, if each has relevant knowledge or skills to contribute, this could become a partnership of equals. Each needs the resources that the other possesses and the outcome depends on that mutual exchange (see Rhodes, 1981, on 'power dependences').

At one extreme, centralised control combines framing and regulating roles, locating all the power to frame and hold others accountable with an elite few. Yet, power does not have to diminish down the stages, or at least not to such an extent. Indeed, if the aim is to support recipients to exercise their autonomy, and widen their scope for social realisation, for it to do so would seem counterproductive. Instead recipients might be given the power to determine the precise form that the good or service takes, in accordance with their particular requirements, so long as this remains within the broad parameters of the intended social meaning and purpose.

Recipients might also be empowered through having rights to challenge decisions resulting from misrecognition. This does, of course, assume that transparent procedures, benchmarks and criteria exist. In such an event, a role for an independent perspective would be implied, to confirm or overturn decisions by reviewing the evidence presented against the criteria. A rights basis to provision shifts the power in favour of recipients, in contrast to dependency on the non-transparent, unaccountable, discretionary whim of an assessor, with power to pass judgement on an individual person's deservingness.

There can be devolution of power elsewhere in the process, too, in fact the distance between policymakers and deliverers can make this, to some degree, hard to avoid. The relationship between policy and delivery can be far from clear-cut. Some argue that policy is only formed at the point of delivery. Those involved may modify – or reframe – the original policy intentions in response to front-line pressures to match unlimited needs to limited resources (Lipsky, 1980, 1993). They may also override criteria and edicts setting out how they are to be assessed by applying, inadvertently or otherwise, other socio-cultural interpretations of indicators.

For recipients to be able to hold others to account and to play a key role in framing the goods and services which they receive would be consistent with an aim of maximising the inclusion of diversity on a basis of empowerment. Moreover, without their involvement, those who do not have their lived experience may not be able to recognise barriers or devise appropriate ways to remove them. The goods they design may be useless to recipients, meaning that they cannot realise intended capabilities, policy does not meet its objectives and funding is wasted.

However, to devolve power to recipients presupposes that they have the information they need to make choices, as well as the capacity and the desire to take responsibility. Information about complex products like pensions, about alternative types of medical treatment or the different providers of community care available in a given geographical area might present challenges of different kinds to making good choices. People who absorb negative cultural (or literal) messages affirming their helplessness, incapacity or inability (not untypically older people, disabled people or young people who fail to thrive at school) may well not have the confidence, or the desire, to exercise choice, take responsibility or engage in the process at all. To hand over (or dump) responsibility without support could be highly disempowering.

This signals that providing appropriate support within the process might be another necessary function. 'Appropriate' in this context might well mean independent of other parties with a (actual or perceived) vested interest, if users are to have the confidence that support is for their benefit rather than that of providers. However it might also have implications for the type of relationship between recipient and provider, whether supportive and person-centred, paternalistic or adversarial, as will be explored in the next chapter.

Levels and spheres

To identify further features that might distinguish a distributive process conducive to the promotion of inclusive equality, it might be helpful to consider it in terms of levels and spheres, their values and systems. Social 'solidarity' issues may be what lie behind the public sector ethos. Market values are evident in funding considerations such as 'value for money' and efficiency. Political considerations apply to powers to frame and the extent of equality of power and voice of different parties within the process. The civil sphere might be represented by the 'witness', audit or regulation function.

In effect, even within the context of process design, the case for a 'separation of spheres' seems to apply. To maximise inclusion and equality (within the process) it might be necessary to decouple the economic from the political (so that funder does not have to equal framer) and devolve power down to the lower level (recipient). It might be important to separate social (support) from civil (policing), if trust is to be built between provider and recipient. The domination of any one sphere could undermine the others. For example, an over-concern for monitoring and scrutiny could generate masses of form-filling bureaucracy that, even if intended to demonstrate value for money, could instead serve to undermine it.

Barriers and limitations

Social barriers

To maximise the accessibility and inclusiveness of distributive processes, it could prove illuminating to take the conceptualisation of social barriers set out in Chapter Four and consider how that approach might be applied. Social barriers could presumably intervene at any stage of a process, to prevent participation in any role, transaction or relationship and prevent the enactment of capabilities. It is irrelevant what income or skills a person may possess, or how willing respective parties are to engage, such barriers can still intervene to exclude them, albeit having an impact on different groups in different ways. It is important to bear in mind that it is not just recipients who may confront such obstacles. Any party involved might encounter them. In some cases it is possible to devise strategies to overcome barriers. Others are more intrinsically problematic. Social barriers, and strategies for their removal are critically important to shaping the social mainstream, who is included into it and how.

For processes to be enacted successfully, parties obviously need to be able to communicate with each other. Given their unique understanding of the barriers they face and what would – or would not – remove them, the voice of recipients needs to be heard at all levels, if goods and services are to be appropriately framed and delivered, and if they are to be empowered within the process and by its outcome. Prospective recipients need information about rights, products and opportunities. They may need physically to demonstrate that they meet criteria in the presence of assessors, in a specified place (for example, hospital appointment). Environmental barriers do not just include physical access issues. The unfamiliarity or formality of a place may be a barrier to mental health service users and others, some environments may be or feel unsafe to women, older people, or people from black or minority ethnic communities (or indeed anyone). Accessible communication methods, physical environments and transport are the 'infrastructure' requirements that enable participation in distributive processes to take place.

Removing social barriers

There is much that can be done to make the infrastructure necessary for participation more accessible. IT has opened up access to information and transaction opportunities. Effective communications, the creation of social networks and the enactment of social relationships increasingly become possible without physical co-presence being necessary, thereby circumventing environmental barriers. However, greater reliance on the internet risks introducing new barriers for those without access to it, or the skills or screen-reading software they need. While information is more available, there may be inherent limits to how much a person can absorb (a contingent limitation). A surfeit may increase the difficulties of distinguishing relevant from irrelevant factors, leading to misrecognition.

There are numerous actions that can be taken to make standard processes more accessible, thereby avoiding potentially stigmatising 'special treatment'. For example, if information leaflets are always in large print, people with visual impairment are not singled out. If all buses are wheelchair accessible, wheelchair users do not have to rely on dial-a-ride schemes or incur the added expense of using taxis, and are thereby brought within the mainstream norm. Moreover, as discussed in Chapter Four, social barriers can cut across groups. This means that changes that benefit one may also help others. To use simple language increases access for people with learning disabilities and people whose first language is not English (not to mention everyone else). Ramps and automatic doors help wheelchair users, students carrying heavy books, and people pushing prams. Flexibility in appointment times might be helpful to people with childcare responsibilities, disabled people or those with religious duties to perform. Re-shaping the mainstream in such ways does not have to be zero-sum – excluding some so that others can take their place – neither is it necessarily at all costly. Such measures also indicate how social categories based on characteristics are formed and can be reframed; how the way in which commonalities cross-sect groups shifts social divisions through realigning the boundaries between sameness and difference.

If social justice requires justification of differential treatment (Williams, 1969), the first thing to establish is whether re-shaping the mainstream removes the need for it. Of course, there may be logical and practical limits beyond which the mainstream cannot be expanded, whether because it ceases to be zero-sum, to remove barriers for the few creates barriers for the many, social meanings and processes disintegrate, or because time and resource limitations intervene. Mainstreaming must not mean reduction to the lowest common denominator, ignoring relevant differences and barriers. Rather, it is a matter of finding the highest common denominator.

Time-based limitations

Time spent on one thing in one place obviously cannot simultaneously be spent on something elsewhere – it is intrinsically limited, in turn imposing limitations on participation and choice for everyone. Commitments like childcare leave less time for other activities (like earning income), or curtail scope for flexibility. Inflexibility in the way services are provided can create barriers. The timing of assistance to a disabled person with washing and dressing can limit work opportunities and make it difficult to attend appointments to access other services (an example of incoherence between processes). Moreover, the time taken to convey and understand complex information has implications for the assessment of prospective recipients by providers and vice versa, undermining the meaningfulness of consumer choice.

One consequence of this is that geographical location can assume major importance. Constraints on travelling time, even if appropriate transport is available, limit choice in situations where physical co-presence is necessary (like schools or hospitals). Coupled with the need to generate profit or to justify expenditure of public funds there will be limits to the number of large institutions such as schools and hospitals that can exist in a given geographical area (whatever sector provides them). Bearing in mind the size of customer-base, time, cost and transport limitations, choice will be contingently limited. Yet it may be the case that choice is not always what is required (a proposition pursued in the next chapter), but rather the reassurance that local schools, hospitals and so on are all of high quality.

As previously discussed (see Chapter Four), there are intrinsic difficulties to accurate recognition and this, too, is exacerbated by lack of time. It is likely to be particularly acute in hierarchical settings, where the voice of recipients is less heard. However, in any situation where parties need to gauge with whom they are dealing, reductionist stereotyping becomes hard to avoid. This may well be two-way – the people delivering welfare goods and services can be just as much subject to it as recipients. What is important is to recognise the indicators and associated assumptions that might inadvertently be made.

As discussed in Chapter Five, 'the exchanges which lie at the heart of social inclusion have a time dimension: they require duration in social relationship – not permanence, but sufficient time for unfolding, repeated interaction to give an experiential meaning to formal commitments'(Sennett, 2000, p 283). It signals the importance of continuity in relationships between particular providers and recipients, to build trust and confidence to engage – a theme that will be further explored in the next chapter.

Distributive institutions

Distribution of welfare goods and services may involve institutions in public (State), private (market) and voluntary sector. While the (very) broad outline of stages of a distributive process might remain common to all, in other respects they differ. Each has advantages and disadvantages (Glennerster, 1997). There are features of each sector that could make a positive contribution to maximising the inclusion of diversity and empowering recipients. Market promises of choice and variety, innovation as a means of attracting more customers, the predominant importance of matching products to customer requirements, the nurturing of customer loyalty, clearly have much to recommend them (whether or not any of this is what actually happens in practice). Yet principles of targeting resources on needs rather than ability to pay, and equitable treatment of people with the same characteristics and circumstances, more usually associated with public sector provision, would also be desirable. Voluntary sector (including community) organisations may be closer to the clients and communities they serve and have a better understanding of their needs. They may have specialist skills, knowledge and contacts pertinent to particular groups. Without the need to make a profit, and avoiding (some of the) political and bureaucratic constraints common to public sector institutions, they are enabled to be flexible.

It is unsurprising that there has been a history of attempts to achieve the best of both private and public sector worlds (see Glennerster, 1997). This has encompassed the introduction of 'quasi-markets', purchaser/provider splits in healthcare services, the issuing of vouchers with which to purchase private sector provision, arrangements for funding to follow patients or students, compulsory competitive tendering and the Private Finance Initiative. Meanwhile, voluntary sector organisations are increasingly looked to as vehicles for delivering publicly funded services (cheaply). They compete alongside private sector bodies, or work in partnership with them to compete with other similarly comprised consortia.[4]

Whether these shifts have really done much to increase user choice, improve efficiency and quality, and better match provision to needs; whether the sole underlying aim has in fact been to reduce public expenditure or redirect it to expand the private sector, are matters for debate elsewhere. Certainly such initiatives have introduced new demands and associated bureaucracy for public sector organisations, surrounding procurement, tendering, contracting, service-level agreements, monitoring and evaluating, and so on. It has added to the complexity of processes and networks, expanded the number of players in the delivery chain and thereby increased the likelihood of inefficiencies creeping in. Taking just the three functions of financing, decision-making and delivery alone results in eight different possible combinations of public/private roles (Burchardt et al, 1999). Provision may be publicly funded, with decisions taken by statutory sector employees, but it is delivered by private or voluntary sector organisations. The three functions may all be contained within statutory organisations, or be carried out by individuals and private sector bodies. Individuals may fund services privately, decide what service they want and select from potential private sector providers. Different roles and stages can be carried out by different institutions in different sectors, or by individuals. Yet, it is not just that there are more functions to contend with, processes can be deconstructed into myriad stages, with the potential to be outsourced.

If the roles of the three sectors are no longer as distinct as they once were, perhaps this is because the best qualities of all have successfully been combined, or at least universally adopted. Another way of construing their increasing similarities and their increasingly complex interconnections might be to see this as an illustration of what happens at meso-level when, at a higher level, one sphere colonises another. In one scenario, the economic sphere subsumes the social as cost becomes the primary driver, and the voluntary sector starts behaving like the private sector in order to attract funds by winning contracts. Public sector delivery bodies diminish as the private sector expands.

While a multiplicity of interconnections might appear to strengthen social cohesion, complexity poses significant challenges to systems and social integration. The more complex the process, the more susceptible it is to incoherence and the greater the risk of breakdown. There are more stages, more players, more goals, constraints and institutional cultures to fit together into a coherent whole. If just one link in the elongated chain breaks, collapse ensues (a process equivalent to catastrophic rupture?). As a device for tackling inefficiency it appears primarily to increase the challenges. The journey between policy formation and delivery lengthens and clear communication – not least of all the voice of end users – risks descending into Chinese whispers. The deliberate decoupling that competitive tendering entails only requires joining them all up again.

However, to focus on the putative merits and demerits of delivery bodies from different sectors risks obscuring rather than illuminating the issues and dilemmas. Instead, it is necessary to abstract further back to identify the processes, relationships, qualities, and so on that are required to construct an inclusive model. The debate needs to be reconfigured to focus on these first and foremost.

Towards an inclusive model

Throughout this chapter and in the preceding discussion, it has been possible to identify numerous barriers or limitations relating to, generated by, or having an impact on, socio-cultural context, processes, groups and individuals. Some can be resolved by the way policy and delivery processes are designed – the criteria and indicators selected, and devolution to lower societal levels. Some have implications for the delivery of policy (access and assessment) – where, how and by whom. Others, such as resource limitations, may vary but will ultimately be unavoidable and will always be factors to take into account, whatever the policy model or thrust of policy direction. Subject to the scope to prevent or remove social barriers, design and deliver empowering, inclusive processes and build the capacity of recipients, the outside parameters of the space for diversity start to become discernible.

Given an underlying importance of ensuring the process matches the good, at one extreme a simple standardised good might be expected to give rise to a simple process with few criteria for categorisation of recipients and a straightforward assessment process. By the same token, a 'complex' good might logically engender a complex process with many variations in what is delivered, reflecting differences in characteristics or circumstances (and possible changes to them), and multiple categories and indicators for assessment. However, to respond to the complexity of identities and associated needs by complicating processes and goods risks a collapse into incoherence.

Challenges for social policy thus include how to square the circle of simplifying assessment and delivery without standardising the good to be delivered – or standardising it in such a way that it allows for multiple applications by diverse recipients – while respecting the purpose of the good. Standardised goods may fail to meet the needs or wants of diverse recipients, particularly if over-specific. The more generic needs are, the more they can be shown to be cross-setting and cross-category, the greater the freedom to use it in different ways to meet the individual's particular version of the need in question, the greater the reduction in stigma and likely improvement in social mobility.

There may also be tensions between the principle of equitable treatment for people with the same circumstances and characteristics and the principle of matching provision to meet individual needs. This may reflect some of the weaknesses inherent to social categorisation. Whereas people may be divided into groups on the basis of a shared characteristic, and it may well be that all group members experience a set of barriers or needs associated with that characteristic, as previously discussed, individuals will have many other characteristics, and therefore may experience additional barriers related to those. Policy needs to respond equitably to samenesses, but flexibly to differences. One solution may be for a two-stage process, the first much broader, perhaps matching a particular social category; the second refining the precise form the good or service will take and the manner of delivery, to suit individual requirements.

To make accurate assessments, it may be necessary to adjust the indicators used and the way in which they are interpreted. Training is likely to be important for assessors, to raise awareness of assumptions and alternative explanations. There needs to be an awareness of symbolic content and a readiness to question it, if assessments are to be accurate. Creative exploration of alternative ways of conveying information about particular qualities might open up access, while remaining faithful to the purpose of the good. However, there will be limitations to the reliability and variability of indicators. The identification of reliable indicators of behaviour is likely to prove problematic, particularly in view of the time constraints under which those delivering some forms of service are compelled to operate.

The nature of relationships between providers and recipients seem likely to be critical to promoting engagement or disengagement. Objective judgement of someone is not necessarily the best means of promoting their subjective engagement, neither is policing their behaviour, scrutinising it minutely to establish desert. Yet it is the recipient who knows best what barriers they face and what they need to address them. A more equal partnership would obviate the need for such intrusion, and get round the need for precise indicators of identity.

There are significant challenges posed by the fact that access to state welfare provision often hinges on negative attributes, like lack of income or incapacity which can lead to participation becoming stigmatising. However, as discussed earlier, by positioning welfare goods as preventative rather than as an emergency safety net for those hovering on the brink of exclusion or destitution, by making them available to meet needs we all have or can reasonably expect to have at some point, associations between welfare goods and recipient inadequacy are diffused.

There is scope to make the nature of interaction more positive, to provide encouragement to recipients and build confidence. If empowerment and choice are necessary to create a good match between good and need, and the better the match the more effective provision is, this implies better value for money. If the purpose of welfare provision is to build and sustain capacity to facilitate participation in wider distributive processes, and it is effective in achieving this purpose, it implies that dependency on some forms of welfare provision should diminish. For example effective employment services mean that people who were on benefit move more quickly into paid work (assuming it exists). If individuals are empowered to manage their own situation, professionals do not have to do it for (or to) them. This being so, a strong case can be made for the promotion of recipients' empowerment and choice on grounds of efficient expenditure of public funds (among many others).

It is important to think holistically about the process and the infrastructure required if people with diverse characteristics (attributed or otherwise) and circumstances are to participate, including how a person acquires information, makes an appointment, attends the appointment, and so on. As discussed, the transactional infrastructure, in or through which processes are conducted, can provide barriers at each stage for any of the parties involved. Institutions therefore need to take concerted action to challenge assumptions, eliminate communication, environmental and transport barriers, and maximise the flexibility of timing. This then needs to become 'business-as-usual'. To maximise inclusion, it may be possible to reframe standard (mainstream) practices so that they accommodate diversity without the need for potentially stigmatising 'special' arrangements. That is not to say the latter will never be required. It is, though, to suggest that the balance between mainstream and 'special' can be altered and that a wide mainstream with few add-ons is intrinsically more inclusive.

Promoting mobility

As discussed in Chapter Five, the systems and processes emanating from different institutions do not always dovetail at all neatly. Poor systems integration can occur between levels and across them. This implies that each institution, system and process needs to be viewed in the wider context of its neighbours, particularly if the aim is to forge and expand connections. The development of a new policy needs to be located within the wider policy context and the different aspects of people's lives and needs. The interface between policies and delivery systems needs to be dovetailed and rationalised, to avoid traps and duplication, to ensure a lack of support in one policy area does not undermine the operation of another, and to maximise social mobility. The structural (institutional) integration of services might be one solution, although there are risks, including that misrecognition could result in 'over-conflation'. For example, although health and social care needs may often go together, it should not be assumed that this will always be the case, that experts in one service are necessarily expert in the other, or that institutional cultures will easily align and processes will be simplified. There may even be fears that integrating those particular services could extend the reach of medical power into other aspects of people's lives. The desirability of strategic coherence between services meeting different needs is not necessarily an argument for fully integrating them into one institutional structure. It remains important to recognise where separation remains appropriate. Depending on the nature of the interface between needs and services, other models and approaches may be indicated (for example, one-stop-shops).

It is not just a matter of deconstructing one process to identify barriers: it is necessary to understand objectives and processes leading to the point of interface from the perspectives of all involved. Thinking back to discussion of network ties (Chapter Five), this may be a matter of enabling recipients to forge new ties on grounds of mutually-enriching difference. If connections are to be successful, awareness is needed of the objectives, needs and constraints pertaining to all actors. Objectives will not necessarily be the same, but they have to be compatible. The needs of one party may be met by the resources of the other. Each may be engaged in separate processes that need to dovetail to allow for transferral. For example, a person who is claiming benefit, unemployed and actively seeking work needs to be able to transfer from that system into work. An employer needs to reach people to fill vacancies through a recruitment process. Both processes need to be considered, and both parties may well need support around the point of transition. Indeed, insufficient attention to smoothing the transition from one service to another, as required by new settings and situations, could provoke major barriers to social mobility, regardless of the merits of each in their own right.

Social mobility is necessary if people are to be enabled to move between settings, exercise autonomy and choice. Settings may be contemporaneous – work, home, leisure, geographical areas – or life-cycle related and connected to age. Policy that is inappropriately 'setting specific' (because needs traverse settings) reduces mobility and scope for inclusion into new settings. If distribution is incapacity-specific, this militates against capacity-building, by requiring the affirmation of negative attributes, contrary to needs for self-esteem. Instead of measuring incapacity – a deficit model – it would be considerably less stigmatising to focus on developing potential and removing barriers to the realisation of capabilities.

The relevant (to the policy issue) features of geographical or spatially-defined areas need to be ascertained. These might include demographic profile, wealth levels, labour market composition, cultural traditions, rurality and transport infrastructure. Inequalities, commonalities and differences between areas can then be identified, indicating where one and the same approach is required, and where different approaches will be needed to equivalise access or outcomes. This could signal what policy, or aspects of policy, need to be devolved downwards. Issues around portability, for example of social care packages, or the avoidance of 'post-code lotteries' (and associated inequalities), might suggest the appropriate level for decision-making.

Potential for connections to new networks may need to be identified and exploited. Barriers unnecessarily preventing access or blocking mobility therefore have to be removed. Policy might also be proactive in promoting connections with new networks and processes, perhaps through events bringing together different parties, or through supporting trial or taster sessions to build the confidence of both. Where a move from one setting to another is to be facilitated, or existing links preserved, the socio-cultural context, processes and individual capacity associated with each may need to be adjusted. To preserve, expand or join new networks, requires the melding of the objectives, needs and constraints of one party with those of another. It necessitates intervention into the processes of the other. An understanding of those processes – and the identification of scope for adjustment – will hence be beneficial.

Support for individuals

Although there is much that can be done to empower recipients by designing and delivering policy as described, unless they have the desire, the capacity and the skills to assume responsibilities within the process, empowerment will remain a token gesture. Capacity-building may therefore be necessary if recipients are to play an active part within the process of welfare design and delivery (to have an input to framing, self-managing, or making choices) as well as beyond. Indeed, while welfare provision contributes to capacity-building for wider participation, capacity-building to participate actively in the process of welfare provision may also be necessary, and have wider application.

Support can be divided into interlinked types. There may be capacity-building in the form of training to give people new skills, or enhance existing ones. Although acquiring skills can in itself boost confidence, without some degree of confidence beforehand in the quality of programmes and capacity to benefit from them, opportunities to acquire skills may not be pursued. The removal of barriers goes in tandem with building confidence. Mechanisms include peer support, mentoring, independent advocacy and access to expert (but accessible) advice and information. Policy therefore needs to focus both on strengthening 'strong' ties with peer group networks as well as opening up access to new, different networks (see Chapter Five), and the former might facilitate the latter. Trial runs in a new setting, to try out new skills, demonstrate appropriate behaviour and build trust, might also serve to boost confidence. It may not just be a matter of strengthening or developing new networks but of maintaining those that people already have, for example when they go into hospital or care home.

The rough summary of an inclusive approach shown in Table 6.1 could be applied to any welfare strategy or policy initiative and used for identifying measures to increase inclusivity and empowerment. Although the sorts of actions proposed are familiar to particular areas of policy, taken as an overall approach there are some significant implications for policy design and delivery, both at an overall strategic level, and with regard to individual policy initiatives. An example of how this approach might be applied to strategy is given in Table 6.2, which summarises what the implications appear to be for health service strategy.

Table 6.1 An inclusive policy framework

	Actions
Socio-cultural context	
	Awareness and accommodation of different objectives and processes Focus on wider participation, transition and connection points Geographical differences and implications for devolution assessed Explore scope to widen the mainstream
Process	
Framing	User need, aspirations and potential barriers as starting point for analysis of commonality and difference Ensure moral justification Remove unnecessary setting and characteristic-specific criteria Involve external stakeholders, particularly recipients Carry out equality impact assessments Wherever possible devolve framing to recipients to achieve a precise match with individual needs
Access	'One-stop-shop' or service integration models – common point of access for various services to meet a likely cluster of needs Information to prospective users about what to expect in advance Removal of barriers in transactional infrastructure
Assessment	Training for assessors to challenge stereotypes and facilitate power shifts Social category (structural) and individual (personal) Quality of face-to-face interaction
Outcomes	Monitor and evaluate against standards and targets Feedback from recipients to inform reframing Scope for recipients to challenge outcome
Support to individuals	
	Quality of relationship with provider Training Tasters/ Trials Peer group support Advice services Independent advocacy Mentoring

Table 6.2 Implications for health-care strategy

	Actions	Implications
Socio-cultural context		
	Different objectives and processes accommodated	Acknowledgement of different objectives for using healthcare services. Interaction with other policies and processes, such as benefits, childcare, housing, transport, education, or community care, analysed and accommodated to avoid traps and inequities.
	Focus on wider participation, transition, connection points	Existing connections preserved, with employers, education, family and community, and proactively created or re-established where unavoidably broken, for example, interface with community care to prevent bed-blocking.
	Geographical differences and devolution	Links between ill-health and poverty – maybe geographical. concentrations. Access to comprehensive, high quality services required throughout (avoidance of 'post-code lotteries'), but different actions may be necessary to achieve this in different locations.
Process		
Framing	Need as basis for analysis of commonality and difference	Services and resource allocations driven by health needs not social categories or geographical location where un-related to need.
	Ensure moral justification	A service for all; everyone likely to need it at some point.
	Remove unnecessary setting and characteristic-specific criteria	Needs and risks may differ by setting (certain types of work) or characteristic (for example, age); others remain constant – structure of services needs to reflect this to avoid gaps and traps (for example, between paediatric and adult provision).
	Involve external stakeholders, particularly recipients	Scope for patients/prospective patients to have an input to health service design and delivery.
	Identify barriers and pre-empt	Carry out equality impact assessments at the outset.
	Devolution of framing to recipients	Professionals advise and present options, provide information to develop patient medical expertise. Patients empowered to take decisions and self-manage.
Access	Removal of barriers in transactional infrastructure	Accessibility of premises and transport, information in different formats, availability of interpreters, avoidance of jargon, flexibility in appointment times as standard.
	'One-stop-shop' models	Access to comprehensive healthcare in one location; siting health services with others; locating other services within health service environments, for example, employment advisers in GP surgeries.
	Advance information to prospective users	Information on service procedures and personnel, routines, and so on.

	Actions	Implications
Assessment	Training for assessors	Not just medical training, also race and disability awareness, links to other services, information giving, how to facilitate patient empowerment, avoidance of unnecessary intrusion. Importance of not making assumptions about quality of life and capacity, based on negative cultural attitudes concerning certain characteristics.
	Social category and individual	Identification of needs associated with social category but also skills to identify individual combinations or needs and flexibility to respond. Avoidance of stereotyping, including assumptions about quality of life.
	Quality of face-to-face interaction	Trust particularly important given personal nature of service. In terms of who treats the patient, continuity likely to be important; cultural or gender factors.
Outcomes	Monitor and evaluate against standards and targets	Target system well established, but to what extent do they reflect the key concerns of patients? Do they provide meaningful information?
	Feed-back from recipients to inform framing	Systems are set up for obtaining and using feedback from patients.
	Scope for recipients to challenge outcome	Complaints procedures, independent reviews, second opinions.
Support to individuals		
	Training	Expert Patient Programmes, Condition Management Programmes so that the recipient has the knowledge and skills to manage their own condition.
	Tasters/Trials	Opportunities to visit hospitals/wards before admittance? Try different GPs?
	Peer group support	Mechanisms to promote communication between people with the same medical condition, or using the same hospital/GP practice. Alcoholics Anonymous model? Role of voluntary sector?
	Advice services	Independent expert advice is made available.
	Independent advocacy	Needs to be widely available (currently mostly confined to mental health field).
	Mentoring	For people with chronic health conditions by people with the same condition.

Conclusion

This chapter has attempted to apply concepts and insights discussed in earlier chapters to the design and delivery of welfare goods in order to reveal how they could best promote inclusive equality. The primary focus has been on the nature of the distributive processes; a recurrent theme throughout the book. To develop the emerging inclusive model still further, the next chapter places under the spotlight the interactions between front-line professionals and people using services, considers how their motivations might be understood and accommodated, and how positive, productive relationships might best be forged.

Notes

[1] See, for example, www.designcouncil.org.uk/about-design/types-of-design/service-design/.

[2] See, for example, coverage of assessments of disabled people carried out by Atos, www.guardian.co.uk/society/2013/apr/17/atos-apologises-long-term-sick.

[3] The concept of framing used here refers to the formal structuring of a process and associated relationships. It bears no similarity to Goffman's (1974) exposition of 'frame analysis', which broadly concerns the analysis of 'strips of activity', and how they can be 'keyed', understood and experienced.

[4] For example, see list of preferred bidders for delivery of the Work Programme, comprised of 16 private sector and two voluntary sector organisations as prime contractors. Amongst the subcontractors there are 289 voluntary sector organisations.

SEVEN

Relationships and identity

Introduction

This chapter explores how incentives or disincentives to engagement can arise due to the way policy is delivered. What occurs at the point of face-to-face interaction is a key factor to inclusion. Without an appreciation of wider needs beyond the immediate focus, how interaction may be experienced, and the threats it can pose, it is difficult to know how to deliver processes in ways that will promote engagement. Without understanding differing objectives and motivations for engagement, parties may pull in different directions, jeopardising the coherence of the process. No matter how coherently structured a process may be, or how positive the intentions of policy-makers, it can fall apart at the point of face-to-face enactment.

Chapter Two suggested that intangible goods like self-respect and power might be better viewed as qualities of relationships rather than goods that can be distributed. Chapter Three explored how needs can take the form of human motivations and how interacting with others is likely to be required, to a greater or lesser extent, in order to meet such needs. Motivations are not just generated by the imperative of bodily survival. They also encompass universal or 'species needs' to belong, for self-esteem and self-actualisation (Maslow, 1943); for work as 'purposive interaction', for meaningful action and to realise potential (distilled from Marxian accounts); for the avoidance of harm (or promotion of well-being); and for autonomy (Doyal and Gough, 1991). Furthermore, theory explored earlier proposed that identity is constructed through socialisation (Chapter Four). It is reflected back through 'dialogical relations with others' (Taylor, 1992, p 34). The nature of interaction should therefore have profound implications for how an individual feels about themselves and the degree to which needs as motivations are fulfilled.

If the intention is that policy should promote engagement, participation and social inclusion, the way in which it is delivered must surely take human motivations into account. If engagement requires the affirmation of incapacity or inadequacy, not only could it adversely affect how recipients feel about themselves, it could also affect how recipients are viewed by others in subsequent transactions. Wherever possible, interactions that underline incapacity, invade privacy, or compromise autonomy, seem likely to be avoided. If welfare provision is broadly intended to build capacity, and to access resources, requires affirmation of incapacity, this obviously poses significant challenges.

Of course, it could be argued that making engagement an unpleasant experience helps to demonstrate the extent of need. If so this is misguided. It seems more than a little counterproductive to promote inclusion by providing disincentives to approach the first hurdle. To seek to empower by disempowering, to build capacity by underlining its absence and destroying confidence in the process, is not the obvious recipe for success.

As previously, the intention is to provide an ideal model to enable deconstruction and analysis – not a literal, empirical description of all social relationships, needs and behaviours.

Transactional needs

Needs and objectives

People's objectives will obviously be extremely variable, depending on individual history and circumstances, socio-cultural pressures and physiological and psychological particularities. Nonetheless, it is possible and useful to explore further what in generic terms might steer decisions to engage in, or disengage from, social processes and relationships. The following describes requirements of the process as much as its outcome.

If it is indeed the case that individual identity is formulated through interaction with the wider environment, there are likely to be direct and indirect social pressures to adhere to the dominant socio-cultural paradigm (see Chapter Five). Micro-level actors may be motivated to acquire goods (economic objectives), and/or by concern for the well-being of family members or fellow citizens (social objectives). Behaviours may be steered by the desire to exert power over others, a commitment to religious beliefs and codes, and by rights and obligations.

People may behave as self-interested actors, calculating costs against benefits to ascertain the most personally advantageous course of action, as rational choice theory emanating from field of microeconomics would suggest. Alternatively, their behaviours may be more instinctively, or emotionally, driven. They may be knights, knaves, pawns or queens (le Grand, 2003) – broadly representative of altruistic, self-interested, passive or proactive roles or motivations respectively. Parties to an interaction may be capable of conforming to any one of these on different occasions, in response to different stimuli or settings. The nature of their interaction may be characterised by each assuming a different role. Alternatively, they may interact as peers; both assuming proactive 'queen-like' roles as they work together towards a shared goal.

The balance between objectives, and the style of relationship engaged in, may vary. It may be contingent on the context in which individuals find themselves, or in which they understand themselves to be. If relationships with others are to be sustained, there needs to be some degree of compatibility between both parties' objectives and understandings of situations. Leeway may be needed for adjustment to synchronise expectations and adopt appropriate styles of interaction. Failure to do so, coupled with imbalances in power and in scope for need satisfaction may jeopardise the cohesion of the relationship.

Personality integration

Building on Lockwood's approach (1992), inclusion may not just be contingent on systems and social integration, but also what could be termed 'personality integration'. Certain factors might strengthen the integrity of the personality while others threaten its disintegration (another way of conceptualising the damaging effects of oppression), acting respectively as incentives or disincentives to engagement. Human motivations for self-esteem, respect and self-actualisation (for example) can be construed as deriving from the imperative to strengthen personality integration, prevent stress and (implicitly) promote good mental health. The extent to which needs are met through the manner in which a distributive process is enacted, as much as by its likely outcome, defines the quality of transactions, the strength of the relationship ties, their impact on identity and hence on motivation to engage.

It seems obvious that the integrity of the personality, confidence and self-esteem will be enhanced by interactions that reflect back positive affirmation (Turner, 2002). To this Turner (2002) adds the gratification of gaining something ('profitable exchange pay-offs'), feelings of being included in the group (Maslow's 'belonging' – to be part of the 'interpersonal flow'); being able to trust the other's sincerity and predict what will happen; and reassurance or endorsement that experiences are commonly held, understandings are shared and all is as it appears (Maslow's 'safety and security' or 'facticity'[1] in Turner's terms). A further factor may be feeling that you have enough control or power to preserve and express autonomy (as per one of Doyal and Gough's 1991 basic needs). If present, these contribute to the positive strengthening of the integrity of the personality and of the relationship, and confidence in the environment (what Giddens terms 'ontological security'). If absent, disincentives to engage will be greater.

There is more to consider. Some situations provoke threats to what Goffman refers to as 'face':[2] 'an image of self delineated in terms of approved social attributes' (1967, p 3). The preservation of 'face' could be described as another transactional need, perhaps the minimum requirement of 'positive affirmation of self'. It may be a means of manipulating behaviour, for example where peer groups exert pressure to do something and declining would mean losing face. More generally, the aim is to avoid becoming embarrassed or flustered: 'to appear flustered, in our society at least, is considered evidence of weakness, inferiority, low status, moral guilt, defeat, and other unenviable attributes' (Goffman 1967, pp 101, 102). It is evidence of incoherence or dissonance – perhaps a form of micro-level rupture – that a person needs to remedy.

There are unwritten rules about status and the degree of familiarity it is appropriate to show. Adherence to these is likely to be another transactional need. Subordinates are generally expected to show greater deference to superordinates, while convention permits the latter to treat the former with greater familiarity (Goffman, 1967). There is a double edge to deference. If it is expressed by the anticipation of needs based on untested assumption (men spontaneously opening doors for women is a classic example) no matter how positive the intention, it can be experienced as disempowering; as confirming the helplessness and inferior status of the recipient. Over-familiarity from strangers, which may be meant as friendliness, can be experienced as disrespectful. This begins to explain why informality is not always the way to diffuse tensions but may instead be received as a failure to take seriously the feelings of others (demonstrating a lack of 'facticity'). The action and the response to it result from misrecognition.

To avoid embarrassment and miscommunication requires not only that the parties understand such expressions of status, what their status is and what consequently is appropriate, they also need to adhere to the 'rituals of interaction' – a micro-level manifestation of ritual as 'society's strongest cement, its very chemistry of inclusion' (Sennett, 2000, p 279). This entails reading and emitting correct behavioural cues such as facial expressions, eye contact, body language, tone of voice and conversational pauses: 'The ultimate behavioral materials are the glances, gestures, positionings, and verbal statements that people continuously feed into the situation, whether intended or not' (Goffman, 1967, p 1).

To get these wrong can be destructive. As noted in Chapter Four, to use a tone of voice when talking to an adult that might be more fitting when conversing with a child will be received as infantilisation (Thompson, 1998), irrespective of the content of what is said. To use an abrupt tone may convey disrespect, failure to make eye contact may exclude or signal lack of interest, while too close a physical proximity might feel invasive or threatening. However, people from different cultures may not just speak another language, they may use different body language, too, bringing risks of misunderstanding and misrecognition of another kind.

Degrees of proximity

Issues of proximity do not just concern physical but also psychological matters. If relationships are to be unthreatening and disincentives to participate avoided, expectations need to be shared about how far into private territory it is acceptable for another to stray. Understanding of how 'psychic preserves' may inadvertently be breached and 'personal-territory contingencies' (Goffman, 1983) occur is clearly important. This indicates, perhaps counterintuitively, that for engagement to be carried out successfully, sometimes the maintenance of distance is required.

It has been suggested (Chapter Five) that it is not enough technically to be included, people need to feel 'subjectively included'. Yet, this should not be taken to imply that inclusion requires relationships to be based on emotional connection: 'Although humans are social...they have never been emotional junkies who seek deep, personal contact with all others in all social relations' (Turner, 2002, p 3). To attempt to forge such connections with everyone would in all likelihood be experienced as profoundly inappropriate and intrusive, constituting a disincentive to engage. To claim, as some have that emotions are social glue (Turner, 2002, discussing Durkheim), is to overlook the possibility that they can repel (and expel) as much as attract. A formal, objective style of engagement may, in some situations, be more cohesive.

As discussed in Chapter Five, it may not just be inappropriate, it can obviously be risky to make an emotional investment in people who are unfamiliar. Even if reciprocated, the tie and the 'personal territory' of both parties are vulnerable to rupture. It ceases to be a strong tie and could become a cause of alienation rather than attachment. The likelihood of this may be increased by asymmetry in emotional investment. The party with less to lose has fewer constraints on transgression. For obvious reasons, symmetry is likely to be particularly important in relationships based on emotional intensity.

Shared understandings about status, degrees of familiarity or formality, closeness or distance, all seem to constitute additional transactional needs. Additionally, an awareness of body language and its interpretation is intrinsic to the successful performance of identity (the conceptualising of identity as performative arises in queer theory, discussed in Chapter Four). Notions of reciprocity and symmetry seem likely to be consistent features of positive social relationships – further manifestations of principles of inclusive equality as equilibrium. Whether symmetry has to imply a mirror image is debatable. It could infer that each party contributes something of different but equal value, that a need or offer on one side is balanced by a different need or offer on the other. Each may be 'tied in' to the relationship by different means but to the same extent: symmetry is differently constituted but ultimately equivalence prevails.

The imperative to satisfy transactional needs can be expected to drive the actions of all involved in the process. While no relationship will necessarily meet all such needs, or necessarily the same needs of each party, social relationships seem likely to be weaker where there is a significant imbalance between the two.

Characteristics

Salience and levels

In order to meet transactional needs and in view of the potential damage incurred by failure to do so, it becomes useful to conceptualise what, in generic terms, comprises a 'self'. Some interactions may be more risky than others, depending on the importance attributed to the characteristics under challenge. As previously discussed (Chapter Four) there are multiple aspects to identity. It seems plausible that some will have more salience than others: 'When self is conceptualized as having multiple identities, these identities are typically seen as ordered into hierarchies of prominence and salience' (Turner, 2002, p 100). Some may be more foundational to identity; others more dispensable.

As previously discussed, characteristics can assume meaning and significance subject to their context. Some come to the fore; others recede or are actively negated. Some have value in one context, but are irrelevant, even negative, in another. Characteristics can even be created by context, as in the social model of disability, or by discourse, as in postmodernist theory. They may be construed as personal, as in the medical model. They might also be described in terms of being, doing and having.

Some aspects of personal identity can be 'adjusted' even if the context is held constant. Certain characteristics are malleable, some removable, others fixed, irrespective of context or capacity-building. If the context changes, the significance of a characteristic may also change, even if the characteristic itself does not. For example, the removal of social barriers means that a person with an impairment ceases to experience disability. The impairment remains, but assumes insignificance (see Chapter Four). However, even if contexts change, it is possible that certain characteristics will consistently dominate and be accorded much the same value and significance in all settings (Turner, 2002).

Salience is thus not only contingent on external context or a given transaction. It is also felt by the individual according to the characteristic's importance for self-image and the integrity of their personality (see Turner, 2002). The identity might be rooted in dominant cultural norms, expectations and values. It might have levels of sorts, with an overarching framework of distilled experiences or values, and intense emotions about the self and how one should be treated which hold firm in any situation. Other feelings might be situation specific or role specific (Turner, 2002). These, too, might be intense, depending on past experience of similar situations or how much sense of self and self-esteem is vested in that role.

No matter how conceived, different aspects of personality need to be broadly consistent. Narratives need to be found to explain apparent inconsistencies, if they are to integrate. However, there is scope for what Turner refers to as 'slippage' between more foundational aspects of 'core self' and more fluid elements. A person may see her/himself as essentially highly competent (and need others to reflect this back), but have no problem accepting their incompetence in a particular situation, confronted with an unfamiliar, atypical task that they would not be expected to perform well.

Sometimes failure to recognise the whole person is detrimental. Capacities, needs or barriers associated with an unacknowledged characteristic impede participation. However, to focus narrowly on a particular aspect of identity, creating distance between it and the whole person, might be a positive thing to do in certain situations. S/he may be able (and need) to distance their core self from an otherwise challenging experience. Sometimes the scope for slippage 'provides insulation against disconfirmation of core self, while potentially offering cognitive and emotional room for defensive strategies to protect the core' (Turner, 2002, p 102). If that ceases to be possible, the nuclear option is rupture, though not necessarily to the sense of self; instead taking the form of rejection of the unsuccessful method of meeting transactional needs that has effectively rejected you, wholesale disengagement and the pursuit of alternative – perhaps illegitimate – means of achieving status and self-esteem. In effect, the personality has mechanisms for accommodating diverse aspects of identity and for keeping itself on an even keel.

Clashes and mismatches

When situations arise which confound culturally derived expectations, the resulting dissonance needs to be worked through. If a satisfactory narrative cannot be constructed within those terms, attitudes and frames of reference need to shift. Contradictions in cultural expectations about different aspects of identity can result in one aspect effectively negating another. If women are expected to be carers and disabled people are expected to be cared for, a disabled mother might find that: 'impairment can *negate* another aspect of *identity*, namely gender and motherhood' (Zappone, 2003, p 135, emphasis in original). For a person with supposedly subordinate characteristics (such as being female, disabled, or from a black or minority ethnic background) to occupy a superordinate role exposes and challenges assumptions: 'as policy analysts and practitioners we need to see the subjects of oppression/subordination, at least potentially, as also and simultaneously constituted in positions of dominance/power' (Lewis, 2002, p 158). In a sense, culturally-induced difference or sameness blindness (see Chapter Two) is exposed. The dissonance created by subconscious, mutually exclusive assumptions flushes them out into full view.

Mismatches between the levels of self each party reveals in an interaction may heighten the risk of harmful encroachment into 'personal territory'. For example, if both are strangers, yet only one is required to reveal private, potentially embarrassing, information about her/himself, a mismatch of levels of identity is occurring. Alternatively, invasion of another's 'core self' can be inadvertent, perhaps because an aspect of it is not recognised and respected as such, causing humiliation, disorientation, or oppression, and hence, once more, disincentives to engage.

Relationship properties

Discussion of transactional needs and threats to identity has suggested a number of qualities that social relationships should have (and pitfalls to avoid) if they are to promote engagement. There would appear to be numerous factors to consider, and different situations may call for different approaches. An emotional basis to a social relationship is appropriate in some circumstances, a more pragmatic basis in others, particularly where engagement with an unfamiliar group, process or network is indicated. The possibility that supposedly 'strong' ties held together by emotional intensity might on occasion provide disincentives to engagement, while 'weak' ties devoid of emotional content may be more successful, suggests that these tags are misleading. What is strong or weak is contingent on with whom the relationship is and its purpose.

The social exclusion literature drew attention to different types of relationship and their respective qualities: 'contract' (market economy) relationships are branded as impersonal, pragmatic and goal driven, while 'compact' (social) relationships are about interdependence, mutuality, solidarity and collective empowerment' (Stewart, 2000). Yet neither contract nor compact relationships necessarily capture all that requires to be considered when designing and enacting processes linking prospective recipients to welfare institutions, or thence onwards to engagement with new processes and networks. Furthermore, relationships associated with public sector welfare providers cannot be assumed to be 'compact' and those with private sector providers will not necessarily always be 'contract'.

Competition for access to public services may be fierce, though the rationale for the way in which resources are distributed may not be obvious to outsiders. There is nothing to say that relationships between those delivering and those receiving services will be distinguished by the qualities Stewart describes, and evidence in Chapter Three showed that they could be experienced as demeaning and dehumanising. Cooperation with colleagues may be necessary for a firm to compete effectively with others. Much time and money is devoted by private sector businesses to advertising that aims to forge emotional connections to products, whether to nurture loyalty to a particular brand or company or to convey that possessing a particular product will bring high social status and self-esteem. According to Sennett cooperation can be used to form the ground-rules within which competition will ensue; a 'combination of cooperation and competition appears in economic markets, in electoral politics and in diplomatic negotiations' (2012, p 5).

It therefore does not appear safe to ascribe particular types of relationship to the sector of organisation with which they happen to be. As in the previous chapter, it might make sense to focus on the properties of relationships that are most likely to promote engagement. It is also worth noting that, as discussed in the preceding chapter, there are different functions to be found within distributive processes. An objective, impersonal approach might be entirely appropriate when it comes to an independent audit or review, when it might be problematic if this characterised face-to-face relationships between providers and recipients.

A range of properties can be extracted from preceding discussions that, in theory, could cluster together in different ways. For the sake of convenience and clarity, they are summarised and loosely grouped in Table 7.1. Although presented as opposites, it is not always the case that those that appear on one side will always be positive and on the other negative. Crucially it depends on the purpose of the relationship. Some may be an entirely necessary part of a distributive process even if they are not all primarily concerned to promote engagement. Moreover, it seems likely, perhaps logical, that some properties will go together, and some will be improbable companions or mutually exclusive.

Reflecting back on discussion of human motivations and incentives for engagement, to a considerable extent those grouped under D seem obviously and normatively likely to discourage while with those grouped under C the converse applies. Bearing in mind earlier discussion on proximity, whether A or B is most likely to be successful seems less clear cut. There are other reasons why certainty regarding these is more difficult.

A recurrent theme of debate has been the need to make the balance of power within a relationship more equal. However, is that always desirable – from either perspective? Would asymmetry not be appropriate in situations where a person needs and wants protection, or others need protecting from her/him? Is coercion not sometimes necessary to prevent destructive behaviours and to the extent that anarchy (social disintegration) is the alterative? While destructive behavior might well indicate a 'catastrophic rupture' of relations between the individual and the mainstream, and removing their power to destroy does not equate to empowering them to behave constructively, at the extreme it becomes necessary to protect others. However, if action stops there, it is likely to strengthen oppositional dynamics, underlining exclusion, possibly in a literal sense in the form of incarceration. The greater the distance from the mainstream, the stronger the need to find ways of promoting engagement and inclusion. This suggests that the process of

Table 7.1 Component properties of relationships

Cluster one: degrees of distance	
A: Distant	***B: Close***
Objective	Subjective
Impersonal	Personal
Formal	Informal, familiarity
Rational, pragmatic	Emotion or faith-based
Personal gain	Collective gain
Disempowerment	Empowerment
Paternalist	Peer-based
Competitive	Collaborative
Conditional	Unconditional
Cluster two: degrees of security	
C: Secure	***D: Insecure***
Predictable	Unpredictable
Overt objectives	Covert objectives
Stable	Unstable
Informed	Uninformed
Trusted	Distrusted
Good communication	Poor communication
Voluntary	Coerced
Uninvasive	Intrusive
Confident	Threatening
Positive affirmation of self	Affirmation of incapacity, inadequacy
Focus on sameness, group membership	Focus on difference
Scope for 'slippage'	Whole person

engagement might go through different phases and that relationships might need to evolve accordingly.

Symmetry might also imply parity in terms of degrees of proximity, objectivity and intrusion permitted. However, are there not risks that the judgement of professionals might be clouded, or their personal territory breached, by subjectivity, proximity and emotional attachment? Do not medical professionals or benefit assessors sometimes need to intrude into privacy, to match the good to the need and to ensure accurate recognition? First, there may be distinctions to draw between the empathy needed to understand the recipient's perspective and emotional attachment. Second, intrusion may to some extent be obviated, if it is left to recipients to make the more detailed refinement of the good according to their individual requirements. Alternatively, intrusion may not be problematic where the recipient trusts the provider and accepts the need for it.

A focus on personal gain may mean ruthlessly discounting the needs and desires of others, or take the more positive form of 'self-help'. Collective gain, or promoting the gain of others, may spell attempts at altruistic empowerment, or paternalism. Altruistic behaviours can still generate personal gain in the form of a positive self-image. Through helping others, the helper may gain self-esteem and a sense of usefulness. However, positive affirmation of their identity could become contingent upon, and increase proportionately to, the neediness of others, reinforcing power asymmetry in the relationship. Formality might be appropriate in an institutional but not a social setting, perhaps because providers and recipients do not know each other and an overly-familiar approach would be experienced as disrespectful. However, formal does not have to mean unfriendly. Objective does not have to mean unempathetic.

This seems to suggest that while properties may be generic or universal, some in particular have the potential to be positive or negative. It might depend on the objective for interaction (not that social interactions in general are always in pursuit of a clearly formed objective) and the degree of pre-existing disengagement. To promote engagement and inclusion without enforcement, relationships that enable human motivations – for self-esteem, autonomy and so on – are indicated (broadly, clusters B and C). Of course, not all forms of interaction have that objective. Some, for example, are concerned with policing. A different cluster of properties would, entirely appropriately, be required. To ensure equitable treatment, or for consistent assessment against a benchmark, a formal, distant, objective stance is likely to be required. In such situations, the power relationship between the assessor and assessed is intrinsically asymmetrical. Yet, unless (for some perverse reason) the aim is to promote the other party's lasting disengagement, it is still necessary to take account of the range of their transactional needs and find ways to accommodate them, if not at the time then through subsequent action as re-engagement occurs and the relationship evolves.

There are various factors that might determine whether the nature of the interaction is 'just'. Echoing discussion in Chapter Two (on the need for balance between distributive principles), it is possible that a property that starts off positive, when carried to extremes becomes negative. Caring for others is a normatively positive quality, yet taken too far risks being transformed into stifling over-protection or paternalism. A further possibility (also illustrated by this example) concerns the different perspectives of the two parties: the gap between what is intended and how it is received, indicating the importance of good two-way communication. Yet perhaps most important is what the nature of interaction conveys about understandings and expectations of the other party and the purpose of the interaction, all of which might be signalled by the immediate context. Injustice occurs when would-be queens are treated as if they were knaves, or when knaves are treated as if they were knights. Once again, accurate recognition appears to be critical to justice.

Two approaches to inclusion

Coercion and conditionality

The obvious dilemma for providers of welfare goods and services is that they may well have two, ostensibly incompatible, objectives. They both want to promote engagement/inclusion and to 'police' – to ensure desert, equitable treatment and the appropriate expenditure of resources. How is this circle to be squared?

Taking a traditional view of equality in terms of resources, capacity, knowledge and skills, and provider objectives such as to move people from welfare to work, to educate, or to promote good health, the relationship between provider and recipient will be very unequal. Asymmetries may also exist with regard to urgency of their respective needs, decision-making powers and ease of exit from the relationship. Inequality may be expected to exist between recipients' starting points and where they aim to be by the end of the process. Goods such as healthcare services and education become 'embodied' in the recipient, to use Bourdieu's terminology (1997), leaving the recipient better resourced. This starts to elaborate on the nature of shifts that can occur during the process, as engagement is strengthened and capacity is built.

The traditional – and in some places, still very current – process of moving people from disengagement to engagement casts the relationship qualities that it has been suggested are usually propitious to engagement as entirely counter-productive to achieving positive changes to an individual's capacity or behaviour. Recipients need to be forced out of their comfort zone, focus on their inadequacy (a deficit model), and surrender all power and initiative to the professionals.

Directive action is necessary to mend the rupture between individuals, groups or neighbourhoods and the social mainstream. Coercion and conditionality, where the only way to meet even basic needs becomes adherence to socially approved behaviours, become necessary to justify public expenditure. They are further justified as the only means of 'helping' the excluded back on the path to inclusion. Intrusion into privacy and surveillance of behaviours naturally follow, transforming the relationship from one of support to one of police and policed, exacerbating inequalities between the two parties. The disempowerment of recipients is affirmed and reinforced, along with their exclusion.

The degree of state scrutiny – of behaviours, morals, resources – experienced by benefit claimants, ex-offenders, refugees, drug addicts, mental health service users, to name just some possible groups, is likely to be particularly high in situations where they are seeking to access public resources or are deemed (or can be presented as) a potential threat, to themselves or to others. While participation in social relationships is generally the means to inclusion, this underlines that some relationships can be indicative of exclusion, or risk of exclusion. It could persuasively be argued that relationships with public service providers are if anything intensified when the risk of exclusion is greatest. Thus, intensive and restrictive relationships with public service providers, and no relationship with them, can both indicate risk of exclusion.

Although 'welfare dependency' usually implies the stagnation of a life on benefits, it might equally apply to passive dependency on teachers or doctors. In all cases, this may be far from what recipients (or providers for that matter) would choose and they may actively resist, prompting a response of further coercion, as ever-widening distance is created between the two parties. The question is whether the inequalities that appear inherent to such relationships leave either party any choice. The answer is that the extent of inequality between them is not inevitable. It follows that neither are the dynamics of demand/ capitulation or resistance/ coercion.

Co-production

A different way of constructing the relationship exists. First, both parties have transactional needs and failure to meet them will always create pressures to disengage. Each is resourced with different types of knowledge, both essential to success. Recipients will be much better placed to define their own situation, what they need, what they would like to achieve, what stops them and what could be done about it.

Professionals might have expert knowledge as doctors, teachers or recruitment specialists. They are well-placed to advise on what resources and options might be available. Working together they refine a vision of the intended outcome. Mixing different types of knowledge and experience enhances the likelihood of creativity in finding solutions. The process becomes one of co-production. As Cahn observes 'without labor from the intended beneficiaries, nothing that professionals do can really work' (2000, p 26).

Of course, it is possible that recipients do not want to work, learn or change their lifestyle to become healthy. Why might this be? Is it really their goal to be poor and unhealthy? Or does fear (or past experience) of failure deter them from trying? Is resistance merely a natural response to enforcement – a response that in other situations (or possibly the same ones) enables us to challenge dictatorship and injustice? If transactional needs include positive affirmation of self, the preservation of 'face', some degree of control, respect for 'personal territory' and a need to maintain the integrity of the personality, then to attempt to engage on any other basis seems destined not to succeed. The shift from an identity and self-esteem defined by opposition to one defined by collaboration entails some reframing, building confidence that effort can bring success, not just affirm failure. It first, though, means taking seriously the very real barriers to engagement that people confront which have nothing to do with their personal capacity and which lie beyond their ability to remove.

Co-production can be defined as 'a partnership between citizens and public services to achieve a valued outcome' (Horne and Shirley, 2009, p 3). According to Boyle and Harris 'Co-production means delivering public services in an equal and reciprocal relationship between professionals, people using services, their families and their neighbours. Where activities are co-produced in this way, both services and neighbourhoods become far more effective agents of change.' (2009, p11).[3] It can be a means of developing policy and strategy, a method of community development and an approach to formulating personalised services, such as care packages.[4] The service provider and recipient may not be peers. However, in many respects this is an equal partnership. The focus is on defining outcomes[5] – the capabilities and freedoms to be achieved, rather than on itemising the inadequacies of the recipient. This may appear to be a semantic quibble, but it positions people very differently: either as lacking and inadequate in some respect, or as wrongly denied the freedoms that should be theirs. Instead of defining and scrutinising what they lack, with obvious consequences for self-esteem, the focus shifts to defining what they could and should be able to do, and identifying the means to enable them to do it.

As discussed, each party brings different knowledge to the table, both of which are necessary for success. Both stand to gain positive affirmation from it. Both need the input and co-operation of the other and both have things to learn from each other. They need to develop trust and to respect each other, finding ways to challenge that will not provoke defensiveness and withdrawal. This is not to suggest that such a relationship will always be feasible on day one, or that it is easy. As discussed in the previous chapter, support of various kinds may be required to enable people who use services to exercise choice and control. In fact, support may be required by providers too, if they are to feel comfortable and confident about devolving power to recipients. Sennett remarks on the dialogic skills required for 'hard' or 'good' cooperation, which include: 'listening well, behaving tactfully, finding points of agreement and managing disagreement, or avoiding frustration in a difficult discussion' (2012, p 6). It would be foolish to assume that such skills are necessarily possessed by either party. Where the parties are not used to working in this way, independent support, advocacy and training might all be helpful to keep the process on an even keel.

Despite its obvious potential to promote user empowerment, a further major caveat remains. Co-production is not the same as co-option. As Byrne observes, the word empowerment can sometimes be misused 'in what one wishes was a cynical but in fact is probably a sincerely and dangerously ignorant fashion as part of a process of real disempowerment through incorporation' (2005, p 177). It must not just become the latest form of oppression: of enticing diverse people to squeeze uncomfortably into an unnecessarily narrowly drawn mainstream. The process should be steered by the recipient's objectives, not the provider's as an instrument of government policy (irrespective of whether delivery has been passed to the private or the voluntary sector). It should be a means of equipping the recipient to forge their own destiny, to live a full life, in keeping with their strengths and interests.

Needs and perspectives

For relationships to work, for the tie to hold, the transactional needs of both parties have to be met. In this case, each is likely to have very different ways of meeting them. To achieve the shift in power that co-production entails could jeopardise current arrangements. There will be a variety of pressures to maintain the status quo, not least the intensification of scrutiny in order to establish desert that funding cuts generate. Furthermore, simply to proclaim that recipients should have more power does not mean that they will. We need to understand from where power might come.

From the perspective of the service provider, 'positive affirmation of self' and 'positive exchange pay-offs' might have pragmatic and emotionally-based aspects. At a pragmatic level, the receipt of a salary might be a positive exchange pay-off, although without (emotionally rather than pragmatically-based) job satisfaction that may be insufficient motivation. Exit, in the form of finding another more satisfying job, may be an option. Positive affirmation might also arise from doing a job well. Job satisfaction might be generated by being instrumental to improving other people's lives, or rather in enabling them to improve their own. However, struggles to meet urgent needs in the context of insufficient resources, having to deal with recipients' anger, disappointment, desperation, cynicism and negativity, all present obvious challenges.

The group to which providers belong might be comprised of members of the administering institution, or fellow colleagues or professionals doing the same job elsewhere. 'Interpersonal flow' might be attributable to the degree of competence with which the institution or team is managed, or by common operating procedures and professional jargon. It is to them that a welfare provider might look for 'facticity'. A professional would want to feel confident that they were prepared to cope with situations that might arise when delivering services. Some degree of predictability in the needs and behaviours of clients would therefore be important, or professional competence (perhaps part of 'core self') might be challenged. However, too great a confidence in the predictability of clients, based on an inadequate assessment of (possibly inadequate) indicators, leads to damaging stereotyping and risks failure to match goods to needs.

While there is scope for recipients to experience 'positive exchange pay-offs' in the form of the gratification derived from meeting basic needs, this has to be weighed against the potential costs. Recipients' transactional needs for 'positive affirmation of self' may be thwarted by the fact that access to many public welfare services is contingent on the demonstration of incapacity and helplessness, providing negative rather than positive affirmation. The possible exception is education, where successful access at a higher level can affirm capacity rather than the reverse. Conversely, school is an environment where repeated tests and exams mean that public judgements on capacity or lack of it are endemic, and where lack of effort becomes the foil for feared inadequacy. To be successful in accessing benefits, public housing or healthcare does not equate to confirmation of self-worth, but potentially its opposite. Empowerment then becomes a critical counterweight.

Along with a process of co-production, where recipients become partners in framing outcomes and strategy, other means of empowerment include improving accountability mechanisms, capacity-building and independent support. For professionals, this rebalancing necessitates a shift in ethos, away from doing things for and to people and towards supporting them to do things for themselves. To transfer power might also entail building their confidence to trust clients and rethinking attitudes to risk. Clearly, if providers' 'core self' is wedded to their ability to exercise power over proportionately powerless clients, achieving such change becomes challenging.

Impenetrable bureaucratic procedures, lack of information, use of jargon, and powerlessness in decision-making processes all militate against feeling part of the 'interpersonal flow' of group inclusion, or in this case of the relationship between provider and recipient. That flow needs to be robust if change is to be achieved. While group inclusion can take the form of peer support, and this can play a valuable role in building confidence to try something new, peers can also apply pressure in the opposite direction, to maintain the status quo – at worst to continue using drugs or commit crime. Voluntary sector organisations catering for particular groups might be a positive source of peer support.

Whatever Sennett's views (2000) on the importance of time for the development of social bonds, and the role of trust in cementing them (Chapter Five) neither may feature in relationships between welfare providers and recipients. Trust may be compromised by unfamiliar environments and procedures, and unpredictable outcomes, and by the conflation of support with policing roles. However, trust is not only engendered by an emotional basis to a social relationship and long-term familiarity. It might also be generated by confidence in a professional's expertise, as may apply in the case of medical diagnosis. Trust may be predicated on objectivity, neutrality and rationality rather than personal familiarity. Nonetheless, continuity of contact with the same professional is likely to be beneficial to building trust and minimising destructive (to the relationship) instability.

Predictability, too, is not only an outcome of prolonged contact, but of confidence in what to expect, perhaps engendered through receiving advance information about the process, hence avoiding experiences of 'flustering' or 'wrong face'. Testimonies from peer group members who have been through it before, or the publication of standards may also assist. Opening up the workings of welfare institutions to external stakeholders, building links with local organisations and communities, involving them in consultations and decision-making, may all help to promote inclusion by making institutions more familiar, more responsive and better equipped to promote social realisation.

Affirmation of the urgency, unfairness or intolerableness of the situation (facticity) will not be forthcoming where providers must adhere rigidly to slow, cumbersome procedures and distance themselves emotionally. The relationship tie between recipient and provider is asymmetrical in situations where the recipient has urgent needs, and hence a strong emotional investment in having those needs met immediately, while the provider is held into the relationship by a contract of employment to work in an environment of complex processes and time-consuming form-filling. The latter may certainly have a desire to help people and to do a good job, but there may be various reasons why a pragmatic approach has to be taken – the need to protect their own 'personal territory' in emotionally charged situations, the challenge of juggling the competing needs of different prospective recipients having insufficient resources to meet all, and so on.

If the strength of emotional involvement is proportionate to the degree of access to 'personal territory' comfortably permitted, this poses significant challenges to those charged with delivering intimate welfare services like health- or personal care, toileting or washing. While the transactional needs of the recipient for trust and predictability might seem more likely to be met by someone familiar to them, such as a partner or family member, this in itself does not necessarily make such an arrangement empowering. For empowerment it is reasonable to suppose that the tie must be voluntarily chosen and that renegotiation and exit are possible. The difficulties of this are considerably greater where there are strong emotional ties.

Although a person may feel more comfortable receiving such assistance from a partner or close relative, should either become dissatisfied with the arrangement and wish it to cease, there can be wider repercussions for the relationship. If, instead, the assistance is provided by someone employed by the person with personal care needs, it is simply a matter of employing someone else. It may not be the degree of emotional investment that determines how comfortable a person is with access to 'personal territory' but the degree of control over who accesses it and on what terms. Control may be easier to exert where there is no emotional investment. To separate the meeting of such needs from primary emotionally-based relationships might also help to distance what both parties might consider an aspect of a person's identity which is irrelevant to their relationship. This may be a means of enabling a person to promote distance – or slippage – between an aspect of their identity and their core self. It also changes the one-way street dynamic of gratitude for altruistic giving to a more equal relationship where one gains a wage and the other the support they need, on the terms they want.

There is clearly considerable scope for the invasion of core self as welfare service deliverers wade into very personal, intimate matters. Healthcare providers may have to relate to people in life or death situations or undergoing the potentially extreme trauma of serious illness. Assessment for disability benefits can require highly personal information about incontinence, inability to use toilets unassisted, wash, and so on – obliging individuals to confront and demonstrate their incapacity. Child support assessors may need information about sexual partners.

Intrusion into private matters may or may not be necessary to ensure that assessments reflect the purpose of the good. For example, if the good is a service to provide assistance with personal care needs, to require information about the nature and extent of those needs seems in keeping with that purpose. However, as previously discussed, it is possible that the assessor can hand over to the recipient responsibility for precise shaping of the service to match needs (having first ensured the recipient has the capacity, support and desire to exercise that responsibility). It may be sufficient for assessors to allocate recipients to broad social categories, in the knowledge that within certain parameters all will have that sort of need. Individuals' specific requirements may differ, but the resource implications for the provider are much the same and the recipient is better equipped than providers to determine a precise match of service to need. This can be conceptualised as restricting the 'policing' role to broad categorisation and ensuring equitable treatment at a level that does not encroach onto personal territory. It is then a matter of working together to achieve outcomes, promote engagement and inclusion.

Different cultures and sub-cultures (not just based on ethnicity but perhaps also age, socio-economic class, even specific organisations) have different social rituals, respond differently to, or recognise different, behavioural cues, use different language, require/expect different levels of deference and express deference and demeanour differently. Even micro-level factors may differ culturally, such as the significance of eye contact or the lack of it, use of gestures, tone of voice, interruptions, and so on. To deliver culturally sensitive (hence inclusive) services is therefore not just a matter of how a process is structured but how face-to-face interaction is conducted. Moreover, to stand up straight, make eye contact and give a firm handshake may generally be understood as signals of confidence, but may be impossibilities for people with certain forms of impairment no matter how confident they are. It may be that social barriers are addressed by the way processes are structured (flexible appointment times and places) yet nonetheless discrimination or misrecognition occurs at the point of enactment.

Personalisation and choice

Finally, there is much that can be done to empower through the way in which policy is structured, as opposed to enacted. Rights to welfare goods and services are important mechanisms for empowering recipients. Alongside social rights, anti-discrimination rights play a key role in empowering individuals to enforce changes to open up access and delivery. They provide benchmarks against which to judge and challenge outcomes, clarity about what to expect and confirmation of entitlement, subject to defined characteristics and circumstances. This is in contrast to provision made on a charitable basis, where people have to depend on the benevolence of others to get their needs met: 'Charity…disrupts equality, places the giver in a superior position and destroys mutuality' (Levitas, 2005, p 108, discussing Macmurray). The mantra of the disability movement in the 1990s was 'rights not charity', reflecting how demeaning it can feel to be on the receiving end of funds generated through pity, awarded on the basis of discretion. That is not to say that all charities are paternalistic, or necessarily were then. They encompass organisations of people who use services themselves as well as large, traditional, unrepresentative institutions. Yet worries about the scope for concealing discrimination in a system of discretionary judgement may be well founded.

The complexity of identity and associated sensitivities may be taken to underline the importance of personalisation (see Leadbeater, 2004, for discussion of personalisation). To fail to recognise individuality or show interest in it, may be experienced as dehumanising. Yet intrusive and insensitive scrutiny may also amount to the denial of the humanity of the recipient and the treatment of her/him as an object. This suggests that, once again, a balance is necessary – or, put another way, the right degree of distance needs to be found. It may also have implications for policy design. If people are very different to each other, to attempt to ensure rights to equal treatment based on shared characteristics becomes an unhelpful constraint. Maybe personalisation is best achieved through giving assessors the power to make discretionary judgement.

Yet, increasing their power and removing rights reduces the power of recipients.

Personalisation is closely linked to the promotion of choice. As discussed, markets are generally viewed as more likely to provide personalised goods and services, and offer wider choice than the traditionally standardised 'one size fits all' approach of the public sector. The current focus is on empowering recipients by giving them choice. However, despite those declared intentions, it is noticeable that cuts to welfare benefits increasingly result in its removal and in the curtailment of autonomy through conditionality. For choices to be worthy of the name, they have to be taken on a basis of information about alternatives, and genuine (relevant) alternatives have to exist. Clearly, no one would knowingly opt for an inferior, poor quality good or service. Yet that may be all that is available locally. As discussed earlier, there may be insufficient time, money or transport to make alternatives practical. Information on alternatives needs to be available and accessible, and this presents obvious challenges when it comes to describing complex services.

How meaningful and useful choice is, and whether it actually means providers choose recipients rather than the reverse, remains uncertain. Particularly when exercising choice over specialist services, like health, education, legal or financial advice, the primary consideration may be confidence in the quality of local providers, rather than a choice of providers. Alternatively, people might not care who empties their bins or want to devote time to researching alternative bin-emptying companies. They just want them regularly emptied. However, in some instances, like the provision of personal care, it may be both desirable and feasible for the individual recipient to have a great deal of choice over who provides it and when they provide it, thereby framing the service they receive. Indeed, it could be argued that choice is particularly important in situations where 'personal territory' has to be encroached upon. Empowerment through increasing choice is therefore not a straightforward matter. It may be important in some situations, less so or near-meaningless in others.

It is not self-evident that choice can only be achieved through marketisation, or that personalisation requires detailed scrutiny and tailoring. If a collective/broad group or universal approach is taken, despite being impersonal, provision may well be experienced as less stigmatising. The risk is that by assessing with a broad-brush the good/service itself is an imprecise match to individual needs. However, it does not have to be a choice between universal provision to reduce stigma or a personalised approach to match provision to individuals. Through co-production and through policy design, it is possible to achieve a more inclusive and empowering approach to service delivery, to achieving the autonomy and well-being that is fundamental to inclusive equality.

Notes

[1] Presumably this applies irrespective of whether what is occurring is 'real' or fantasy (for example, a film or a play) – the confirmation required is of the appropriate frame, to use Goffman's term (1986).

[2] This includes, in Goffman's terms, to be in 'wrong face' (when a person is unable to integrate information about her/his social worth) or 'out of face' (when unexpectedly unprepared for or caught out by a situation).

[3] For more on co-production see for example Slay et al (2010) and Needham and Carr (2009).

[4] See, for example, the Social Care (Self-directed Support) (Scotland) Act 2013

[5] See, for example, Talking Points www.jitscotland.org.uk/action-areas/talking-points-user-and-carer-involvement/

EIGHT

Conclusion

This book began by setting out a tentative proposition; a vision for mainstream society and for social justice, where diversity – of people, cultures, forms of contribution, and so on – is recognised, valued, and accommodated to the maximum extent possible. It followed that inclusion had to be on a basis of empowerment to express difference, rather than conditional on its oppression. However, it was acknowledged that there would be limits to what can be included without jeopardising social cohesion. It was proposed that exclusion on other grounds would contravene social justice.

We are now in a position to understand more about the meaning that underlies that initial snapshot. In the course of exploration, this book has ranged from the depths of abstract theory through to the development of proposals for policy and practice, while attempting to illuminate the path from one to the other. The discussion journeyed from macro-level concerns around the nature of society, to the operation of meso-level institutions, down to factors in micro-level interactions, considering the impact on inclusion of inequalities of different types. It traversed different academic areas of study in the quest to develop the 'richest possible synthesis' (Askonas, 2000) of relevant material. This methodology, the knitting together of themes across literatures and disciplines, echoes the quest to find a theoretical basis for the richest possible social synthesis. Both methodology and aim have entailed the breaching of boundaries (between literatures or social categories respectively), the extraction of commonalities, the detection of coherence, and cross-fertilisation between different perspectives. Echoing the fact that people have many characteristics, and thus many options for categorisation exist, it is possible to align themes from the literatures around a framework provided by the structuring and enactment of distributive processes within a wider socio-cultural context.

Key themes from the literatures

The raw materials used to develop the theoretical framework were the key themes extracted from existing theory around disadvantage and exclusion. The first challenge was to consider each separately, attempt to find coherence between them and align them in accordance with the book's goal. This necessitated some degree of theory development. It became clear that each area encompassed themes relevant to others. However, not all relevant themes featured in all the literatures. Even where themes spanned literatures, important insights about them did not. It was then a matter of considering how themes could be positioned in relation to each other to form an overall framework.

There were recurrent indications that the social (particularly distributive) processes and relationships through which individuals are 'attached' to wider society might constitute a fruitful line of inquiry. The proposition that socially just distribution cannot be achieved without accurate recognition, rather than these two being separate considerations, was a fundamental starting point. The literature on poverty and need contributed a variety of approaches to determining what resources people needed to have and what they should be able to do if they are to participate in customary norms. The importance of accommodating emotional needs (for example, for self-esteem) as well as pragmatic, practical needs (for food, money to pay bills) was a key insight. Moreover, it was clear that there were circumstances in which resources of any type or quantity could not grant access to inclusion. The discrimination literature shed light on the social barriers that also need to be addressed. This suggested three 'sites' for investigation, where changes might be possible to promote inclusion: macro-level socio-cultural context; meso-level processes, and micro-level capacity, interactions and identity. It was noticeable that poverty literature seemed primarily concerned with matters of distribution and discrimination literature with issues around recognition. The social exclusion literature then took us back to a focus on the processes and relationship networks through which inclusion is achieved.

Alongside these distinctive contributions, each of the literatures tackled in different ways questions around the structuring and operation of society. There was much discussion, in different contexts, of whether a generic, universal approach was appropriate – or indeed feasible. To try to define the ideal society is perhaps an intrinsically oppressive and imperialistic act. To focus on the physiological needs we all share as human beings risks overlooking the way in which those needs could be requisitioned and reconstituted by dominant ideologies and groups in order to strengthen the status quo. The imperative to conform to the norms they set can override all others, so that needs become relative to whatever those norms are. Where they are narrowly drawn, inclusion becomes conditional on the oppression of difference. Reflecting the image of whomsoever the dominant group happens to be, the attitudes that prevail and the way society operates create barriers for other groups and thereby underscore their inferiority.

These norms and barriers are expressed through the design of processes and/or the enactment of relationship networks which connect people to institutions and to each other. Institutions are of different types, in different spheres of public life – economic, political, social and civil – and they exist at all levels. Different types of goods, distributive principles, values and relationships could be associated with each. Inclusion requires the existence of infrastructure through which multiway communications and accountability can take place, and through which distributions can be enacted. Those processes need to be accessible and integrated. It is through such processes that social structure and cultural issues find expression, and the interface with individual capacity issues occurs. It is through them that socio-cultural barriers need to be removed, and individual resources need to be increased. However, it is not just structural factors that can work against inclusion. How people feel about engaging, or the prospect of it, was argued to be of critical importance.

These are broadly generic approaches to conceptualising the structure of society and its consequences. There was also much to be found that focused more specifically on capitalism as the dominant contemporary ideology within Western societies. Academic research into relative poverty is inevitably situated within a particular context, itemising the resources and customary activities that are regarded as the norm. In so doing, they also describe – if not prescribe – the norms in question. The structuring of the labour market does not just create 'vertical' divisions in terms of socio-economic classes. It also results in 'horizontal' divisions, in the form of devalued groups who, for whatever reason, are not in a position to be economically productive. Levitas's three discourses of exclusion can be seen as reflecting different facets of capitalism; the need to redistribute to redress the inequalities it creates, the reinforcement of paid work as the route to inclusion (and generating profit), and the moral condemnation of a so-called underclass, who allegedly choose not to work, preferring instead to live off benefits funded by the taxation of virtuous, hard-working families.

Discussion of inequality that featured in each of the literatures enabled different forms of inequality to be identified, along with their implications for social inclusion. There was discussion of complex equality – the importance of separating out different types and forms of distribution – what theoreticians more inclined to abstraction would describe in terms of the separation of economic, political, social and civil spheres. It was also a matter of separating, rather than conflating, primary goods of power, wealth and opportunity. In effect, complex equality diffuses the accumulative dynamics of inequality (both vertically and horizontally).

The theme of equivalence was closely related, in that it was proposed that forms of contribution associated with each, while different, could have equal value. The principle of equivalence – the equal valuing of difference, was of wider importance to the pursuit of including diversity. Of course, this implies accurate recognition. Inequalities can arise from failure to identify difference or sameness, and to level the playing field or ensure equal treatment accordingly. Similarly, the theme of equilibrium or balance, between 'spheres' and distributive principles was implied. Equal voice and greater empowerment in decision-making – particularly of those directly affected – was reflected in approaches to co-production. This could constitute a means of separating the (commonly conflated) primary goods (Rawls 1973) of power, resources and liberty as they cease to be contingent on each other. Publicly funded service providers devolve power to recipients, who have an equal say in defining the outcomes (or social realisation) they want to achieve. The provider and recipient might differ with regards to their objectives, knowledge, powers, needs and so on, but there were various strategies to make more equal the degree to which the range of the transactional needs of both might be met. Finally, a key principle of inclusive equality concerns the recognition of the worth of all human beings, by virtue of our shared humanity.

In the blatantly dysfunctional form of capitalism we currently endure it is not just that extremes of inequality pervade all aspects of society and that inequalities arise and accumulate due to the way it operates. To a considerable extent inequalities of different types and degrees articulate and demarcate the very structures of society. They delineate the location of unequal concentrations of power and resources and the barriers to inclusion that result. It is not just that such social barriers have an impact on different groups, they create those groups, carving out social divisions. They create social distances that weaken – and sometimes tear apart – the social fabric of relationship networks.

Across the literatures, potential was revealed for clashes – or false dichotomies. To establish a universal benchmark does not preclude relativity. Very different priorities and actions could be required in relation to it, reflecting very different circumstances. Relative is not the antithesis of universal. To argue that the focus should be on structural issues rather than on the feelings and motivations of individuals is to overlook the need to address both if the concern is to tackle social exclusion. Distinctions between objective and subjective are murkier than might be implied – subjectivity will always be present even where conscious attempts are made to minimise it. Dialogue – through public reasoning or co-production – can be a means of understanding not just others' perspectives but also our own, through the eyes of others. It is not a matter of focusing either on perfecting institutions (in order to promote socially just behaviours) or on social realisation (what people can actually do), as this risks missing the possibility that socially just institutions are those that maximise the scope for social realisation. Finally, social cohesion does not require homogeneity. Integration (of different groups, policy areas or themes from different literatures) does not have to mean conflation. It can mean establishing connections between separate entities; each providing a context for the other, enabling coherence to be forged and a better understanding of differences, samenesses and alternatives to be achieved.

A vision for inclusive equality

The aim throughout was to develop theory around social justice as social inclusion, to explore the role/s of inequality/ies in promoting social exclusion. This goes beyond a notion that inequalities are unjust in their own right (and arguments may well hold to that effect). The aim here was to explore their impact, and to gauge the extent of their injustice according to the extent to which they inhibit social inclusion on non-oppressive terms and compromise social cohesion. This means that not all inequalities are de facto unjust and not all take the form of sameness. Indeed, in a variation of Rawls' difference principle, inequalities of certain sorts and to a certain extent might not just be tolerable; they might even be necessary to enable choice, social change and diversity to flourish. However, where the wrong type of equality is imposed and/or that extent is exceeded, social cohesion and sustainability are jeopardised.

We saw how, theoretically, a dominant yet imbalanced socio-cultural configuration of 'spheres' at a higher societal level can permeate downwards to lower levels. That imbalance plays out in a reduction in the scope for complex equality. Instead of many goals, forms of contribution and characteristics having equal value and being necessary for social cohesion, value narrows to one goal (profit), form of contribution (paid work) and the characteristics most fitting to achieve it. The narrower the goal and associated notions of value, the more likely that competitive dynamics will be exacerbated, as will the exclusion of those not equipped for that particular competition.

While globalisation challenges the notion of society, it remains possible to identify distributive communities of varying scales. Lower-level socio-cultural context was argued to be vital in determining the meaning of goods and priorities. Nonetheless, some generic or universal approaches began to sketch out the space for social realisation, the capabilities and liberties that should, or could in principle, be equally and universally available to all. The promotion of autonomy and well-being (reframing Doyal and Gough's basic needs), Baker et al's (2004) five dimensions of inequality (respect and recognition; resources; love care and solidarity; power; working and learning) are augmented in Burchardt and Vizard's 'Domains of central and valuable capabilities'.[1] These provide a potential framework of universal liberties. It is noticeable that they include capabilities that imply economic, political, social and civil inclusion, along with the generic capability of 'skills to participate in society'. Human rights provide another such approach (and were drawn upon by Burchard and Vizard). Meanwhile others have identified generic human motivations that need to be accommodated (for example Maslow and Turner). The aim of promoting capabilities and respecting human rights signals the need for processes connecting people to economic, political, social and civil institutions at all levels. It also signals the nature of relationships: that they need to take account of human motivations. However, social barriers – negative attitudes, inaccessible environments, inflexible organisation and so on, can intervene at any point to bar access and create inequalities. Very different action may be required in different settings to achieve the same (or equivalent) outcomes, or rather opportunities for people to determine their own. In many respects, this conceptualisation describes the precursors to freedoms, not instructions for how they should be used.

Thus, to understand social inclusion entailed consideration of the nature of inclusion and of what inclusion was into. It was proposed that it could best be construed as inclusion into social processes through the relationships required to enact them. Processes are structured and delivered through institutions located at different societal levels. Social mobility, to move between settings, is implicit to inclusion. Settings may change 'vertically' (chronologically) through the life-course and 'horizontally' (contemporaneously) at any point. The challenge for social policy becomes to open up access, smooth points of transition and increase and/or maintain points of connection.

It was therefore necessary to identify and address the factors that can compromise inclusion. These were shown to arise at macro-, meso- and micro-levels and at each of the three sites for intervention. By exploring social structure, processes and relationships through these different lenses, at different degrees of proximity, further challenges arose. They include inaccessible transactional infrastructure, poor dovetailing of processes, unnecessarily rigid access criteria, inadequate indicators for the purposes of assessment, artificially constructed scarcity, insufficient material resources or skills, and invasive, disempowering, stigmatising interactions. The prospect of such interactions provides incentives to disengagement. The experience of them reinforces exclusion.

If a policy of singling out a group for special (different) treatment is de facto exclusive, the challenge becomes how to avoid 'including by excluding' people with aspirations, needs, cultural norms, combinations of characteristics and circumstances, which differ from the majority. To deny those differences would amount to, and result in, oppressive exclusion. This points to the importance of how 'mainstream' is conceptualised, and its implications when applied to society and social policy design.

To be part of 'the mainstream' implies having something in common with a majority. To widen the mainstream thus entails finding uniting points of commonality. Instead of separating out the population into discrete one-dimensional social categories, it is necessary to acknowledge the multiple characteristics and circumstances of which identities are composed. It follows that each individual has access to multiple peer groups, and that there are many possible points of commonality and hence options for attachment. Inclusion does not have to be as simple as one or more points of commonality uniting the majority, but can be achieved through the existence of many potential points of commonality and mutually enriching difference through which individuals can be 'attached'. However, a key insight was that networks can form around difference too, to access new resources, opportunities and so on that the peer group does not possess. Society can be envisaged as a shifting mass of interconnected relationship networks, formed around shared points of commonality.

Generic features can emerge once the artificial boundaries of social categories are breached – not that the latter are redundant – they remain important devices for ensuring that people with a certain characteristic are not disproportionately disadvantaged by cross-cutting structural barriers. Furthermore, 'weak tie bridges' between peer groups, enabling mutual enrichment, should play a key role in promoting social cohesion, accommodating – and valuing – diversity. Strengthening peer groups and supporting the development of connections with new, different networks might both be useful goals for social policy.

Structurally, society can accommodate diversity within a macro-level framework of commonality, devolving powers down the levels. Power may be a positional good, but it is still possible to dilute concentrations by providing multiple settings within which it might be exercised by different people and by narrowing the span between more and less powerful. Social policy design can accommodate diversity, promote social mobility and forge cross-group alliances by taking a needs/aspirations/barriers analysis as its starting point. Subject to the nature of these, different shapes of 'mainstream' are created.

Empowerment and inclusion are symbiotically connected. Disempowerment restricts the expression of diversity, provokes disengagement, or engagement through oppressing certain aspects of identity and/or passivity. By eroding autonomy, personal responsibility and decision-making capacity, it deprives people of confidence and experience, thereby reinforcing dependence. It can mean that people already ill-equipped to forge new social connections become even less well-equipped. If the social meaning of welfare provision revolves around promoting inclusion and empowering disadvantaged people, it is clearly important that its design and delivery do not inadvertently exacerbate exclusion and disempowerment. Empowerment is an intrinsic part of successful outcomes, if the aim is to increase resources for participation.

The theoretical model enables conclusions to be drawn about the types of society, processes and relationships most likely to be conducive to inclusion on the desired basis. For example, an inclusive society would be one in which there is equilibrium, separation yet coherence between economic, social, political and civil systems, where many forms of contribution are recognised and commonly valued, and consequently so, too, are different goods and characteristics. Cultural norms value difference *and* commonalities, challenge rather than passively accept stereotypes. Competition is diffused as people pursue different objectives and types of good. Equal status can be achieved in many ways. Social mobility is supported by policy that is rationalised to remove unnecessary complexity and dovetailed to avoid gaps and traps. Transactional infrastructure is accessible as standard.

In an inclusive distributive process the general social meaning and purpose of the good are unambiguous while allowing for many alternative forms of expression. Instead of a tight association between meanings, access criteria and links to characteristics, as procedural justice might imply, inclusive equality requires maximum flexibility in the ways available to achieve the purpose of the good and this is reflected in access criteria. Attempts are made to minimise reliance on unreliable indicators of identity, and to avoid stereotypical judgements. Where possible, the exact framing of the good to meet individual needs is devolved to recipients in order to achieve a precise match. Recipients receive support to engage in the process. Rights, national standards, accountability and redress further help to remove power imbalances between provider and recipient. The nature of the networks leading to and from welfare institutions require particular consideration, if disincentives to take up services are to be avoided and the capacity of welfare institutions to play a pivotal role in promoting wider societal inclusion is to be realised. Otherwise, they cease to be routes to inclusion and instead become dead-ends, this itself acting as a disincentive to engagement.

The quality of relationships between individuals and collective institutions, recipients and providers may appear to be compromised by unavoidable asymmetries in power, knowledge, capacity, sense of urgency, among other features. However, co-production enables the contribution of different yet equally necessary knowledge of recipients. Without their active engagement, teachers cannot teach, doctors cannot enforce healthy behaviours and so on (Cahn, 2000). Co-production can be used to develop strategies and policies, for community development purposes or to define individual outcomes and services.

The greater the distance from the mainstream, the increased likelihood there is of an oppositional dynamic, as failure (or fear of it) to acquire self-esteem or to have power in legitimate settings leads to the pursuit of illegitimate alternatives. To turn this dynamic round – to change destructive behaviours rather than reinforce the status quo – compulsion might seem the obvious route – and in extremis it might be necessary to prevent wider social disintegration. However, this rides rough-shod over transactional needs. It serves to humiliate and compound disempowerment. It risks entrenching resistance and alienation rather than promoting engagement

Limitations

In the course of theory development, various tensions and dilemmas arose: how both to respect the diversity of individual identities and keep track of inequalities between social categories; how to secure social cohesion while promoting the expression of diversity and social mobility, to name but two. The extent of room for manoeuvre, limitations and constraints to the widening of the mainstream and to empowerment were noted throughout. Limitations were of different types: logically unavoidable; inevitable consequences contingent on other factors, or artificially constructed, perhaps to generate profit (for example, by manipulating supply and demand) or control behaviour.

To propose that an 'ideal' socio-cultural context is one which removes inequalities in order to promote inclusion and maximise collective liberty is not a proposition that many cultures, and the elites whose power-base rests on their perpetuation, would endorse. This exposes the most significant limitation to inclusive equality. It concerns how to deal with people whose 'difference' is that they do not want equality; how (and if) cosmopolitan tolerance can extend to tolerating the intolerant. There are cultures characterised by the belief that some groups are innately inferior to others and that people who do not conform to their narrowly defined approved norms should be prevented from expressing that difference. While the implications of carrying the model of inclusive equality to an extreme have been explored in terms of its internal logical and practical limitations, it needs to be set in the external context of competing cultural models built on inequality. Such cultures are to be found throughout the world.

As with the proposition that other extremes (libertarianism or economic egalitarianism, for example) can result in social conflict and disintegration, it seems so, too, could a rigidly enforced model of inclusive equality. While its very essence concerns negotiation between differing perspectives, inclusive equality could still fall foul of the challenge that any ideal model is infeasible and imperialistic because consensus will never be achieved. Yet that is a long way from confirming its redundancy.

Looking ahead

The financial crisis lifted the stone that covered the functioning of the financial markets, the location of power and the extent of inequality. The 'invisible hand' that led the natural functioning of a free, unregulated market comprised of self-interested participants to generate outcomes mutually beneficial to all (Adam Smith, 1776) was instead revealed to be proactively and disproportionately directing wealth towards the already very wealthy.

Yet, five years on, little of any significance has obviously changed. Economies remain flat, or in recession, yet the rich continue to get richer, while the rest of us endure an era of austerity. The growth of inequality remains unchecked as the system appears increasingly to work against the interests of the majority. It is not just the least advantaged who fail to benefit from escalating inequality, in contravention of Rawls' difference principle. The middle classes too have found themselves increasingly squeezed, as testified by falls in median income.[2] The scope for 'vertical' alliances between working and middle classes, the potential reconfiguration of socio-economic categorisations implied, has perhaps still to be fully realised.

People who are not economically productive are cast aside or pummelled into marginal jobs. They might have potential to be very productive in other ways within their communities, yet only one form of productivity counts. However, cutting public sector funding, removing all options other than 'do it yourself', merging voluntary, private and public sectors into one and failing to find ways to reward voluntary effort do not seem to be kick-starting economic recovery.

There are glimmers of positive developments. Co-production has increasingly been recognised as a valuable approach. That is not to say it is an easy process, or that it necessarily takes place even when there are commitments to it. For example, Beresford comments on the irony that involving service users and increasing their choice and control has been the mantra of personalisation, yet service users and their organisations generally do not feel they have had a say in its shaping or development (2009). Moreover, while policy in the social care field has increasingly sought to promote user choice and control,[3] the impact of massive cuts to local authority budgets look set to undermine scope to deliver that goal, or for that matter social care of even minimally acceptable quality to those who need it.[4] Alongside swinging cuts to welfare benefits, the prognosis for those with urgent needs and without the personal resources to pay for them is bleak indeed.

A brief survey of our current situation thus reveals a world massively out of kilter. The market, its values and libertarian principles dominate to such an extent that even the sustainability of the planet is in jeopardy. Yet far from attempting to rebalance, markets seem destined to penetrate ever more deeply into our lives. Public money is increasingly used, not to fund essential services that we all need, but to expand the perimeters of the market and prop up crumbling, dysfunctional financial infrastructure. As countries in the Eurozone totter on the brink of bankruptcy, the apparently unstoppable market dynamic is to push them over the edge, as the interest rates on loans increase in proportion to their poverty. Politicians, even at international level, seem incapable of altering that course. The first test of every government policy has become, not what the electorate make of it, but how the markets respond.

What might continuing down this path entail? As inequality increases, the centralisation and concentration of power and resources necessitates greater social control and surveillance to contain unrest. Taxation becomes little more than a compulsory private sector subsidy. Profits continue to be made out of essential needs, as private sector companies receive public money to provide work programmes, care homes and education, and/or costs are transferred onto individuals. Policing and the army become privatised (and there are already precedents for this). As personal resource needs increase, so poverty increases exponentially – as does the wanton destruction of the environment in pursuit of profit. The role of social policy remains relegated to mitigating the worst effects, monitoring behaviours and subsidising employers by providing free labour or topping up low pay. If co-production features at all, it is with an aim of incorporation, of diffusing opposition.

Other scenarios are, of course, possible. The path might unexpectedly make a u-turn back to a more equal, more sustainable form of capitalism. It might take us all over a precipice, or gradually lose definition as the system unravels. Whichever is the case, as opposition to austerity measures strengthens across Europe, we can be assured that 'The exploitative rich certainly act in their own interests. The interesting question is whether the rest of us will act in ours' (Byrne, 2005, p 71). Another interesting question is where we should look for leadership. None of our mainstream political parties appears currently to be offering anything beyond shades of the same political hue. Yet it is up to us whether we just sink into apathy or limit our protests to angry posts on various blogs. How we treat each other, what we do in our communities, whether or not we attempt to jump on every passing fashionable bandwagon, hold our local politicians to account, take at face value everything we are told, have the courage to protest against injustice; all these are up to us.

At a time marked by extremes of inequality in resources, power and voice, this book has tried to conjure up a vision of a more positive alternative and to indicate approaches to policy and practice that should take us in that direction. It is admittedly a broad-brush outline on a wide canvas, the features of which will be too blurry for the comfort of some. On occasions, the distance may indeed have been too great to capture meaning and misrecognition may have crept in. Moreover, although this book has drawn heavily on the reasoning of others, it is not a product of public reasoning. It reflects the thoughts and perspective of just one person. To take this project forward would require the input and action of others. It is now necessary to move in closer, to explore in more detail aspects of the landscape revealed. There is much that would lend itself to empirical investigation, such as the impact of social barriers on different groups, or understandings of value and equivalence. It needs skilful, courageous, selfless politicians to challenge and transform the current direction of travel. Most importantly, a voice in shaping the way forward needs to be given to people 'on the sharp end'; voices that all too often go unheard.

Notes

[1] These domains were 'being alive', physical security, health, skills to participate in society, a comfortable standard of living, engagement in productive and valued activities, enjoyment of individual, family and social life, participation in decision-making (having voice and influence), expressing yourself and having self-respect, protection and fair treatment by the law (discussed in Chapter Three).

[2] See, for example, www.marketwatch.com/story/household-income-falls-as-46-million-in-poverty-2012-09-12; and www.ons.gov.uk/ons/dcp29904_279770.pdf

[3] For example, the system of direct payments which gave people who use services money to buy in the support they wanted. Originally introduced in the UK by the Community Care (Direct Payments) Act 1996.

[4] See for example, www.adass.org.uk/index.php?option=com_content&view=article&id=914:social-care-funding-bleak-outlook-bleaker&catid=160:press-releases-2013&Itemid=489

References

Anderson, J. (1999) 'Social and system integration and the underclass', in I. Gough and G. Olofsson (eds) *Capitalism and social cohesion: essays on exclusion and integration*, Basingstoke: Macmillan.

Archibugi, D. (2010) 'The architecture of cosmopolitan democracy', in G.W. Brown and D. Held (eds) (2010) *The cosmopolitanism reader*, Cambridge: Polity Press.

Askonas, P. (2000) 'What kind of hope for the future?', in P. Askonas and A. Stewart (eds) *Social inclusion possibilities and tensions*, Basingstoke: Palgrave.

Baker, J., Lynch, K., Cantillon, S. and Walsh, J. (2004) *Equality: from theory to action*, Basingstoke: Palgrave Macmillan.

Banton, M. (1994) *Discrimination*, Buckingham: Open University Press.

Barnes, C. and Mercer, G. (1996) 'Introduction: exploring the divide', in C. Barnes and G. Mercer, *Exploring the divide: illness and disability*, Leeds: Disability Press.

Barry, B. (2001) *Culture and equality: an egalitarian critique of multiculturalism*, Cambridge: Polity Press.

Barry, B. (2002) 'Social exclusion, social isolation, and the distribution of income', in J. Hills, J. Le Grand and D. Piachaud (eds) *Understanding social exclusion*, Oxford: Oxford University Press.

Bauman, Z. (2000) 'What it means "to be excluded": living to stay apart – or together?', in P. Askonas and A. Stewart (eds) *Social inclusion possibilities and tensions*, Basingstoke: Palgrave.

Begum, N., Hill, M. and Stevens, A. (1994) *Reflections: views of black disabled people on their lives and community care,* London: Central Council for Education and Training in Social Work.

Beresford, P. (2009) 'Whose personalisation?', *Think pieces*, London: Compass.

Beresford, P., Green, D., Lister, R. and Woodard, K. (1999) *Poverty first hand: poor people speak for themselves*, London: CPAG (Child Poverty Action Group).

Berghman, J. (1995) 'Social exclusion in Europe: policy context and analytical framework', in G. Room (ed) *Beyond the threshold: the measurement and analysis of social exclusion*, Bristol: The Policy Press.

Bertram, C. (2008) 'Globalisation, social justice and the politics of aid', in G. Craig, T. Burchardt and D. Gordon (eds) (2008) *Social justice and public policy: seeking fairness in diverse societies*, Bristol: The Policy Press.

Blackless, M., Charuvastra, A., Derryck, A., Fausto-Sterling, A., Lauzanne, K. and Lee, E. (2000) 'How sexually dimorphic are we? Review and synthesis', *American Journal of Human Biology* vol 12, no 2, pp 151–66.

Bourdieu, P. (1997) 'The forms of capital', in A.H. Halsey, H. Lauder, P. Brown and A. Stuart Wells (eds) *Education: culture, economy, and society*, Oxford: Oxford University Press.

Boyle, D. and Harris, M. (2009) *The challenge of co-production: How equal partnerships between professionals and the public are crucial to improving public services,* London: NEF/NESTA.

Bradley, H. (1996) *Fractured identities: changing patterns of inequality*, Cambridge: Polity Press.

Bradshaw, J., Middleton, S., David, A., Oldfield, N., Smith, N. Cusworth, L. and Williams, J. (2008) *A minimum income standard for Britain: what people think*, York: Joseph Rowntree Foundation.

Brock, G. (2009) *Global justice: a cosmopolitan account*, Oxford: Oxford University Press.

Brooks, T. (2008) *The global justice reader*, Oxford: Wiley-Blackwell.

Brown, G.W. and Held, D. (eds) (2010) *The cosmopolitanism reader*, Cambridge: Polity Press.

Burchardt, T. (2008) 'Monitoring inequality: putting the capability approach to work', in G. Craig, T. Burchardt and D. Gordon (eds) (2008) *Social justice and public policy: seeking fairness in diverse societies*, Bristol: The Policy Press.

Burchardt, T. and Craig, G. (2008) 'Introduction', in G. Craig, T. Burchardt and D. Gordon (eds) *Social justice and public policy: seeking fairness in diverse societies*, Bristol: The Policy Press.

Burchardt, T. and Vizard, P. (2007) *Definitions of equality and framework for measurement*, Final recommendations of the Equalities Review Steering Group on Measurement, Paper 1, CASE paper 120, London: Centre for Analysis of Social Exclusion.

Burchardt, T., Hills, J. and Propper, C. (1999) *Private welfare and public policy*, York: Joseph Rowntree Foundation.

Burchardt, T., Le Grand, J. and Piachaud, D. (2002a) 'Introduction', in J. Hills, J. Le Grand and D. Piachaud (eds) *Understanding social exclusion*, Oxford: Oxford University Press.

Burchardt, T., Le Grand, J. and Piachaud, D. (2002b) 'Degrees of exclusion: developing a dynamic, multidimensional measure', in J. Hills, J. Le Grand and D. Piachaud (eds) *Understanding social exclusion*, Oxford: Oxford University Press.

Butler, C. (2002) *Postmodernism: a very short introduction*, Oxford: Oxford University Press.

Butler, J.P. (1990) *Gender trouble: feminism and the subversion of identity*, London: Routledge.

Byrne, D. (2005) *Social exclusion*, Maidenhead: Open University Press.

Cahn, E. (2000) *No more throwaway people: the co-production imperative*, Washington, DC: Essential Books.

Cahn, E. (2008) 'Foreword: a commentary from the United States' in L. Stephens, J. Ryan-Collins, D. Boyle (authors) *Co-production: a manifesto for growing the core economy*, London: New Economics Foundation.

Cantle, T. (2001) *Community cohesion: a report of the independent review team chaired by Ted Cantle*, London: Home Office.

Care Quality Commission (2011) *Dignity and nutrition inspection programme: national overview*, Newcastle upon Tyne: Care Quality Commission.

Chodorow, N. (1978) *The reproduction of mothering*, Berkeley: University of California Press.

Commission on Social Justice (1994) *Social justice: strategies for national renewal*, London: Vintage.

Crow, L. (1996) 'Including all of our lives: renewing the social model of disability', in C. Barnes and G. Mercer (eds) *Exploring the divide: illness and disability*, Leeds: Disability Press.

Deacon, A. (2002) *Perspectives on welfare: ideas, ideologies and policy debates (introducing social policy)*, Buckingham: Open University Press.

Deacon, B. (2007) *Global social policy and governance*, London: Sage.

Dean, H. (2010) *Understanding human need*, Bristol: The Policy Press.

Doyal, L. and Gough, I. (1991) *A theory of human need*, Basingstoke: Palgrave and Macmillan.

Dworkin, R. (2000) *Sovereign virtue*, Cambridge, MA: Harvard University Press.

EEC (1985) *On specific community action to combat poverty* (Council Decision of 19 December 1984) 85/8/EEC, Official Journal of the EEC, 2/24.

EHRC (Equality and Human Rights Commission) (2010) *How fair is Britain? Equality, human rights and good relations in 2010 – the first triennial review*, London: EHRC.

EHRC (2011) *Close to home: an inquiry into older people and human rights in home care*, London: EHRC.

EHRC (2011) *Hidden in plain sight: Inquiry into disability-related harassment*, London: EHRC.

European Commission (1992) *Towards a Europe of solidarity: intensifying the fights against social exclusion, fostering integration*, Communication COM (92) 542, Brussels: European Commission.

Flaherty, J., Veit-Wilson, J. and Dornan, P. (2004) *Poverty: the facts*, London: CPAG (Child Poverty Action Group).

Foucault, M. (1980) *Power/knowledge: selected interviews and other writings 1972–77* (ed C. Gordon), Brighton: Harvester Press.

Foucault, M. (1981) *The history of sexuality. Volume 1: an introduction*, Harmondsworth: Penguin.

Foucault, M. (1986) 'On the genealogy of ethics: an overview of work in progress', in P. Rabinow (ed) *The Foucault reader*, Harmondsworth: Penguin.

Fraser, N. (1997) *Justice interruptus: critical reflections on the 'postsocialist' condition*, New York and London: Routledge.

Fraser, N. (2003) 'Social justice in the age of identity politics: redistribution, recognition and participation', in N. Fraser and A. Honneth (eds) *Redistribution or recognition? A political–philosophical exchange*, London: Verso.

Giddens, A. (1984) *The constitution of society: outline of the theory of structuration*, Cambridge: Polity Press.

Giddens, A. (1998) *The third way: the renewal of social democracy*, Cambridge: Polity Press.

Giddens, A. (2002) *Runaway world: how globalisation is reshaping our lives*, London: Profile Books.

Gittins, D. (1993) *The family in question*, London: Macmillan.

Glennerster, H. (1997) *Paying for welfare*, Hemel Hempstead: Prentice-Hall.

Goffman, E. (1967) *Interaction ritual: essays on face-to-face behavior*, New York: Pantheon Books.

Goffman, E. (1983) 'The interaction order', in *American Sociological Review*, vol 48, pp 1–17.

Goffman, E. (1986) *Frame analysis: an essay on the organization of experience*, second edition, Boston, MA: Northeastern University Press.

Gordon, D., Adelman, L., Ashworth, K., Bradshaw, J., Levitas, R., Middleton, S., Pantazis, C., Patsios, D., Paynes, S., Townsend, P. and Williams, J. (2000) *Poverty and social exclusion in Britain*, York: Joseph Rowntree Foundation.

Gore, C. (1995) 'Social exclusion and social change: insights from the African literature' in G. Rodgers, C. Gore and J.B. Figueiredo (eds) *Social Exclusion: Rhetoric Reality Responses*, Geneva: International Labour Organization.

Gore, C., Figueiredo, J.B. and Rodgers, G. (1995) 'Introduction: markets, citizenship and social exclusion', in G. Rodgers, C. Gore and J.B. Figueiredo (eds) *Social exclusion: rhetoric reality responses*, Geneva: International Labour Organization.

Granovetter, M. (1973) 'The strength of weak ties', in *American Journal of Sociology*, vol 78, no 6, pp 1362–80.

Gray, J. (2000) 'Inclusion: a radical critique', in P. Askonas and A. Stewart (eds) *Social inclusion possibilities and tensions*, Basingstoke: Palgrave.

Greenfield, S. (2008correct) *ID: the quest for meaning in the 21st century*, London: Hodder and Stoughton.

Grosz, E. (1994) 'Experimental desire: rethinking queer subjectivity', in J. Copjec (ed) *Supposing the subject*, London: Verso.

Habermas, J. (2010) 'A political constitution for the pluralist world society?', in G.W. Brown and D. Held (eds) (2010) *The cosmopolitanism reader*, Cambridge: Polity Press.

Hayek, F.A. (1976) *Law, legislation and liberty. Volume 2: the mirage of social justice*, London and New York: Routledge.

Held, D. (2010) 'Reframing global governance: apocalypse soon or reform!', in G.W. Brown and D. Held (eds) (2010) *The cosmopolitanism reader*, Cambridge: Polity Press.

Herrnstein, R.J. and Murray, C.A. (1994) *The bell-curve: intelligence and class structure in American life*, New York and London: Free Press.

High Pay Commission (2011) *Cheques with balances: why tackling high pay is in the national interest*, final report of the High Pay Commission, published 22 November 2011, http://highpaycentre.org/files/Cheques_with_Balances.pdf.

Hills, J. (2002) 'Does a focus on "social exclusion" change the policy response?', in J. Hills, J. Le Grand and D. Piachaud (eds) *Understanding social exclusion*, Oxford: Oxford University Press.

Hirsch, F. (1977) *The social limits to growth*, London: Routledge & Kegan Paul.

Hirst, P., Thompson, G. and Bromley, S. (2009) *Globalization in question*, third edition, Cambridge: Polity Press.

Honneth, A. (2003) 'Redistribution as recognition' in N. Fraser and A. Honneth, *Redistribution or recognition? A political-philosophical exchange*, London and New York, NY: Verso.

Horne, M. and Shirley, T. (2009) *Co-production in public services: a new partnership with citizens*, London: Cabinet Office.

Howard, M. (2003) *An interactionist perspective on barriers and bridges to work for disabled people*, London: IPPR (Institute for Public Policy Research).

Hutton, W. (1996) *The state we're in*, London: Vintage.

Hutton, W. (2011) *Them and us: changing Britain – why we need a fair society*, London: Abacus.

Killin, D. (1993) 'Independent living, personal assistance, disabled lesbians and disabled gay men', in C. Barnes (ed) *Making our own choices*, Derby: The British Council of Disabled People.

Kirsch, M.H. (2000) *Queer theory and social change*, London: Routledge.

Kymlicka, W. (1995) *Multicultural citizenship: a liberal theory of minority rights*, Oxford: Clarendon Press.

Kymlicka, W. (2008) 'Multiculturalism, social justice and the welfare state' in G. Craig, T. Burchardt, & D. Gordon (eds) *Social justice and public policy: seeking fairness in diverse societies*, Bristol: The Policy Press.

Le Grand, J. (2003) *Motivation, agency and public policy*, Oxford: Oxford University Press.

Leadbeater, C. (2004) *Personalisation through participation: a new script for public services*, London: Demos.

Levitas, R. (2005) *The inclusive society? Social exclusion and New Labour*, second edition, Basingstoke: Palgrave Macmillan.

Lewis, G. (2002) 'Categories of exclusion: "race", gender and the micro-social in social services departments', in E. Breitenbach, A. Brown, F. Mackay and J. Webb (eds) *The Changing Politics of Gender Equality in Britain*, Basingstoke: Palgrave.

Lipsky, M. (1980) *Street-level bureaucracy: dilemmas of the individual in public services*, New York: Russell Sage Foundation.

Lipsky, M. (1993) 'Street-level bureaucracy: an introduction', in M. Hill (ed) *The Policy Process: A Reader*, London: Harvester-Wheatsheaf.

Lister, R. (2000) 'Strategies for social inclusion: promoting social cohesion or social justice?', in P. Askonas and A. Stewart (eds) *Social inclusion possibilities and tensions*, Basingstoke: Palgrave.

Lister, R. (2004) *Poverty*, Cambridge: Polity Press.

Lister, R. (2008) 'Recognition and voice: the challenge for social justice', in G. Craig, T. Burchardt and D. Gordon (eds) *Social justice and public policy: seeking fairness in diverse societies*, Bristol: The Policy Press, pp 105–22.

Lister, R. (2010) *Understanding theories and concepts in social policy*, Bristol: The Policy Press.

Llewelyn, A. and Hogan, K. (2000) 'The use and abuse of models of disability', *Disability and Society*, vol 15, no 1, pp 157–65.

Lockwood, D. (1992) *Solidarity and schism, 'the problem of disorder' in Durkheimian and Marxist sociology*, Oxford: Clarendon Press.

Lupton, R. (2003) *Poverty street: the dynamics of neighbourhood decline and renewal*, Bristol: Policy Press.

Lupton, R. and Power. A (2005) 'Disadvantaged by where you live? New Labour and neighbourhood renewal' in J. Hills and K. Stewart (eds) *A more equal society? New Labour, poverty, inequality and exclusion*, Bristol: Policy Press.

Lyotard, J-F. (1984) *The postmodern condition: a report on knowledge*, Manchester: Manchester University Press.

Mack, J. and Lansley, S. (1985) *Poor Britain*, London: George Allen and Unwin.

Mack, J. and Lansley, S. (1992) *Breadline Britain in the 1990s*, London: Harper Collins.

Malik, K. (1996) *The meaning of race: race, history and culture in Western society*, London: Macmillan.

Mandle, J. (2006) *Global justice: an introduction (key concepts)*, Cambridge: Polity Press.

Marshall, T.H. (1950) *Citizenship and social class*, London: Cambridge University Press.

Maslow, A. (1943) 'A theory of human motivation', *Psychological Review*, vol 50, no 4, pp 370–96.

Maslow, A. (1970) *Motivation and personality*, New York, NY: Harper and Row.

Miles, R. and Brown, M. (2003) *Racism*, second edition, London: Routledge.

Miller, D. (2001) *Principles of social justice*, London: Harvard University Press.

Moore, J. (1989) 'The end of the line for poverty', Speech delivered by the Rt Hon John Moore, Secretary of State for Social Security, to the Greater London Conservative Political Centre on 11 May.

Morrell, G., Scott, S., McNeish, D. and Webster, S. (2011) *The August riots in England: understanding the involvement of young people*, London: NatCen.

Morris, J. (1991) *Pride against prejudice*, London: Women's Press.

Mouzelis, N. (1991) *Back to sociological theory*, London: Macmillan.

Mouzelis, N. (1999) 'Differentiation and marginalization in late modernity', in I. Gough and G. Olofsson (eds) *Capitalism and social cohesion: essays on exclusion and integration*, Basingstoke: Macmillan.

Murray, C. (1996) 'The emerging British underclass', in R. Lister (ed) *Charles Murray and the underclass: the developing debate*, London: IEA (Institute of Economic Affairs).

Needham, C. and Carr, S. (2009) *Co-production: an emerging evidence base for adult social care transformation*, Research Briefing 31, London: Social Care Institute for Excellence.

New Economics Foundation (2008) *Co-production: a manifesto for growing the core economy*, London, New Economics Foundation.

Nozick, R. (1974) *Anarchy, state and utopia*, Oxford: Blackwell.

Nussbaum, M. (2000) *Women and human development: the capabilities approach*, Cambridge: Cambridge University Press.

OECD (Organisation for Economic Co-operation and Development) (2011) *Society at a glance 2011: OECD social indicators*, Paris: OECD, www.oecd.org/els/social/indicators/SAG.

Office for National Statistics (2011) *Labour market statistics*, November 2011, Crown copyright, published 16 November 2011 (see www.ons.gov.uk).

Oliver, M. (1990) *The politics of disablement*, Basingstoke: Palgrave Macmillan.

Oliver, M. (1996) *Understanding disability: from theory to practice*, Basingstoke: Palgrave Macmillan.

Olofsson, G. (1999) 'Embeddedness and integration', in I. Gough and G. Olofsson (eds) *Capitalism and social cohesion: essays on exclusion and integration*, Basingstoke: Macmillan.

Park, A., Curtice, J., Clery, E. and Bryson, C. (eds) (2010) *British social attitudes: the 27th report*, London: Sage/NatCen.

Park, A., Clery, E., Curtice, J., Phillips, M. and Utting, D. (eds) (2011) *British social attitudes 28: 2011–2012*, London: Sage/NatCen, www.natcen.ac.uk/BSA28.

Perri 6 (1997) *Escaping poverty*, London: Demos.

Phillips, A. (1997) 'From inequality to difference: a severe case of displacement?', in *New Left Review*, no 224, pp 143–53.

Piachaud, D. (2008) 'Social justice and public policy: a social policy perspective', in G. Craig, T. Burchardt and D. Gordon (eds) (2008) *Social justice and public policy: seeking fairness in diverse societies*, Bristol: The Policy Press.

Polanyi, K. (1957) *The great transformation: the political and economic origins of our time*, Boston: Beacon Press.

Powell, F. (1995) 'Citizenship and social exclusion', *Administration*, vol 43, no 3, pp 22–35.

Pudney, S., Hancock, R. and Sutherland, H. (2005) *Stigma, claim costs and means-tested pensioner benefits*, ESRC End-of-award Report, www.esrc.ac.uk/my-esrc/grants/R000239105/read

Quarmby, K (2011) *Scapegoat: how we are failing disabled people in Britain*, London: Portobello Press.

Ratcliffe, P. (2000) 'Is the assertion of minority identity compatible with the idea of a socially inclusive society?', in P. Askonas and A. Stewart (eds) *Social inclusion possibilities and tensions*, Basingstoke: Palgrave.

Ravallion, M. (1992) *Poverty comparison: a guide to concepts and methods*, Washington, DC: The World Bank.

Rawls, J. (1973) *A theory of justice*, Oxford: Oxford University Press.

Rhodes, R.A.W. (1981) *Control and power in central–local relations*, Farnborough: Saxon House.

Rodgers, G. (1995a) 'What is special about a "social exclusion" approach?', in G. Rodgers, C. Gore and J.B. Figueiredo (eds) *Social exclusion: rhetoric reality responses*, Geneva: International Labour Organization.

Rodgers, G. (1995b) 'The design of policy against exclusion', in G. Rodgers, C. Gore and J.B. Figueiredo (eds) *Social exclusion: rhetoric reality responses*, Geneva: International Labour Organization.

Room, G. (1995) 'Poverty and social exclusion: the new European agenda for policy and research', in G. Room (ed) *Beyond the threshold: the measurement and analysis of social exclusion*, Bristol: The Policy Press.

Room, G.J. (1999) 'Social exclusion, solidarity and the challenge of globalization', *International Journal of Social Welfare*, vol 8, no 8, pp 166–74.

Rousseau, J-J. (1762, translation published 1968) *The social contract*, London: Penguin Books.

Sandel, M.J. (2009) *Justice: what is the right thing to do?*, London: Allen Lane.

Sandel, M.J. (2012) *What money can't buy: the moral limits of the markets*, London: Allen Lane and Penguin Group.

Seabrook, J. (1988) *The race for riches: the human cost of wealth*, Basingstoke: Marshall Pickering.

Sen, A. (1983) 'Poor, relatively speaking', *Oxford Economic Papers*, New Series, vol 35, no 2, pp 153–69.

Sen, A. (1985) *Commodities and capabilities*, Oxford: North-Holland.

Sen, A. (1999) *Development as freedom*, Oxford: Oxford University Press.

Sen, A. (2000) *Social exclusion: concept, application and scrutiny*, Manila: Asian Development Bank.

Sen, A. (2010) *The idea of justice*, London: Penguin Books.

Sennett, R. (2000) 'Work and social inclusion', P. Askonas and A. Stewart (eds) *Social inclusion possibilities and tensions*, Basingstoke: Palgrave.

Sennett, R. (2012) *Together: the rituals, pleasures and politics of cooperation*, London: Allen Lane and Penguin Books.

Shakespeare, T. (1996) 'Disability, identity, difference', in C. Barnes and G. Mercer (eds) *Exploring the divide: illness and disability*, Leeds: Disability Press.

Sibeon, R. (1992) *Towards a new sociology of social work*, Aldershot: Avebury.

Silver, H. (1994) 'Social exclusion and social solidarity: three paradigms', *International Labour Review*, vol 133, nos 5–6, pp 531–78.

Skellington, R. (1996) *'Race' in Britain today*, London: Sage.

Slay, J., Sherwood, C., Coote, A. and Boyle, D. (2010) *Right here, right now: taking co-production into the mainstream*, London: NEF/ NESTA.

Smith, A. (1776) *The wealth of nations*, 2003 edition, New York: Bantam Dell.

Stewart, A. (2000) 'Never ending story: inclusion and exclusion in late modernity', in P. Askonas and A. Stewart (eds) *Social Inclusion Possibilities and Tensions*, Basingstoke: Palgrave.

Stiglitz, J. (2002) *Globalization and its discontents*, London: Penguin.

Stocking, G.W. Jr. (1982) *Race, Culture and Evolution: Essays in the History of Anthropology*, London: Collier-Macmillan.

Stuart, O. (1992) 'Race and Disability: What Type of Double Disadvantage?', *Disability, Handicap and Society*, 7, 2.

Swain, J. and French, S. (2000) 'Towards an Affirmative Model of Disability', *Disability and Society*, Vol. 15, No.4, pp 569–82.

Taylor, C. (1992) *Multiculturalism and "The Politics of Recognition"*, Princeton, NJ: Princeton University Press.

Thompson, N. (1998) *Promoting equality: challenging discrimination and oppression in the human services*, London: Macmillan.

Touraine, A. (1991) 'Face à l'exclusion', *Esprit*, vol 169, pp 7–13.

Townsend, P. (1975) *Sociology and social policy*, London: Allen Lane.

Townsend, P. (1979) *Poverty in the United Kingdom*, Harmondsworth: Penguin.

Townsend, P. (1981) 'Guerrillas, subordinates and passers-by: the relationship between sociologists and social policy', *Critical Social Policy*, vol 1, no 2, pp 22–34.

Townsend, P. (1983) 'The pursuit of equality', *Poverty*, pp 11–15.

Townsend, P. (1985) 'A sociological approach to the measurement of poverty – a rejoinder to Professor Amartya Sen'. *Oxford Economic Papers*, vol 37, pp 659–68.

Townsend, P. (1993) 'Underclass and overclass: the widening gulf between social classes in Britain in the 1980s', in M. Cross and G. Payne (eds) *Sociology in action*, London: Macmillan, pp 91–118.

Turner, J.H. (2002) *Face to face: towards a sociological theory of interpersonal behavior*, Stanford, CA: Stanford University Press.

United Nations (2000) *Programme of action of the world summit for social development Copenhagen*, 1995.

UPIAS (Union of the Physically Impaired Against Segregation) (1976) *Fundamental principles of disability*, London: UPIAS.

Veblen, T. (1899) *The theory of the leisure class*, New York, NY: Random House.

Veit-Wilson, J. (1998) *Setting adequacy standards: how governments define minimum incomes*, Bristol: The Policy Press.

Waddell, G., Aylward, M. and Sawney, P. (2002) *Back pain, incapacity for work and social security benefits: an international literature review and analysis*, London: The Royal Society of Medicine Press.

Walker, A. (1997) 'Introduction: the strategy of inequality', in A. Walker and C. Walker (eds) *Britain divided: the growth of social exclusion in the 1980s and 1990s*, London: CPAG (Child Poverty Action Group).

Walker, R. (1995) 'The dynamics of poverty and social exclusion', in G. Room (ed) *Beyond the threshold: the measurement and analysis of social exclusion*, Bristol: The Policy Press.

Walzer, M. (1983) *Spheres of justice: a defence of pluralism and equality*, Oxford: Basil Blackwell.

Wasserman, S. and Faust, K. (1994) *Social network analysis: methods and applications*, Cambridge: Cambridge University Press.

Wharton, A.S. (2005) *The sociology of gender: an introduction to theory and research*, Oxford: Blackwell.

WHO (1980) *International classification of impairments, disabilities and handicaps: a manual of classification relating to the consequences of disease*, Geneva: World Health Organisation.

WHO (2001) *International classification of functioning, disability and health*, Geneva: World Health Organisation.

Wilchins, R. (2004) *Queer theory, gender theory: an instant primer*, New York: Alyson Publications.

Wilkinson, R. and Pickett, K. (2010) *The spirit level: why equality is better for everyone*, London: Penguin Books.

Williams, B. (1969) 'The idea of equality', in J. Feinberg (ed) *Moral concepts*, Oxford: Oxford University Press.

Williams, G. (1996) 'Representing Disability: some questions of phenomenology and politics', in C. Barnes and G. Mercer (eds) *Exploring the divide: illness and disability*, Leeds: Disability Press.

Wilson, W.J. (1987) *The truly disadvantaged: the underclass and public policy*, Chicago, IL: University of Chicago Press.

Witcher, S. (2003) *Reviewing the terms of inclusion: transactional processes, currencies and context*, London: Centre for Analysis of Social Exclusion, London School of Economics.

Witcher, S. (2005) 'Mainstreaming equality: the implications for disabled people', *Social Policy and Society*, vol 4, no 1, pp 55–64.

Wolff, J. (2008) 'Social justice and public policy: a view from political philosophy', in G. Craig, T. Burchardt and D. Gordon (eds) (2008) *Social justice and public policy: seeking fairness in diverse societies*, Bristol: The Policy Press.

Xiberras, M. (1993) *Les théories de l'exclusion*, Paris: Meridiens Klincksieck.

Yépez del Castillo, I. (1994) 'Review of the French and Belgian literature on social exclusion: a Latin-American perspective', *Discussion Paper Series*, no 71. Geneva: International Institute of Labour Studies.

Young, I.M. (1990) *Justice and the politics of difference*, Princeton, NJ: Princeton University Press.

Young, I.M. (2008) 'Structural injustice and the politics of difference', in G. Craig, T. Burchardt and D. Gordon (eds) *Social justice and public policy: seeking fairness in diverse societies*, Bristol: The Policy Press.

Zappone, K.E. (2003) 'Conclusion: the challenge of diversity', in K. Zappone (ed) *Re-thinking identity: the challenge of diversity*, Belfast: Joint Equality and Human Rights Forum.

Zola, I. (1989) 'Towards the necessary universalizing of disability policy', *Milbank Memorial Quarterly*, vol 67, no 2, pp 401–28.

Index

D

Q

R

S

T

U